Creating the New Woman

WOMEN IN AMERICAN HISTORY

Series Editors

Mari Jo Buhle

Nancy A. Hewitt

Anne Firor Scott

Stephanie Shaw

A list of books in the series appears at the end of this book.

Creating the New Woman

The Rise of Southern Women's Progressive Culture in Texas, 1893–1918

Judith N. McArthur

UNIVERSITY OF ILLINOIS PRESS

URBANA AND CHICAGO

© 1998 by the Board of Trustees of the University of Illinois
Manufactured in the United States of America
1 2 3 4 5 C P 6 5 4 3

This book is printed on acid-free paper.

Library of Congress Cataloging-in-Publication Data
McArthur, Judith N.
Creating the new woman : the rise of southern women's
progressive culture in Texas, 1893–1918 / Judith N.
McArthur.
    p.   cm. — (Women in American history)
Includes bibliographical references and index.
ISBN 10: 0-252-02376-5 (alk. paper). — ISBN 10: 0-252-06679-0
(pbk. : alk. paper)
ISBN 13: 978-0-252-02376-7 (alk. paper). — ISBN 13: 978-0-252-06679-5
(pbk. : alk. paper)
1. Women social reformers—Texas—History. 2. Women
in politics—Texas—History. I. Title. II. Series.
HQ1438.T4M35   1998
305.42'09764—dc21   97-21067
CIP

For Hal, with love and thanks

Contents

Acknowledgments

It is a pleasure to acknowledge the contributions of the many people who gave advice and assistance as I worked on this book. Ellen C. Temple and the Foundation for Women's Resources sparked my interest in Texas women while I was a graduate student. Norman D. Brown directed the original dissertation at the University of Texas at Austin; Patricia S. Kruppa, Emily F. Cutrer, and Myron P. Gutmann served on the committee. Anne Firor Scott, whose scholarship was my inspiration, graciously donated her time as a long-distance member. I owe a special debt to Professor Scott for years of generous mentoring that stretched from the dissertation proposal through the final book draft.

Numerous friends provided material and moral support. Megan Seaholm lent a manuscript copy of her dissertation on the Texas Federation of Women's Clubs. Elizabeth Hayes Turner shared her dissertation and several conference papers, fed and sheltered me during research trips to Houston, and sat up late talking about southern women's history. Elizabeth York Enstam answered innumerable requests for information about Dallas women, shared portions of her own work, sharpened my ideas, and pruned my prose. Jackie McElhaney opened her files on "Pauline Periwinkle" and offered encouragement at every turn. Marjorie Spruill Wheeler helped refine my understanding of the southern suffrage movement and enabled me to see Texas suffragists in regional context.

Among the many librarians and archivists who assisted me at the University of Texas libraries, I am especially indebted to Ralph Elder and Trudy Croes at the Center for American History, and to Cheryl Malone at the Perry-Castenada Library. My thanks as well to Mike Green, Texas State Library Archives; Ellen K. Brown, Baylor University; Elizabeth Snapp, Texas Women's University; Mike Hazel, Dallas Historical Society; and the public services staffs at the Houston Metropolitan Research Center, Houston Public Library, and the Austin History Center, Austin Public Library. I am indebted to the Texas Congress of Parents and Teachers for granting access to its archives and library and to

Bernice Sehnerr for making me welcome. Lillian Watts Green graciously permitted me to examine the papers of her mother, Lala Fay Watts, and extended warm hospitality.

It has been a pleasure to work with the editors and advisory editors at the University of Illinois Press. I am indebted to Karen Hewitt for shepherding the manuscript through review; to Nancy Hewitt for her kind encouragement; and to Theresa Sears and Louis Simon for their expertise and efficiency.

Most of all, I am grateful to my husband, Harold L. Smith, for steadfast support and for the inspiration of his example.

Creating the New Woman

Introduction

Attending the first Texas Congress of Women, held during the state fair in 1893, convinced Austin journalist Bride Neill Taylor that women in Texas and other former Confederate states no longer dwelt in an isolated cultural backwater. Midway through the week of speeches and papers examining women's changing social role, Taylor concluded optimistically: "It has been said that the Southern woman is too painfully conservative, but I find she is up with the procession."[1] The first half of Taylor's observation was considerably more accurate than the second. Southern women were notoriously slow to espouse women's rights and lagged far behind their northern sisters in organizing to work for social and moral reform. Those in Texas had been struggling for a decade to build a viable Woman's Christian Temperance Union and had yet to form a federation of women's clubs. A tiny state suffrage association—the first ever attempted—was only a few months old and would not long endure. Texas women were hardly "up with the procession" in 1893, but over the next quarter century they would gain ground rapidly and join the vast numbers of progressive women seeking to reform politics and society.

The fact that few women could vote notwithstanding, the years between 1890 and 1920 constituted "a great age for women in politics," in historian Suzanne Lebsock's apt phrase. Using their separate voluntary associations to forge a female public culture, disfranchised women introduced their concern for domestic and social welfare into the political discourse. Middle-class women living in congested and dirty cities discovered that the personal was political: they became municipal housekeepers in order to secure pure food, safe milk and water, and sanitary sewage disposal. In an era of rapidly expanding industrial capitalism, they worked to strengthen the state's power to prevent the exploitation of the vulnerable. The results were evident in laws mandating compulsory education, the restriction of child labor, factory safety, and minimum wages and maximum hours for female workers. Women so dominated the social justice side of progressivism that William Chafe has argued for the existence of two Progressive Eras, one based on the politics of men and the other on the cultural politics of women.[2]

This dichotomy is notably evident in the historiography of progressivism in Texas. Historians of the period emphasize the agency of farmers, organized labor, and politicians in pursuit of goals such as railroad and insurance industry regulation, electoral reform, labor safety laws, and prohibition. Only recently has research on the state's women begun to uncover female-inspired efforts to restrict child labor, reform the juvenile justice system, protect the food supply, secure minimum wage and maximum hour legislation for employed women, establish settlement houses and abolish red-light districts. A generation of research in southern women's history has partially revealed the outlines of this second, female, progressive culture throughout the New South. The "well-dressed, well-spoken southern ladies," whom Anne Firor Scott inadvertently discovered during her disseration research in the 1950s, were on the front lines of social reform, just like their better-known counterparts in the North.[3]

In a fine biography of Florence Kelley, Kathryn Kish Sklar has postulated that weak government, combined with a strong tradition of citizen volunteerism, enabled disfranchised women to carve out this significant political role. The roots of women's public culture, she stresses, reach back to the anti-slavery agitation of the pre–Civil War decades. The Progressive-Era cohort of women found its own voice at a time when the conflict between capital and labor had supplanted slavery as the national preoccupation and the proscriptions against female political activism were becoming less stringent. Women such as Florence Kelley and Jane Addams, who came to maturity in the 1870s as the ideology of separate "spheres" for the sexes was losing force, widened the road opened by the antebellum generation of women activists.[4]

While such a model astutely captures the experience of northern women, it has less explanatory power for their sisters below the Mason-Dixon line. Southern women, living in a deeply patriarchal society structured and sustained by hierarchies of race and gender, had no comparable tradition of antebellum activism. In the South, hostility toward abolitionism stifled public dissent and severed the evangelical churches from their northern counterparts, turning them into defenders of human bondage and "southern rights." Women who openly denounced slavery, such as Angelina and Sarah Grimké, had to leave the region and make their public careers in the North. At the same time, the South's lack of industrial development and its reliance on slave labor prevented the structural separation of home and workplace, precluding female domination in a separate domestic sphere. Isolated in rural households supervised by men, antebellum southern women had few opportunities to translate a Victorian concept of distinctive womanhood into an ideology for social activism.[5]

Thus for southern women, the construct of separate spheres eroded much more slowly after the Civil War. On the one hand, urban expansion and the developing passion for an industrialized New South fostered an environment more conducive to the growth of women's organizations and female public culture.[6] On the other hand, the cult of the Lost Cause, which celebrated the ideals of the defeated Confederacy, urged elite women to uphold the model of antebellum southern ladyhood. Consequently middle- and upper-class southern white women negotiated public roles tentatively. In church and benevolent societies they expressed woman's supposedly "natural" inclination toward piety and kindness without offending strong cultural prescriptions about her "place."

Post-Reconstruction Texas reflected this heritage: female organizational networks that could nourish sisterhood and encourage a female (not to mention feminist) public presence were barely visible. Not a tradition of religious activism but a network of secular voluntary associations dating from the 1890s pulled southern women out of their cultural isolation and into progressivism. The General Federation of Women's Clubs and the National Congress of Mothers, which stimulated local organizing while emphasizing a national outlook, proved far more effective than the Woman's Christian Temperance Union in encouraging Texas women to public activity. Initially avoiding controversial issues, these elite and self-described conservative women helped "domesticate" politics, using voluntary associations to advocate the concerns of household and family.[7] Multiple layers of organization enabled them to combine community-level activism with pressure-group lobbying at the state level for statutory change.

This book assesses the origins and effects of the women's public culture that emerged between the 1890s and World War I on the western border of the New South, a region united by its peculiar history but divided by distinct subcultures, economies, and racial-ethnic clusterings. Focusing on a single state permits close attention to how women were energized, how they organized themselves, how they behaved in a particular political-social environment—and how some of them gradually developed feminist consciousness. As Nancy Cott has pointed out, not all female political activity is feminist, even when undertaken in the name of women's interests. "Female consciousness," rooted in awareness of gender difference and acceptance of a sex-based division of labor, can operate for either conservative or radical ends; "feminist consciousness," which challenges male hegemony, grows only from the latter.[8] "Feminism" was a term of opprobrium in the South, and Texas women avoided it, but their maternalist politics raised challenges to male dominance and facilitated a transformation of consciousness among some.

Chapter 1 examines the dramatic expansion of Texas women's public culture that began in the 1890s, spurred by the World's Columbian Exposition in Chicago and by the rise of federated voluntary associations, especially the General Federation of Women's Clubs. Quickly surpassing the women's temperance movement in numbers and influence, the federated club movement introduced Texas women to the agenda of northern progressivism and offered them a public forum akin to the male political party. Chapters 2 and 3 describe how clubwomen used the emerging "sciences" of home economics and child development to manipulate traditional images of femaleness and subvert gender roles. In women's and mothers' clubs, middle-class women discovered the inseparability of home and community, translating knowledge gained from study courses into justification for seeking female power as municipal housekeepers and child welfare advocates. The impetus for women to run for school board seats developed within the club movement, which shaped a female perspective on school reform that differed significantly from that of the male-dominated Conference for Education in Texas.

At the same time, studying "social economics" turned middle-class women toward investigating the underlying economic causes of social problems. Chapter 4 examines their efforts to rid their rapidly growing cities of red-light districts and to reach across class (but not race) divisions through settlement houses and YWCAs. In the process they claimed new areas of the public domain for women. Chapter 5 describes the evolution of ladies into suffragists within the space of two decades and through the nonfeminist agency of voluntary associations. Conjoined to the maternalist values of the progressive reform agenda, suffrage acquired a new image and a broad following in the 1910s. Women who had hesitated to use the rhetoric of equality readily adopted domestic arguments, asking for the ballot as mothers on behalf of children and as housekeepers on behalf of the public.

By World War I, voluntarist women could even argue for the vote as patriotic wives and mothers on behalf of absent husbands and sons. Chapter 6 explores the effect of the Great War on gender and racial boundaries and argues that it advanced the progressive agenda of female voluntary associations. Wartime mobilization created new opportunities for women to do public work and new agencies through which to do it. The war emergency gave voluntarist women a new partner, the federal government, in their longstanding battles to safeguard child health and welfare, abolish legal prostitution, and banish saloons. It also provided an unlikely coalition of Texas legislators with a rationalization—not a motive—for granting women the right to vote in primary elections. Texas women in 1918 became part of the very small group in the South who secured significant voting rights before Congress passed the Nineteenth Amendment.

For southern women, the Progressive decades were thus seminal ones for what historian Glenna Matthews has called "the rise of public woman." In the 1890s much of public space was still sex-segregated or proscribed to genteel women in the South. Even public speaking, a taboo that northern women had shattered in the antebellum era, required courage and frequently provoked censure. Over the next quarter century Texas women claimed public roles spatially and culturally, by speaking and acting in the public domain; legally, by working to overturn coverture for married women; and politically by securing partial suffrage.[9]

As white women increased their public presence, that of black women was forcibly constricted. The Progressive Era marked the nadir of race relations: Texas and other southern states took advantage of northern indifference to disfranchise the majority of black men and codify racial segregation. At the same time that Jim Crow restricted African Americans' access to public space, demographic change reduced their relative numbers in Texas. African Americans had been nearly one-third of the state's population at the time of the Civil War, but large white in-migration during the succeeding decades steadily reduced the black percentage. In 1890 the state had the smallest proportion of African Americans in the former Confederacy—21.8 percent—and it continued to decline, dropping to 17.7 percent by 1910. Texas had no black belt; of the state's 245 counties, just 12, in the old plantation districts of the east and southeast, had black majorities. Among the state's major cities only Houston, which drew rural migrants from East Texas, had a disproportionately large black citizenry—30 percent in 1910.

The relatively small size of the African American population in Texas and tiny proportion of middle-class blacks make documenting black women's public culture more difficult. The sources are fragmentary and reveal virtually nothing about African American women's attitudes toward their white counterparts. Only the WCTU extended membership to black women (in separate unions); other organizations excluded and largely ignored them. For middle-class African American women, issues of sex and race were inseparable. Motivated by what Elsa Barkley Brown has called "womanist" consciousness, they used their own voluntary associations to do "race work" and to expand female influence within the black community.[10] Yet however much white women distanced themselves from black, racial polarities structured and constrained their efforts for social and political change. Texas suffragists never argued for the vote on racial grounds, but they confronted the politics of race at every turn; their opponents disingenuously invoked the specter of black women flocking to the polls as a ruthlessly effective argument against the female ballot.

A third group of women, Mexican Americans, lacked a female public culture and voluntary association tradition comparable to that of Anglo and African

American women. In the late 1940s Mexican Americans would displace African Americans as the largest ethnic minority in Texas, a demographic shift that has reoriented the cultural perception of the state as more southwestern than southern. In 1890, however, Hispanics made up only 4 percent of the population. Within the next two decades the beginning of sustained migration from Mexico raised the proportion to 8 percent, but Hispanics remained heavily concentrated in the far south and along the southwestern perimeter. Few Mexican American women worked in urban industries before 1920. Predominantly rural, unskilled, and unacculturated, this group lacked the urban middle class that in the African American community formed charitable societies, temperance unions, study clubs, and eventually a settlement house and a YWCA.[11]

Historians have for decades debated the issue of continuity or discontinuity between the Old and New South, almost entirely without reference to the female half of the population. Yet one of the newest things about the New South was surely its activist new women, the wives and daughters of the emerging town-based middle class. Few were educated single women in the mold of Jane Addams or Julia Lathrop; the progressive women leaders in Texas were typically married women with children. Most shared the class elitism and racial biases of the time and place and believed themselves essentially conservative. Like the men of their class, they looked to the North for a model on which to pattern a rising New South.

But unlike the boosters of industrialism, voluntarist women were inspired by different, female models of progress: Hull House and the Children's Bureau. Through federations of women's and mothers' clubs they protested the southern tradition of minimalist cheap government and advocated a proactive state; as suffragists they sought to expand the franchise that the Bourbon Democrats had constricted. Like all generations of southern women, those of the Progressive Era have been "half-sisters of history." The challenge of making them full members of the family is to search out the shared meaning of their separate stories in the vast and varied New South.[12]

"The Coming Woman in Politics" 1

IN 1886 a San Antonio woman published an impassioned newspaper appeal to the Christian women of her city, urging them to join the Woman's Christian Temperance Union, which was struggling for a foothold in Texas. "The women of the South may be slow to undertake this work because of a false idea, born of their conservatism, that it is unwomanly," she conceded. But "the W.C.T.U. says silence is no longer golden." Organizing against the saloons that impoverished their homes and debauched their menfolk was "a higher, holier realization of a woman's duty and influence." While she hoped that "the hearts of our Southern women will echo and take up the cry of women elsewhere," the writer unwittingly revealed one reason for their hesitation: as a modest southern lady, she submitted her plea anonymously. Meanwhile, in the town of Tyler, a band of women had overcome fears of unwomanliness and formed a WCTU chapter, but all shrank from being in the public eye as president; a Baptist minister assumed the office.[1]

Although women in the Northeast and Midwest had been flocking to the WCTU since 1874, enthusiasm for religious-inspired reform in the South was tempered by the region's ingrained conservatism. Like their counterparts throughout the former Confederacy, the majority of Texas women lived in a patriarchal, evangelical culture that discouraged the formation of independent women's networks among the white middle class. A newspaper editor in Denison, Texas, voiced his disapproval of the WCTU by delineating the narrow boundaries of woman's place: "the parlor, the nursery, the flower garden, the kitchen, the ladies' bower, and the places where human sufferings could be alleviated by acts of charity." Within these confines lay "the peculiar empire of woman."[2]

Even in urban areas, few Texas women in the 1870s and 1880s experienced any public role beyond local work for charitable societies and church missionary unions. When WCTU President Frances Willard began a series of southern organizing tours in the early 1880s, the majority of her audiences had never heard a woman speak in public. Although Willard was one of the most famous and admired women in America, her lecture offended the Denison editor because she "had stepped out of the sphere in which her Creator placed her and taken upon herself the duties belonging solely to a man."

Despite the fact that WCTU women advocated a pious cause, southern clergymen were as likely as not to invoke St. Paul's dictum that women should keep silent. According to tradition, when Willard arrived in the town of Paris, Texas, the first stop on her initial visit to the state in 1881, she spoke in an opera house because no minister would sponsor her appearance in his church. Theologically and socially conservative, southern churchmen restricted female congregants to subordinate and auxiliary roles. Women's missionary societies were required to turn over their annual reports for men to read at state church conventions, and women as individuals were denied the laity rights of serving as delegates and voting. As late as 1896 the Baptist Mission Board of Texas threatened to cease contributing to the salary of the Woman's Missionary Union's state organizer if she continued to address mixed audiences of men and women.[3]

In the WCTU women took their semi-private church work into the public arena and liberated it from male oversight, expanding "the peculiar empire of woman" well beyond what many southerners felt comfortable with. Regarded as suspiciously radical because it supported woman suffrage, the WCTU did not germinate in the South until Frances Willard deliberately sowed the seeds of sectional reconciliation by traveling to Dixie. Her visits to Texas in 1881 and 1882 resulted in a state WCTU that grew slowly until 1888, when it followed the national organization and endorsed the ballot. Membership plunged from 1,500 to 539 and remained nearly flat for the next five years.[4]

While some southern women progressed from missionary and benevolent societies into the WCTU, the number in Texas was not large; even after the turn of the century, total WCTU membership remained under 2,500. None of the state's four largest cities—San Antonio, Dallas, Houston, and Fort Worth—ever counted more than two functioning temperance unions, although nearly every Protestant church had a women's society. In Houston, for example, the 1887–88 city directory listed more than a dozen ladies' aid and missionary societies, but only one WCTU, with twenty-five members. By 1913, church societies were listed by the dozens and twenty-three of them had united to form the Houston Federation of Missionary Societies, yet there were only two temperance unions with a total of fifty-two members.[5]

Undoubtedly, as has been argued, church societies and the WCTU did offer southern women opportunities for self-development, but the strength of religious conservatism kept many from enlisting in Willard's white ribbon army. In

1892 this largest and most influential women's organization of the nineteenth century counted only 769 members in Texas, a state larger than the Carolinas, Alabama, Georgia, and Florida combined. "It is hard to get our women to do public work," the state's corresponding secretary lamented. "They dislike anything that savors of suffrage. They are afraid of public criticism and afraid that if they join the W.C.T.U. they will be ushered into politics or made to speak in public."[6]

Instead, leisured women were forming study clubs. Self-culture clubs had developed rapidly in the North after the Civil War, but not until the 1880s did groups such as the Ladies' Reading Club of Houston begin to appear in the South.[7] Organized in 1885, the club drew its membership from more elite social and religious strata than the evangelical WCTU. More than half of the charter members worshiped at Christ Episcopal Church or First Presbyterian, and their husbands were prominent business and professional men. Originally called the Ladies' History Class, the Reading Club sought "intellectual and social culture" beyond that which the members had acquired at institutions such as Miss Brown's Young Ladies' Boarding and Day School in Houston.[8]

The women had no intention of challenging gender conventions or undertaking public work, but through club discussion they moved gradually toward both. By 1893 the Ladies' Reading Club was debating the question of whether education for careers rendered young women unfit for marriage and motherhood; it decided overwhelmingly in the negative. The president used the club's tenth anniversary in 1895 to ask whether the group was exercising influence "as largely as we might" and to urge that it turn its energies toward community improvement.[9]

Around the state and across the nation women's clubs forming in communities of every size were pondering the same question. The 1890s saw an unprecedented expansion in women's public culture, one that southern women as well as northern would embrace and influence. Two pivotal developments in that decade helped bring forward the "new women" of the Progressive Era: the uniting of individual clubs and societies into national federations, and women's participation in the World's Columbian Exposition of 1893. Before the 1890s only the Woman's Christian Temperance Union had attempted to organize in every state as a national federation of women. In the nineties federations suddenly began to appear in quick succession: the General Federation of Women's Clubs in 1890, the National Council of Jewish Women in 1893, the National Association of Colored Women in 1896, and the National Congress of Mothers in 1897.

More dramatically, women around the country cooperated during 1891–92 to celebrate female achievement at the Columbian Exposition, popularly known as the Chicago World's Fair, by erecting a Woman's Building and organizing a week-long Women's Congress. The Board of Lady Managers that directed the effort was a network that reached into every state and territory soliciting funds for the Woman's Building and collecting examples of women's industry and art to fill it.

The Columbian Exposition and the proliferating federations were a remarkable energizing force for women. Lady managers and female visitors alike came home from Chicago optimistic about women's opportunities in the approaching new century. Inspired by the rhetoric of the Woman's Congress, some, including a group of enthusiastic Texans, organized smaller-scale congresses in their own states. And the new federated voluntary associations, like great rivers formed from tributary streams, magnified the energy of individual organizations in the single states and redirected it along a broader channel. Women in the sparsely populated West and culturally isolated South were pulled into a national network with the Northeast and Midwest, where voluntary associations were already studying "social economics" and investigating community problems. We can trace in Texas the process of becoming politically aware and collectively outspoken that put women at the heart of the municipal housekeeping and social welfare campaigns of the 1910s. It began with inspiration from the great fair in Chicago in the summer of 1893.

❀

Women's public culture was so much in evidence at the Columbian Exposition that *Harper's Monthly* took notice. The event could almost be called "a woman's fair," the magazine acknowledged, noting that "whatever they took hold of went." Such had not been the case at the 1876 Centennial Exposition in Philadelphia. In 1876 a Woman's Pavillion had been erected after the Women's Centennial Executive Committee was denied exhibit space in the main building. The women had to raise their own funds and the pavillion was designed by a man, after a fruitless search for a female architect. The National Woman Suffrage Association's request to read a declaration of women's rights at the Fourth of July celebration had been refused: Susan B. Anthony and an entourage of suffragists crashed the ceremony in order to be heard, and repaired afterward to a nearby Unitarian church to hold a suffrage meeting.[10]

In 1893, by contrast, prominent suffragists appeared on the speakers' platforms. The Board of Lady Managers (which Congress created rather than accede to Anthony's demand for equal female representation on the Exposition's planning commission) received a federal appropriation. The board's diligence and chairwoman Bertha Honoré Palmer's gift for prying money and commitments from Congress and the commissioners yielded impressive results. The Lady Managers, representing the women of their states, filled the elaborate Woman's Building with exhibits that showcased not only careerism but women's industrial wage labor and volunteer activism. Julia Morgan, who designed it, was chosen through a national competition for women architects; other contests selected women to create the sculptures, paintings, and additional finishing designs.[11]

Lady Manager Ellen Henrotin of the Chicago Woman's Club saw to it that women were also included in the two hundred auxiliary "congresses" at which experts delivered papers on every conceivable subject. About one quarter of the speakers were female, but the president of the National Council of Women, suffragist May Wright Sewell, wanted a gathering that focused on woman as a subject. She arranged a Woman's Congress to emphasize "the revolution wrought in recent years in the world's concept of woman's natural capabilities." In the regular congresses women would speak as members of various professions; in the Woman's Congress they would examine their shared experience as women. Every aspect of women's public and private work would be discussed: housekeeping, wage labor, social service, and political activism.[12]

Opening at the grand Memorial Art Palace in mid-May, the World's Congress of Representative Women lasted for a week, running as many as eighteen sessions a day. It drew huge crowds to hear papers on women's contributions to education, arts and literature, science, moral and social reform, civic life and politics, religion, philanthropy, and industrial labor. The 330 scheduled speakers, and an almost equal number of unscheduled ones, included Jane Addams, Mary Kenney of the American Federation of Labor, and the venerable leaders of the woman suffrage movement: Lucy Stone, Susan B. Anthony, Elizabeth Cady Stanton, and Anna Howard Shaw. May Wright Sewell gave the welcoming address wearing a skirt eighteen inches off the ground—with knee-high gaiters to preserve modesty—as an example of "reformed" dress designed to permit women complete freedom of movement.[13]

Additional women's meetings went on throughout the weeks as organizations such as the Woman's Christian Temperance Union, the National and International Councils of Women, the National American Woman Suffrage Association (NAWSA), and the International Kindergarten Union scheduled their annual conventions to coincide with the Columbian Exposition. The General Federation of Women's Clubs, which had celebrated its first biennial convention the year before, held a council meeting. The National Council of Jewish Women was born at the Jewish Women's Congress. All in all, some two hundred papers were read at auxiliary congresses that convened in the Woman's Building over the course of the summer. Titles like "Women in Journalism," "Women as Political Economists," "The Legal Profession for Women," and "The Medical Profession for Women," emphasized the New Woman's ambitions.

There was so much activity that Rebecca Henry Hayes of Galveston decided to go to Chicago in May and stay until the end in order "to take it all in." She arranged to rent a flat with friends "on the co-opperative [*sic*] plan," reveling in the prospect of freedom from housekeeping duties and the liberty of dining "wherever we find ourselves." They joined the "army of women . . . who diligently went about the buildings . . . day after day, taking notes," *Harper's* reported. "Everywhere were the women with notebooks, determined to see everything, to understand and to jot down everything for future study." And like countless other women among the 27 million American and foreign visitors, Hayes went to the Columbian Exposition to participate as well as to observe. As president of the newly founded Texas Equal Rights Association (TERA), the state's first suffrage organization, she was a NAWSA convention delegate and a speaker at one of the government congresses the suffragists sponsored.[14]

Women like Rebecca Hayes and Dr. Ellen Lawson Dabbs of Fort Worth were responsible for the burst of organizing energy that radiated through the states after the Chicago Exposition.[15] What happened in Texas was a classic example of the fair's ripple effect. Dabbs, like Hayes an officer in TERA, went to the fair as a NAWSA convention delegate and carried the inspiration of the women's congresses home. She organized a small-scale replica—two dozen speakers representing a handful of women's organizations—that convened during the Texas State Fair in Dallas that October on the heels of the Columbian Exposition. Attendance for the first afternoon's papers was modest; the *Dallas Morning News* described the audience as "so small as to cause some of the criticizing lords of creation to smile." But the curious crowds grew larger, and by the fourth day three hundred people filled the hall nearly to capacity.[16]

For her own paper, "Professional Women from a Physician's Standpoint," Dabbs followed May Wright Sewell's lead in encouraging dress reform. She stressed that the "weaker sex" was created by culture, not biology: if boys had for generations been squeezed into corsets, hobbled by voluminous skirts, and kept indoors for fear of injuring their complexions, they too would have grown up pale and listless. Dr. Fanny Leak, who combined a medical practice in Austin with an active role in the Texas Farmers' Alliance, reinforced the point with a speech on "The Evolution of Woman," a subject that future NAWSA president Carrie Chapman Catt also favored for public lectures.[17]

Women who had been to the Chicago fair were prominent on the program. One speaker reviewed "Women's Work in Connection with the Columbian Exposition." Dallas clubwoman Mary Kittrell Craig, who in Chicago had presented a paper on the evolution of American literature, this time discussed the club movement itself. Elizabeth Fry, who had been president of the San Antonio Board of Lady Managers and vice president of the Texas board, disputed the theological argument for female subordination. Rebecca Henry Hayes spoke optimistically of "The Coming Woman in Politics," an individual whose arrival seemed fairly remote in Texas in 1893.[18]

The Texas Woman's Congress differed in two important respects from the World's Congress of Representative Women. It was to be a permanent organization that would reconvene annually, so a secretary received membership applications at the end of the daily sessions. And as was to be expected in a state that celebrated its Confederate history, all of the participants were white. At the Columbian Exposition the Board of Lady Managers had voted not to bar African American women, although only a few were speakers and a white woman was appointed to represent black women's organizations. Southern board members had made derogatory remarks during the racial policy debate, including a Texas Lady Manager who asserted: "The darkies are better off in white folks' hands. The Negroes in my state do not want representation."[19]

White southern women would continue to defend racial segregation and rationalize the African American's "place" even as they challenged the constraints of their own. Ellen Lawson Dabbs's progressive daughter Junia, at school in Massachusetts, was "dumbfounded" when someone at a church entertainment attempted to introduce two African American women to her and another southern student. Like gender boundaries, racial boundaries were porous, but the crossing points were carefully delineated. While the Texas Woman's Congress was in progress, black women were helping prepare for the parade and entertainments staged on "Colored People's Day," when African Americans were admitted to the fair.[20]

After its debut in 1893, the Texas Woman's Congress held three more annual conventions during the state fair. At their second meeting in 1894 the Texas women received telegrams of greetings from women's congresses in Tennessee and California. New England's noted club leader and suffragist, Julia Ward Howe, presiding over the annual convention of the Association for the Advancement of Women, wired greetings from Nashville: "This, the first women's congress, congratulates the new one." The Texas Woman's Congress voted that year to affiliate with the National Council of Women and change its name to State Council of Women of Texas.

The members also laid plans to erect a building on the Dallas fairgrounds like the one the Lady Managers had put up at the Columbian Exposition. The Texas Woman's Building, however, was to be a permanent edifice with an assembly room that could seat one thousand people and separate meeting and reading rooms for the member clubs and organizations. The women voted to raise a construction fund by selling shares in the structure and authorized Ellen Lawson Dabbs to appoint local building committees to canvass. Plans designed by a woman architect in Chicago were on display at the following year's convention in 1895, and every woman's organization in Dallas participated in the cornerstone-laying ceremony. Despite generous contributors like El Paso's Current Topics Club, which sent double the ten-dollar assessment in the hope that others would do the same and "enable the committee to put up at least a $5,000 building," money turned out to be an insurmountable obstacle. The nationwide economic depression that had begun in 1893 dragged on until 1897, crippling the fundraising campaign, and the Woman's Building never progressed beyond the sketches and the cornerstone.[21]

Nevertheless, the renamed Woman's Congress did have a permanent legacy. By making individual women's groups aware of each others' activities, it helped produce a state federation of women's clubs. In the late 1880s there had been perhaps two dozen women's clubs in Texas.[22] The enthusiasm generated by the World's Congress of Representative Women and its Dallas echo stimulated a flurry of organizing. In response to the Woman's Building fund drive, the Current Topics Club, a handful of women who had been meeting informally to study literature and current events, organized formally under an inclusive new name and with a new purpose. It became the Woman's Club of El Paso and soon had more than one hundred members. Over the next decade the women would sponsor a massive municipal cleanup drive, and prod El Paso into establishing a public library, a city playground, and a home for delinquent boys.[23]

More clubs appeared at each annual convention of the State Council of Women, and although Ellen Lawson Dabbs always retained the presidency, clubwomen filled the other offices and made up the executive board. By the spring of 1896, clubs in the northern part of the state were numerous enough to convene a regional Congress of Clubs in Dallas.[24] The State Council of Women of Texas met for the last time at the State Fair that fall.[25] The dominant clubwomen formed their own statewide organization in the spring of 1897, and the new Texas Federation of Women's Clubs (TFWC) carried forward the momentum generated by the Congress of Women.

❀

The preparations for the Columbian Exposition had brought women together temporarily; federation united them in enduring networks. Just as local clubs had gathered isolated individuals, federation brought together the isolated clubs. Each formed a link in a chain that reached around the state, the separate state chains joining to form a national federation. Like Robert Wiebe's "island communities," the small towns being drawn into the expanding web of urban industrial life in the late nineteenth century, clubs shifted their perspective beyond pure localism; they became part of a national, more formal and bureaucratic social system. Not all clubs chose to affiliate, of course, but the trend, as in the business world, was away from isolated independence and toward conglomeration. And like corporate business, the federated club movement grew spectacularly. "The whole country is budding into women's clubs," Charlotte Perkins Gilman observed without exaggeration in 1898.[26]

Federation, which brought women together in regular district, state, and national conventions, created ties that bridged distance and difference. The national meetings also enabled delegates from small towns and isolated areas to hear noted social reformers such as Jane Addams and Florence Kelley, Owen Lovejoy of the National Child Labor Committee, and juvenile court pioneer Judge Ben Lindsey of Denver. Clubwomen who wanted to work for such causes found new power in federation. The local club's range of influence was limited; state and national federations could speak with the authority of thousands of women.

For once the southerners did not have to be coaxed or prodded to join. The WCTU, through its Superintendent of Southern Work, and NAWSA, with its Southern Committee, had acknowledged the regional limitations of their appeal.[27] In Texas the WCTU added members by hundreds, while the TFWC grew by thousands. By 1901 the TFWC claimed 3,400 members, or more than twice as many as the state WCTU; by 1910 it had reached 10,000, more than four times the WCTU's size. The TERA barely increased by tens. Founded in 1893, it ceased functioning in 1896; like the other southern suffrage associations that NAWSA tried to establish in the 1890s, it was a victim of the region's entrenched hostility toward feminism. By contrast, the GFWC flourished without a southern outreach department, quickly outstripping the WCTU to become the nation's largest women's organization.[28]

With the dramatic growth of the federated club movement, the voluntary association tradition turned a corner away from the Victorian era's phalanxes of praying women and took a new direction. Clubwomen were church-going women but not churchwomen like the organizers of the moral reform societies, missionary circles, and temperance unions that predominated in the 1870s and 1880s. In Texas, women did not progress from temperance in the 1880s to clubs in the 1890s; the two movements remained largely separate. The WCTU and the TFWC shared no state leaders and local studies reveal little overlap in the rank and file membership.[29]

For women in Texas and the other states of the former Confederacy, the rise of the GFWC proved much more significant than Frances Willard's carrying the WCTU into the South in the early 1880s. Willard had brought northern and southern women together in a single organization by enshrining localism as the WCTU's operating principle, allowing states leeway to ignore the national body's more controversial pronouncements, such as support for suffrage. Each union adopted as much or as little of the national program as it chose. By the 1890s the national WCTU had established over forty departments of work under the influence of Willard's "Do Everything" policy, but the state organizations had the option of doing only a few things. The Texas WCTU usually worked in about half of the departments and its local unions in far fewer. Thus while the national WCTU championed a multiplicity of progressive social causes, local Texas chapters continued to operate in the older moral reform tradition; they focused primarily on defeating liquor in local option elections, evangelism, and alcohol education.[30]

The WCTU's localism, frequently cited as an organizational strength, at the same time conceded the geographic limitations of its appeal. Local autonomy notwithstanding, prosuffragism was a drag on the WCTU's growth in the South.[31] Willard and the presidents who succeeded her were northern women, as was the bulk of the membership. The GFWC, by contrast, elected its first southern president, Rebecca Douglas Lowe of Georgia, before the organization was a decade old, and Texas's Anna Pennybacker became the second in 1912. While the WCTU accommodated a relatively small number of southern women, the GFWC attracted them in representative numbers. An early policy of avoiding "political questions" such as suffrage and prohibition brought in the members; rejecting local autonomy ensured that they were fully integrated and active.[32]

Although the federated club movement would have more influence than the WCTU in advancing southern women's public culture, it was in one respect— interracial cooperation—a large step backward. Frances Willard had spoken to African American audiences during her visits to the South and other southern lecturers did likewise, organizing black women into separate chapters (as was usually the case in the North as well). The Paris, Texas, union had a "Negro" counterpart as early as 1882, presided over by "the colored pastor's wife." White women oversaw "colored work" until black leaders could be found, and six black unions had formed in Texas before the first African American organizer was appointed in 1886. When Lucy Thurman became president of the Colored Division of the national WCTU she began serious organizing in the South. In 1897 Thurman's efforts in Texas resulted in fifteen unions and a state organization, the Texas "Number Two" or "Thurman" Union; two years later it reported sixty-two active and thirty honorary members.[33]

Historians have justly criticized the WCTU for segregating and subordinating African American members, but temperance women were far in advance of the GFWC, which excluded black clubs. The WCTU anticipated Booker T. Washington's dictum that the races could live closely but separately, like the fingers on one hand. The "WCTU Notes" column on the woman's page of the *Dal-*

las Morning News printed the activities of Mrs. Eliza Peterson of Texarkana, state president of the black union from 1898 to 1909. The only account of a Texas Thurman convention (1909) yet discovered reported "many white people" in attendance.[34] By contrast, the state's white and black club federations were separate hands, the white hand taking no notice of what the black one was doing.

African American leaders built their own federation, the National Association of Colored Women (NACW), which may have been even more important for black southern women than the GFWC was for their white counterparts. When Eliza Peterson wanted to establish an African American kindergarten in Texarkana in 1899, she confronted the double isolation of race and region: she could not turn for assistance to the TFWC's kindergarten committee, and there was no state federation of black clubs. Instead, Peterson wrote to her "dear friend" Margaret Murray Washington (Mrs. Booker T.) of the Tuskegee (Alabama) Woman's Club and the NACW, a kindergarten advocate who had previously sent her reading matter. To help draw black women like those in Texarkana into its national network, the NACW gathered two hundred southern African American clubwomen in Montgomery, Alabama, in December 1899 to form the Southern Federation of Colored Women's Clubs. Margaret Washington, who presided over the meeting, defined its purpose as uniting black southern women "for greater usefulness in their own section of the country."[35]

No clubwomen from west of Alabama attended the organizing meeting in 1899, and only one Texas group, the Phyllis Wheatley Club of Fort Worth, yet belonged to the NACW. But by the 1901 convention in Vicksburg, Mississippi, delegates from Texas and other states of the old southwest were present. Through the Southern Federation, black Texas clubwomen were drawn into the NACW; they formed the Texas Association of Colored Women's Clubs (TACWC) in 1905 and affiliated with the NACW a year later. It seems likely that proportionally more black clubs than white remained unfederated; paying extra dues and traveling to state and national conventions were significant burdens for African American women. The TACWC grew slowly, minus the unaffordable luxuries of a state magazine and yearbook that abundantly document the white club movement, until the 1920s, when membership reached some 1,800.[36]

The NACW's motto, "Lifting as We Climb," reflected a tradition of self-help and social responsibility that was generations old. The NACW did not separate club work from the older traditions of benevolence and religion; it had departments of charities and of religious work, and a special one called Ministers and Bishops Wives. In the NACW black women promoted temperance without white guidance: it was a department of work and the WCTU's Lucy Thurman was an NACW officer. Nor did African American clubwomen have the option of claiming to be apolitical; they spoke out from the beginning against lynching and segregation. In the name of racial progress and uplift the NACW did everything: arts and literature, kindergartens and day nurseries, rescue and reformatory work, mothers' meetings and neighborhood missions.[37]

Although white clubwomen's vision remained narrower, the GFWC, too, gradually widened its focus beyond literature and the arts. As it took up the study of social issues in the late 1890s, state federations followed suit. The TFWC, originally called the Texas Federation of Literary Clubs, changed its name to reflect its broadening interests and steadily added new committees and subcommittees: Education, Village Improvement, Household Economics, Civics, Parks and School Grounds, Kindergartens, and Child Labor. Small town clubs that lagged behind drew severe criticism from Isadore Callaway, president of the Dallas Federation of Women's Clubs and editor of the woman's page of the *Dallas Morning News* and its sister publication, the *Galveston Daily News.* "Of what can sane women be thinking," she scolded in her weekly column, "when they deliberately choose for their club work 'Julius Caesar' or the 'Pippa Passes,' while all the streets and alleys of their town breed unsightliness if not actual pestilence?"[38]

By the mid-1910s, when the GFWC abandoned its policy of avoiding "political" issues and endorsed suffrage and prohibition, clubwomen had fully appropriated the WCTU's old "Do Everything" approach. But because federated clubs were required to replicate the GFWC's agenda and standing committees, policies formulated at national biennial conventions were carried out on both sides of the Mason-Dixon line. The GFWC's turn toward social reform pulled "conservative" women from "backward" southern states like Texas away from the tradition of localism and limited government and toward the concept of an activist state.

Innumerable examples can be cited; the crusade against child labor offers one of the earliest. The GFWC Biennial in 1898 included a session on "The Industrial Problem as It Affects Women and Children." Chaired by Claire DeGraffenreid, noted as an investigator of cotton mill labor in her native South, the panel also featured Britain's Beatrice Webb. A committee then formed under DeGraffenreid to draft a set of resolutions recommending minimum age and maximum hours requirements for child workers. These were adopted in convention, along with a resolution laying out a practical, three-pronged plan of action. Each club was to appoint a standing committee to investigate the working conditions of women and children locally; each state federation was instructed to appoint another to survey its state's labor ordinances and enforcement provisions. The General Federation itself was directed to create a Committee on

Isadore Sutherland Miner Callaway, named editor of the "Woman's Century" page of the *Dallas Morning News* in 1896, was better known to readers as "Pauline Periwinkle." A clubwoman and suffragist, Callaway used her weekly column to champion women's rights and the progressive agenda, especially public health, child welfare, and school reform. (From *Who's Who of the Womanhood of Texas*, vol. 1, 1923–24 [N.p.: Texas Federation of Women's Clubs, 1924])

Legislation for Women and Children to collect the state reports and present a summary at the 1900 Biennial.[39]

Child labor reform was thereafter part of federated club work. After the 1900 Biennial, Florence Kelley, the former Illinois factory inspector who was executive secretary of the newly established Consumers' League, was appointed chair of the Industrial Problems Committee. Kelley mailed each club a pamphlet of child labor facts, complete with bibliography and resource list, and asked that at least one meeting be devoted to discussing the industrial problem. She urged clubwomen to investigate their state regulations. Was there a factory inspector? What was the legal age for employing children and the length of the working day? Was home manufacturing licensed? At the 1902 Biennial a circular tabulating child labor statutes in the states was distributed; each delegate could see how her state compared to the rest of the country. Jane Addams of Hull House and the Chicago Woman's Club spoke on the suffering behind the statistics, detailing the social, moral, and mental waste that child labor inflicted on the nation.[40]

As inspiration and information flowed from the General Federation to its state branches and their member clubs, southern ladies were drawn into social investigation. The Dallas Federation of Women's Clubs encountered a revealing difficulty in its attempt to discuss the industrial problem: there were no statistics on the number of children working in the city's cotton mill district because the state had no child labor law and therefore no factory inspector. When the mill owners denied entry to a federation committee, the women stood outside the gates on both shifts and counted the children as they went to and from work. Their findings went into a paper that Isadore Callaway (who had reported the child labor discussion and resolutions of the 1902 GFWC Biennial in her newspaper column) delivered at the TFWC convention in 1902. After President Anna Pennybacker's forceful speech on the need for legislation, the convention endorsed the state federation of labor's demand for a bill prohibiting the employment of children under twelve and "most earnestly" urged the legislature to act in the upcoming session.[41]

Organized labor did most of the actual lobbying that secured the first Texas law in 1903, raising the age for factory and mill work to twelve. The TFWC had not yet formed a legislative committee and become a forthright lobbying presence. But the Dallas Federation paid to have copies of the child labor bill printed and mailed to every club in the TFWC so that the members could publicize the issue and coordinate letter writing campaigns to state legislators. As the General Federation continued to investigate and agitate, joining forces with the Consumers' League and with the National Child Labor Committee (NCLC) that formed in 1904, the Texas Federation followed its lead, even trying to secure Jane Addams as a convention keynote speaker. Since the state lacked a branch of the

NCLC, the TFWC created its own child labor committee; it persuaded the state commissioner of labor to draft a bill barring children under fifteen from factories and mills and requiring higher safety and sanitation standards. The clubwomen secured legislative sponsors (a member's husband introduced the bill in the Senate) and lobbied the measure through the 1911 legislative session.[42] In state after state club federations mounted similar campaigns.[43]

The "coming woman in politics" of whom Rebecca Henry Hayes had spoken in 1893 thus arrived well ahead of the vote. She entered unintentionally by the back door, through voluntary associations like the TFWC. The Dallas Federation's advocacy of "a state law such as they have in all the Northern and New England States" to regulate child labor bespoke the education that such women acquired through GFWC membership. The six clubs that had formed the Dallas Federation in 1898 had only the most uncontroversial purpose in mind: combining forces to build a public library. None anticipated that four years later the members would be engaged in cotton mill "espionage," as one delicately put it, standing against the men of their own class who advocated the New South creed of unfettered industrial development. Without intending to, the club federation had introduced more women to social reform than the Dallas WCTU, which according to the city directory counted only forty-six members, even though it had existed for thirty years.[44]

❀

It is a truism that increasing impatience and frustration with politicians who ignored their petitions and requests helped turn many clubwomen into suffragists. Clubs, a contemporary observed shrewdly, were "the primary schools which lead to the university of politics."[45] But the well-documented transition from self-culture to social reform is only half the story. The nature and structure of the federated club movement itself taught women to think and act politically, ultimately enabling many to envision themselves as voters. Counting membership by thousands in the states and hundreds of thousands nationally, federations provided a vast public space in which women learned to run for office, court votes, manage campaigns, hold conventions, negotiate and compromise, debate policy, and build consensus. In short, they found the opportunity to practice in their own network much that men did in political parties.

Contesting for places in the strata of federation offices—city, district, state, and national—a corps of ambitious women honed their political skills. Short election cycles (presidents could serve two two-year terms in the GFWC, two one-year terms in the TFWC) guaranteed regular turnover of both elected officers and committee chairwomen, who were presidential appointees. Such openness to advancement contrasted sharply with the static pattern of the WCTU, which retained presidents and department chairs for years. Between 1897 and 1918 the Texas WCTU elected only four presidents while the TFWC chose eleven, each administration providing dozens of other opportunities for office seekers. In an era when women had few other routes to public recognition and influence, they could build the equivalent of "careers" in federated clubwork, rising through the ranks to state and national prominence.

Convention decreed that the office should seek the woman, but the private politics of building public careers was evident in the TFWC by the turn of the century. The queenmaker was Mary Young Terrell, doyenne of Fort Worth's clubwomen. The daughter of transplanted South Carolinians, Terrell grew up in the East Texas plantation country, graduating from Marshall Masonic Female Institute, of which her father was a founder and trustee, in 1864. After spending more than two decades as a teacher, she married a wealthy widower and assumed the role of stepmother to his five children. In this second phase of her life, Terrell channeled her energy into the rising club movement. She became a leader in the Woman's Wednesday Club of Fort Worth and a member of the executive board of the State Council of Women of Texas. At the organizing meeting of the TFWC, Terrell was elected first vice president; she succeeded to the presidency in 1899, when she was fifty-two.[46]

Mary Terrell's TFWC portrait shows a diminutive woman in a high-necked black bodice, severe bun, and spectacles—the very image of a self-effacing Victorian grandmother. In reality she was strong-willed and assertive, with a shrewd understanding of power and the instincts of a professional politician. Terrell was determined that her protégée, Anna Pennybacker, would succeed her as president in 1901, even though Pennybacker was not yet forty and had never held state office. Like Terrell, Pennybacker traced her origins to the coastal South—she liked to refer to herself as a daughter of Virginia—and had deep roots in East Texas and years of experience in the teaching profession.

Since her school days, Anna J. Hardwicke Pennybacker had been an ambitious high achiever. She had won a scholarship (with a perfect score on the entrance exam) to the first class to enter Sam Houston Normal Institute (now Sam Houston State University) and graduated with honors in 1880. Within four years she had become principal of the high school in Tyler and married the superintendent, a former classmate from Sam Houston Normal. She went on to organize the town's first woman's club, and within a few years had produced both the Tyler Federation of Women's Clubs and a school history of Texas. The textbook, which was regularly revised and adopted year after year in Texas classrooms, brought her reputation and enough wealth to cushion the shock of being widowed young and left with three children to rear.[47] Petite and pretty, she was at ease on a podium and a compelling public speaker.

Anna J. Hardwicke Pennybacker, president of the Texas Federation of Women's Clubs (1901–3) and the General Federation of Women's Clubs (1912–16), found a "career" and a national reputation in the club movement. Despite Pennybacker's ambivalence, the GFWC endorsed woman suffrage at the beginning of her second term in 1914. (From *Who's Who of the Womanhood of Texas*, vol. 1, 1923–24 [N.p.: Texas Federation of Women's Clubs, 1924])

Standing between Pennybacker's desire for the TFWC presidency and Terrell's determination to make it a reality was the first vice president and heir apparent, sixty-four-year-old Mary Eleanor Brackenridge of San Antonio. The never-married Brackenridge was wealthy and socially prominent, thanks to her millionaire bachelor brother, George, over whose mansion she presided. A generous philanthropist like her brother, "Miss Eleanor" was a reliable patron of San Antonio's schools and civic projects. In addition to sitting on the boards of her brother's two banks, she was the founding president of the Woman's Club of San Antonio, the state's first nonliterary or "department" club.[48] It hosted the TFWC convention in 1900, allowing Brackenridge to shine on her home stage; she appeared poised to succeed to the presidency in 1901.

President Terrell moved indirectly and subtly to position Anna Pennybacker to advantage against Brackenridge. She saw to it that Pennybacker made an address on education during a plenary session at the 1901 convention, and instigated a change in the procedure for electing officers. Although the new method, a nominating committee instead of floor nominations, was ostensibly proposed to prevent "hasty" election of officers, Terrell almost certainly hoped to boost Pennybacker's chances and perhaps keep Brackenridge off the ballot entirely.

The necessary revision of the by-laws was approved only after a heated floor debate and protests that the change would create a nominating "machine." The press account of the election is tantalizingly suggestive and incomplete: somehow, Pennybacker appeared on the platform and appealed for harmony, begging the delegates not to "wrangle" over the matter. Brackenridge, who presided while Terrell went onto the convention floor to defend the proposal, seems to have kept silent, apparently torn between the desire for office and repugnance at the prospect of having to campaign for it openly and immodestly.[49] Three presidential candidates were ultimately nominated (using the old floor method because the new forms failed to arrive from the printer). When the votes were tallied Pennybacker ranked first and Brackenridge third, only two votes behind the second-place finisher, who immediately withdrew to keep her from being eliminated. A second ballot delivered victory to the Terrell-Pennybacker faction.[50]

Clubwomen suppressed evidence of such disputatious proceedings; minutes reported outcomes without elaboration, and club-written reports emphasized consensus and goodwill. A few years later Pennybacker published a description of the 1906 GFWC Biennial conveying the impression that several thousand proper ladies had merely conducted a large parlor meeting: "The order was excellent. The report of the officers and working committees were clear and concise, while the minutes were models of their kind. The revision of the By-laws was accomplished with no loss of time or temper. Even the nominating committee and the election of officers passed without an unpleasant word. . . . There was honest difference of opinion, but there was almost no personal feeling."[51] "Personal feeling," like "wrangling," was the kind of behavior men regularly displayed at political conventions, and clubwomen carefully avoided the appearance of such. They stressed cooperation, decorum—waving delicate white handkerchiefs in the famous "Chautauqua salute" instead of masculine clapping and cheering—and above all, harmony.

Yet however reluctant they were to acknowledge it, women learned to politick in their federated networks, to seek power, to enjoy recognition and influence— in essence to have a public existence. After Pennybacker captured the Texas presidency, both she and her mentor moved on to positions of prominence in the GFWC. At the 1902 Biennial in Los Angeles, Terrell was elected to the board of directors, the first Texas woman to hold a federation office. Pennybacker, leading the Texas delegation, made an auspicious debut. She delivered the state's report so forcefully that the *Los Angeles Times* dubbed her "the Texas Cyclone." A *Herald* reporter, in a humorous appreciative poem, noted her success in bringing rambling floor debates back to the point by rising repeatedly to move the previous question.[52]

Anna Pennybacker's star rose a little higher at each successive Biennial. She was elected treasurer in 1904, auditor in 1906, and chaired the program committee in 1908. When the GFWC decided in 1910 to raise a $100,000 endowment to expand its programs and services, Pennybacker chaired the Field Committee. The position was demanding and required considerable travel, but it brought correspondingly high visibility. Her appeal for the endowment prompted the Texas convention to pledge the state's entire assessment—$2,000—in less than twenty minutes, enhancing her reputation as a woman who got things done.[53]

By 1912 Pennybacker was fifty-one and ready to seek the national presidency. When the GFWC *Bulletin* announced in April that she had decided to "accept the earnest solicitation of her friends throughout the country and allow her name to be placed in nomination," a cadre of Texas clubwomen directed by Mary Terrell had already been busy for months.[54] Terrell's Woman's Wednesday Club in Fort Worth had petitioned the TFWC president to send a delegation to Pennybacker's home in Austin to "ask" her to run. Isadore Callaway applauded the prospect in her popular "Pauline Periwinkle" column. Borrowing the phrase Theodore Roosevelt had just used to announce his presidential candidacy, Callaway exulted privately that "assuredly Mrs. Pennybacker's hat is in the ring."[55]

The TFWC leadership quickly mobilized to promote her candidacy "by all dignified and laudable means." The crucial "means" was an eight-member campaign committee euphemistically called the Special Committee. Mary Terrell chaired it, mapping strategy with two younger lieutenants: Secretary-Treasurer

Ida Saunders and Callaway, who planned newspaper publicity. The Special Committee raised a campaign fund by levying a surcharge on each club in the state federation, and it urged clubs not enrolled in the GFWC to do so promptly. More memberships would entitle the state to send additional delegates to the Biennial in California: "the stronger the delegation at San Franciso, the better our chances of success." At the same time, members were requested to write to friends "prominent and active" in other states to solicit support for Pennybacker and pass their names on to Secretary Saunders.[56]

Meanwhile, the clubwomen of New York State were promoting their own candidate, Fanny Hallock Carpenter, a Yonkers attorney and the first woman to win a case before the New York Court of Appeals. Years after graduating from Mills College in California and marrying a lawyer, she had earned a law degree from New York University, joined her husband's practice, and helped organize the Woman Lawyer's Club of New York. Carpenter had been president of the New York State Federation of Women's Clubs and was the immediate past president of New York City's famous Sorosis Club, which put forward her name. A former GFWC board member, she had chaired the program committee for the 1910 Biennial and been elected chair of the important Outlook Committee, the organization's legislative lobbying arm.[57] In short, Carpenter was impressively qualified, and Pennybacker's supporters did not underestimate the challenge ahead. "The contest may be a friendly one," Isadore Callaway wrote privately; "it will be to a finish at all events."[58]

As the Republican and Democratic parties prepared for their upcoming national conventions and partisans boomed Taft and Roosevelt, Bryan and Wilson, a similar process unfolded in the GFWC. As Pennybacker's campaign manager, Mary Terrell undertook to see that no delegate arrived in San Francisco ignorant of her candidate's merits. She and Ida Saunders mailed an announcement to every address in the General Federation directory and to the various state federation magazines. Anticipating heavy turnout from the western clubs, Terrell also secured lists of those that had affiliated since the directory appeared. ("They are as the flies of Egypt," she lamented, addressing envelopes to the California newcomers.) Isadore Callaway prepared a biographical sketch and distributed it, with Pennybacker's photograph, to colleagues who edited women's pages in metropolitan newspapers around the country. Final publicity sketches were timed to reach the West Coast papers just before the Biennial opened in late June.[59]

They dared not prosecute the campaign too aggressively, however, for fear of alienating the substantial number of clubwomen who found overt politicking distasteful. Two former GFWC presidents close to Pennybacker and Terrell cautioned that overactivity had proved the undoing of some past candidates.

Pennybacker and Carpenter (who were in fact friends) repeatedly professed their mutual admiration and disclaimed personal rivalry. Isadore Callaway, however, declined to let the courtesies override political good sense. She fed a journalist complimentary remarks (supposedly uttered by Pennybacker) about Carpenter and then advised her candidate: "Before sending a clipping to Mrs. C., clip off the Mich. paragraph, as it may simply give her lieutenants a tip as to where they ought to be getting in good work."[60]

Pennybacker and her advisers struggled for weeks to work out a politically viable stand on suffrage. After several years of agitating, the prosuffrage element of the GFWC had succeeded in getting the subject on the program of the 1910 Biennial. An evening had been devoted to discussing both sides of the issue, and more than a thousand women attended a suffrage reception; a survey of the delegates had shown that over half endorsed the movement.[61] Many of the prosuffragists had in past years concurred with the GFWC's refusal to take sides on a "political" issue, but sentiment in favor of endorsement was mounting. The issue was expected to come to a head at the San Francisco Biennial. California women were still exulting over their suffrage victory in 1911, and a constitutional amendment was pending in neighboring Oregon. Many of the western delegates would represent states that had given women the ballot.

Moreover, the New York delegation was strongly prosuffrage. Carpenter's campaign manager, NYFWC President Mary Garrett Hay, was president of the New York Equal Suffrage League and a longtime associate of Carrie Chapman Catt, with whom she also shared a house. The New York Federation had a standing committee on suffrage and before the end of the year the membership would vote to endorse the movement.[62] Texas, by contrast, lacked a functioning state suffrage association in 1912, and Pennybacker's sentiments were no more than lukewarm. Her advisers in Fort Worth and Dallas were divided. Mary Terrell and Ida Saunders adamantly opposed any stand that might alienate other conservative southerners; Isadore Callaway, a northern emigré, was an outspoken suffragist. After endless consultations, Pennybacker settled on a position calculated to draw votes from both camps: she declared herself personally in favor of suffrage but opposed to "injecting" it into the GFWC.[63]

As the Texas delegation prepared to leave for California, Saunders reassured the candidate that Terrell was "gathering up the loose ends and tying them all in one firm knot." The sixty-five-year-old "general," as Terrell was known to the rest of the Special Committee, worried over the details of last minute publicity and reported herself "squeezed dry" of ideas. In a last missive to Pennybacker, she voiced a cautious politician's optimism: "Our chances seem good, if some suffragist from the West doesn't arise & stampede the convention—then we'll sure get *swatted*."[64]

But when the sixty-seven delegates assembled in Fort Worth for departure by Pullman car, General Terrell reviewed her troops with dismay. "*Such green stuff!* and to go up against N.Y.! . . . The names I called some of our women who should have been there are best unwritten." The opposition proved as formidable as she anticipated: ninety-four New Yorkers led by Mary Garrett Hay, and accompanied by the twenty-two delegates from New Jersey, disembarked in San Francisco from their chartered "Federation Special" train. Both delegations wore white badges emblazoned with Carpenter's name.[65] Badges, delegations, and campaign managers were the stuff of partisan politics, and the GFWC Biennial resembled a political nominating convention in ways that no observer could have failed to notice.

Locked in competition for what one journalist called "the highest office a woman can hold in America," Anna Pennybacker and Fanny Carpenter behaved like experienced vote seekers. Both candidates had highly visible campaign entourages. The Texans distributed flyers for Pennybacker from a parlor suite provided by her fellow members of the Austin American History Club. The New Yorkers handed out Carpenter badges: Mary Garrett Hay claimed to have seen three Texas delegates wearing them, provoking vehement denials from Pennybacker headquarters. Every state delegation was allowed one representative on the Nominating Committee, and states with divided sympathies—California was reported among them—were lobbied intensively by both camps. Carpenter's publicist predicted victory to the press; Terrell said Pennybacker's nomination was assured. Each side vowed to nominate from the floor if its candidate were not selected.[66]

Ultimately, the Nominating Committee extricated itself from a difficult situation with an unprecedented decision to nominate both candidates. For the record, it cited geographic balance as the rationale and stressed that its meeting had been "most harmonious." The election itself was less so. Civility was openly strained when one of Carpenter's delegates demanded from the convention floor that New York should be entitled to an inspector on the election board because Texas had one. The Texas inspector, Olga Kohlberg of the El Paso Woman's Club, immediately pointed out that New York had a teller and Texas did not, making them even. When New York implied that it doubted Kohlberg's integrity by continuing to press for an inspector, she retorted that Texas would gladly withdraw, eliciting murmurs of sympathetic indignation from the assembly. After voting to keep the original list of inspectors and tellers, the convention elected Pennybacker by a comfortable margin.[67]

Terrell thought two factors had been decisive: a strong candidate and a posture of being "above" politics. Pennybacker's charisma and skill as a public speaker were advantages that her managers had counted on from the beginning.

(Ida Saunders had advised her to "make a short, clear, distinct 'Pennytexas' speech and lay Mrs. C. in the shade!") Equally important, a number of delegates apparently found Mary Garrett Hay's campaign techniques too heavy-handed. Quickly recognizing "that we were no match for our opponents in the game of politics," Terrell proved the contrary by outmaneuvering them. She deliberately adopted a lower profile than Carpenter's people and followed a calculated strategy of "being good, straight & above board."[68]

This was the image clubwomen valued. While presiding over a session on the endowment fund, Pennybacker had drawn an ovation from the crowd by leading Carpenter to the front of the platform and laughingly pledging to serve under her rival if defeated. As the two stood clasping hands, Carpenter affirmed the same: "we are sisters and nothing could make us otherwise."[69] The *General Federation Bulletin* conciliated the defeated candidate's supporters by praising the "fine impression" that Carpenter, "one of the most gifted women in the country and an orator of rare ability," had made at the Biennial. Her address, it noted, had been received with "the greatest interest and delight," a compliment at odds with Mary Terrell's impression that Carpenter lost in part because she spoke from text rather than extemporaneously.[70]

By disavowing and concealing their political side and emphasizing genteel sorority, clubs avoided alienating members who feared participating in "unwomanly" activity. Clubwomen became a force in social reform by essentially the same strategy: disclaiming any intent to "mix in politics" and stressing motherhood as their motivation. "We have no platform unless it is the care of women and children, and the home, the latter meaning the four walls of the city as well as the four walls of brick and mortar," GFWC President Eva Perry Moore proclaimed in 1910. Journalist and clubwoman Rheta Childe Dorr, in a much-quoted metaphor, likened community to home, citizenry to family, and public school to nursery, all of them badly in need of a mother's attention. When critics such as former president Grover Cleveland complained that club life was taking women too far outside their homes, the president of the Dallas Federation of Women's Clubs, could counter that it was precisely "love of home and children" that prompted women's activity.[71]

Women thus appeared in legislative halls as concerned mothers rather than "lobbyists." When the TFWC created a legislative lobbying arm in 1906 it was euphemistically called the Outlook Committee, in accordance with GFWC policy. Clubwomen called petitioning and persuading "educating public opinion" and insisted that their nonpartisanship was proof of being "above politics."[72] Club leaders, as the wives and daughters of influential businessmen and politicians, nevertheless knew the value of good connections and political aptitude. When TFWC President Birdie Robertson Johnson privately solicited suggestions for committee appointments in 1905, she sought the kind of woman "who can go before the legislature if necessary and who has influence."[73]

The GFWC's strategy of studying and debating social problems and waiting for consensus to evolve before endorsing controversial issues brought thousands of apolitical women to public activism. Anna Pennybacker's rise from small-town clubs in rural East Texas to become president of the Texas and General Federations epitomized the development of the South's "new women" in the previous two decades. In the aftermath of the Columbian Exposition, women's club federations formed in every southern state, and by 1910 all had joined the GFWC.[74] Through them, southern women acquired a social vision that extended beyond the community and across the Mason-Dixon line. They learned to think nationally and act locally in pursuit of progressive goals shared with a network of women that extended from New England to the Pacific.

Only three Texas clubs had been represented at the first GFWC Biennial in 1892; two decades later a state federation claiming more than ten thousand members successfully promoted one of its own for the national presidency. The GFWC had not yet endorsed suffrage, but the members had advanced through the primary school of literary clubs into the university of politics. They were committed to an ever-lengthening agenda of municipal housekeeping and social welfare reforms. And they could read in the *General Federation Bulletin* in the autumn of 1912 articles on the roles that women were playing in the Democratic, Republican, Socialist, and Progressive parties. The latter's special outreach to the network of women's voluntary associations was evident in Jane Addams's "Why Every Woman Should be a Progressive," which included a clip-and-mail membership form.[75] Avowed suffragists were not yet numerous in Texas and the other southern states, but "the coming woman in politics" had already arrived.

Domestic Revolutionaries 2

THE EXPANSION of women's public culture in the 1890s brought correspondingly new motivations for voluntarist politics. Victorian women had ventured into public space on the strength of superior moral virtue, a useful strategy that Progressive Era women did not by any means abandon. But by the 1890s new "scientific" approaches to homemaking and childrearing, topics of intense interest to women's study clubs, opened additional routes to social activism by linking the private home to society. Middle-class women, united in believing that home and children were a natural female responsibility, discovered in the emerging field of household economics the rationale for claiming new public roles as municipal housekeepers. Fired with the progressives' passion for efficiency and scientific rationalism, the first home economists sought to free women from drudgery and elevate traditional women's work into a professional coequality with that of men.

Such women were not home economists as the term has since come to be used. Ellen Swallow Richards, the guiding spirit of the early household economics movement, taught "sanitary chemistry" at Massachusetts Institute of Technology and specialized in analyzing drinking water. At the University of Chicago her former student, Marion Talbot, offered courses in "sanitary science"—including the new germ theory of disease—through the department of sociology. From such programs, Richards and Talbot hoped, would come "trained women" equal to the challenges of urban life in the approaching new century, whether they chose to pursue careers or marry and rear families. (Few people thought women could do both.) Bertha Palmer articulated this vision when she opened the Woman's Building at the Columbian Exposition. Her speech stressed the need to educate women not only for industrial and professional work, but for "enlightened" homemaking. Subsequent discussion of the subject in the congress on household economics led its organizers to found the

National Household Economics Association to promote housekeeping "on a scientific and hygenic basis."[1]

The new science and technology displayed at the Columbian Exposition suggested the complexity of such homemaking. In the Massachusetts Building, Ellen Richards demonstrated the link between food and energy. Visitors to her Rumford Kitchen (named for Massachusetts-born Count Rumford of Bavaria, who had pioneered the study of nutrition) could observe every preparation stage of the foods offered for lunch and dinner in the kitchen's adjoining cafe. The amounts of protein, fat, and carbohydrate—terms then unfamiliar to the public—were printed beside each dish on the menu, along with the amount of nutrients it supplied toward the body's daily requirement. Charts and exhibits illustrated the chemical composition of basic foods and of the human body; a model home chemistry lab showed housewives how to test food and water for impurities.[2]

In the model kitchen of the Woman's Building, home economists gave cooking demonstrations twice a day on a gas stove. The Horticultural Building featured a complete model house in which gas also powered a refrigerator, a hot water heater, and an automatic dishwasher. The home on display in the Electrical Building promised even more: stove, hot plate, washing machine, iron, dishwasher, fans, and carpet sweeper all operated electrically. Most of the women who marveled at these innovations cooked on coal and wood stoves and cooled their butter and milk with blocks of ice; gas and electricity were still used mainly for illumination in the homes of the wealthy. But by the end of the century gas stoves, water heaters, and furnaces were being marketed on a limited scale. Chairing the first Lake Placid Conference on Household Economics in 1899, Ellen Richards announced that its mission would be "to raise teachers and housewives to an appreciation of what the same kind of scientific intelligence might do for them that had planned railroads and machines."[3]

The proponents of reinventing homemaking as an applied science always included some voices hopeful that elevating the housewife's status might keep women from running after careers.[4] A larger number, however, had exactly the opposite in mind: they envisioned household economics as a partial solution to women's limited career options, which lagged far behind their greatly expanded access to higher education. Texas women were among the privileged minority of southern daughters not barred from attending their state universities; the University of Texas had been coeducational since its founding in 1883. Women made up slightly more than a third of its enrollment in the 1890s, when the State Council of Women of Texas nevertheless pointed out the need for a state vocational college for women.[5] Most business and professional careers remained closed to women, and those who graduated from the University of Texas had few realistic prospects beyond marriage or teaching.

Numerous educators within the Association of Collegiate Alumnae (now the American Association of University Women) therefore advocated supplementing pure academics with vocational courses like business methods and household economics. Largely due to student interest, the latter had by 1910 gained a place in the curriculum at more than one hundred colleges and universities.[6] Although the content and value of such courses was by no means uniform, Ellen Richards and Marion Talbot envisioned more than turning out cooks who understood chemistry. As chair of the ACA's Committee on the Economic Efficiency of College Women, Richards advocated scientific and technological training that would fit women to help solve the problems of industrial society. She contended that public health menaces—dirty markets, unsanitary dairies, garbage-choked alleys—could be controlled "if all housewives would combine in carrying out the knowledge which some of them have and which all may have." Volunteers could work through their clubs; professional women would put a new face on government authority. Slum landlords would find that "when [the tenement housewife] has a woman sanitary inspector to appeal to, matters will take on a different aspect."[7]

This was the heart of Richards's agenda: professionals and trained housewives would collaborate in raising the level of public health and making cities fit habitations. The new college courses would prepare young women for specialized work, while their mothers educated themselves through study clubs and translated their knowledge into civic activism. Clubwomen were eager to cooperate when the National Household Economics Association introduced the subject into the program at the GFWC Biennial in 1896. By the next convention the GFWC had created a Committee on Household Economics and Sanitary Science; eventually this committee absorbed the NHEA.[8]

A syllabus for clubwomen was one of the earliest projects of Ellen Richards's annual Lake Placid Conference (which became the National Home Economics Association in 1908). After a Massachusetts domestic scientist named Maria Daniel reported on her enthusiastically received teaching-demonstration tours in Texas in 1903 and 1904 (sponsored by the TFWC's Committee on Household Economics and Sanitary Science) the Lake Placid Conference extended membership to all household economics chairwomen in the GFWC. The recommended booklists laid out a course of serious reading; Richards suggested titles such as *How to Drain a House, Home Sanitation, The Chemistry of Cooking and Cleaning,* and *Food Materials and Their Adulteration.*[9]

Household economics led middle-class women directly into municipal housekeeping. Learning the dangers of living in a house that drained toward the well, carried drinking water in lead pipes, and lacked vents and fans to remove airborne microbes that spread diseases such as tuberculosis was a first step. Discovering the interconnectedness of domestic and municipal sanitation followed. The link was readily apparent to mothers who dreaded the summer "sickly season," when infants and young children were at greatest risk of death from high bacterial levels in milk and water. The need to eliminate dirt and germs at the source helped women redefine the city as a larger home in need of "outdoor" housekeeping and expand a private role into a public one.

The Dallas Federation of Women's Clubs launched a crusade for a water filtration plant after the women studied and found wanting the authorities' plan to improve the municipal water system. The city fathers proposed building a new reservoir and allowing the new water from purer sources to mix with the supply in the old reservoirs, and treating the whole with chemicals when circumstances required it—in other words, if a typhoid epidemic broke out. The city mothers were appalled and undertook a three-year campaign to persuade the male electorate to approve a bond issue for a filtration plant. When the water facility opened in 1913, the clubwomen set to work to secure a sewage disposal plant.[10]

In Galveston, the Women's Health Protective Association paid for a sanitation survey of the city. It demanded and got sanitation ordinances governing groceries and bakeries, and one requiring property occupiers to clean regularly the abutting sidewalks and alleys. WHPA volunteer committees checked to see that the ordinances were enforced.[11] Such women, following Ellen Richards's advice to take their housekeeping to the streets and markets, appropriated for themselves a broad new authority for public activism. By virtue of education and experience, "trained women" asserted themselves uniquely qualified to guide the government toward higher standards of "housekeeping."

Enthroning science and efficiency as their household gods, turn-of-the century women attempted to reshape domesticity in a form that would strengthen their position inside the home and their influence outside it. The patriarchal husband, to whose comforts and wishes the Victorian wife had been expected to render service, was nowhere to be found in the new housekeeping treatises. Household economics put the husband in the wings as an invisible source of income and moved the wife to center stage with new roles as budget analyst, sanitary engineer, and dietician—with time left over for herself. The efficient modern woman "believes that the laundry, the bakery and cannery have taken the place of eighteenth-century methods," announced an article in *Texas Motherhood Magazine.* "She investigates and tests to find the most wholesome and sanitary conditions and then buys intelligently," using the time saved to pursue her own extra-domestic interests.[12]

Mass production and distribution also added a social dimension to the housewife's role. Responsible buying, as advocated by the National Consumers' League, was as important as finding good value and high quality. Marion Talbot and Sophonisba P. Breckinridge in *The Modern Household* emphasized "the household as a social unit," pointing out that "those who spend determine the fate of those who make." Buying clothing should be more than a matter of style and price, they advised. The consumer should consider whether the garment was made by sweated labor. Was it produced under sanitary conditions? Did the workers receive a "reasonably adequate" wage? Were they permitted to join a union?[13]

Individual homemakers could hardly obtain such information unassisted; they needed to form local consumers' leagues or make such investigations a club project. As voluntary associations became more involved in public housekeeping, they began to criticize the old-fashioned, stay-at-home, "domestic" woman as more misguided than devoted. Isadore Callaway, whose "Pauline Periwinkle" columns in the *Dallas Morning News* had been promoting household economics since the late 1890s, advised women to spend *less* time in the kitchen. Most men hardly noticed what was on their plates as long as it was filling, and "in this age of dyspepsia the woman who knows how to make more than three kinds of cake knows too much anyway, and ought to be suppressed." Parlor crafts—"the mania for gilding bread-toasters to hold photographs"—and endless hours of fancy sewing had even less merit.[14] The new housekeeping merged indoors and outdoors, private and public spaces. A conscientious mother's time was better spent helping investigate the dairies that supplied her children's milk than in embellishing layettes with embroidery and lace.

"Scientific" housekeeping likewise enabled women to contend for recognition in the "culture of professionalism" created by white-collar males seeking to upgrade the status of their occupations with formal educational and credentialing requirements. Whether the home economics departments women established within the academy should be considered beachheads or ghettoes depends very much upon the point in time from which they are viewed. Texas women pressing for their own state vocational college and a household economics department at the University of Texas saw both as beachheads, hard-won female spaces pried from reluctant state legislators and university administrators.

When WCTU president Helen Stoddard prepared a bill in 1897 proposing a state college for white women, the Grange had already failed three times in pursuit of the same legislative goal. The Grangers had been seeking vocational opportunities for country girls, who were barred from the Agricultural and Mechanical College of Texas (now Texas A&M University). Stoddard modified the original bill (modeled on the enabling legislation for Mississippi's State Industrial Institute and College for Women) to make household economics a centerpiece of the curriculum. The new provision specified that the college would be required to offer instruction in "scientific and practical cooking, including a chemical study of foods," as well as "practical housekeeping," nursing, and "the care and culture of children."[15]

At the turn of the century, before the existence of packaged foods, nutritional labels, vitamin supplements, and antiseptic household cleaners, these phrases were invested with meanings now somewhat difficult to appreciate. "Scientific and practical cooking" taught the home economics gospel of eating for health instead of pleasure, a concept not always well received by those who had few other gratifications. ("I'd ruther eat what I'd ruther," a Hull House neighbor told Jane Addams, turning up her nose at the cheap, nutritious food sold from the settlement's public kitchen modeled on the prototype Ellen Richards had established in Boston. "I don't want to eat what's good for me.") Nutrition research even suggested that the solution to women's long struggle with male intemperance might lie in their own kitchens. The national WCTU's new Department of Scientific Cooking and Nutrition distributed a pamphlet by Ellen Richards suggesting that a balanced, energy-producing diet was likely to reduce craving for stimulants.[16]

The "care and culture of children," too, had special significance at a time when 18 percent died before age five, two-thirds of them before their first birthday.[17] The biographical directories of Texas club leaders reveal how common was the loss of a child, even among these elite women. Gastroenteritis killed many infants and accounted for the progressives' almost obsessive concern with proper baby feeding. Every mother was essentially her own pediatrician; few doctors yet specialized in pediatrics, and the mortality rate of physicians' children was only a few percentage points below the national average. Women held life and health in their hands, "Pauline Periwinkle" pointed out, yet homemaking and motherhood were "classed with the unskilled trades, to be learned only by hard experience."[18]

Isadore Callaway, who penned these sentiments, was hardly a conservative apologist for full-time motherhood. A professional journalist all her life, she had been an editor of Dr. John Harvey Kellogg's *Good Health* magazine in Battle Creek, Michigan, and a staff writer for the *Toledo Commercial* before coming to the *Dallas Morning News*.[19] No Sarah Josepha Hale or Catharine Beecher pursuing her own vocation while prescribing domesticity for other women, Callaway was an outspoken suffragist, a champion of careers for women, and a wickedly witty critic of gender inequality. For Callaway and Stoddard, a former mathematics instructor at Fort Worth University, household economics was an integral part of their feminist protest against women's subordinate status.

The Texas legislature saw it in precisely that light. Helen Stoddard found that the domestic science provisions provoked the "fiercest" of all the "bitter battles" fought over the women's college bill. In claiming public acknowledgment for their domestic work, women implicitly demanded recognition of their worth and sought to advance their status. Legislators insisted that there was no science of homemaking, that instinct made women good wives and mothers. Stoddard, who had buried a child, countered that untrained maternal instinct kept the graveyards filled with babies. The men's real objection to the bill, she suspected, was that "they saw female rights written all over it!"[20]

It took three biennial legislative sessions of hard lobbying before women's groups finally secured their Girls' Industrial College (now Texas Woman's University) in 1901. In 1899, the WCTU was joined by the Texas Woman's Press Association and the TFWC. "Pauline Periwinkle" promoted the college in her column and printed the text of the bill (a practice that she would follow for numerous others that the TFWC supported over the years). In 1901 Eleanor Brackenridge took charge of legislative liason work for the TFWC, whose more affluent, fast-growing membership gave the organization more political clout than the WCTU. Even with the prestige of Brackenridge's name, the Democratic party's endorsement, and the combined pressure of the women's organizations, the Girls' Industrial College bill barely passed; the presiding officers in both chambers had to cast tie-breaking votes.[21]

Helen Stoddard was the only woman appointed to the thirteen-member commission charged with selecting a location for the college. She served as secretary through fourteen site visits and seventy-six ballots. The honor eventually went to the small town of Denton, near Fort Worth, which had the moral advantage of being saloon-free by local option. (It is not recorded if the reception the Denton Woman's Shakespeare Club gave for the commissioners affected the decision. The group literally emptied its treasury and had to assess each woman a fifteen-cent head tax to cover the bills.) Stoddard, Eleanor Brackenridge, and future TFWC president Birdie Johnson became the first female college regents in the state when they were appointed to the seven-member board. Brackenridge was elected vice president and Stoddard secretary.[22]

The campaign to create the Girls' Industrial School (renamed the College of Industrial Arts in 1905) and the ongoing struggle to secure adequate funding created the state's first coalition of activists dedicated to advancing women's interests. The three women regents kept their organizations lobbying at full strength for the financially shaky institution. Every biennial legislative session found Stoddard (who headed the WCTU until 1907) and the TFWC's president and education committee chairwoman at the capitol, asking for larger appropriations and expanded facilities. They were backed by members throughout the state who undertook grassroots letter-writing campaigns. The lack of dormitories that forced students to seek expensive town lodging was the most immediate concern; it took the women three additional legislative sessions to pry loose the money for the first one, Stoddard Hall. They headed off attempts to cut faculty salaries, eliminate the physician's position, and eviscerate the liberal arts portion of the curriculum. Appropriations for summer sessions were granted only after Eleanor Brackenridge personally put up a thousand dollars to fund one in 1907.[23]

The TFWC made the college an official project. Every club was directed to promote the C.I.A. locally; to facilitate the task, the federation assumed the cost of sending each one a copy of the quarterly college bulletin. During Regent Birdie Johnson's 1905–7 term as TFWC president, every club president received a copy of the board of regents' report, and the federation's Committee on Education made a campus inspection visit and a full report in convention. So close were the ties between the C.I.A. and the TFWC that the college bulletin printed speeches by federation presidents and reports of its committees in special "women's club" issues.[24]

In defending and promoting the college, many otherwise conservative clubwomen found themselves for the first time agitating a woman's cause. They were keenly aware that "their" college was the poor stepsister of the large and prosperous Agricultural and Mechanical College, and the competition for influence soon exposed underlying gender conflicts. As they kept a watchful eye on the physical plant and curriculum, organized white women also built the College of Industrial Arts into a woman's space from which they would challenge the authority and dominance of the men at A&M.

African American women experienced home economics very differently, the consequence of the state's stinginess and of white southerners' refusal to admit them to the privileges of ladyhood. They were very much a part of A&M's "Negro" counterpart, Prairie View State Normal and Industrial College, modeled on Hampton Institute in Virginia, which had been established to teach practical skills to the freedmen. As Glenda Gilmore has pointed out in her study of North Carolina, African Americans would have been unlikely to choose single sex institutions that denied admission to women even if state legislatures had been willing to fund them. Most African Americans realized that the majority of black women would have to spend part or all of a lifetime in paid labor; coeducation was the norm at both teachers' and industrial colleges.[25]

Consequently, Prairie View, like Hampton, and later Tuskegee Institute in Alabama, was coeducational and domestic science was included in its vocational training mission. The first classes in cooking, sewing, and hygiene were introduced in the 1880s, apparently at the instigation of the school's male president. Young black women were being trained "for the duties and responsibilities of home and social life," while white women were still pressuring the legislature to create the C.I.A. When Prairie View adopted a college-level curriculum in 1908, the Female Industrial Department offered a two-year course in dress-making and a one-year course in cooking; the B.A. in Domestic Art and Science was approved in 1916.[26]

Black clubwomen promoted scientific homemaking with as much zeal as their white counterparts, investing it with special significance in their agenda of racial progress. They urged elevated standards of homemaking—"better homes"—as the bedrock of community improvement and the cultivation of "finer womanhood" as a strategic response to white supremacy. "If there is anything we are lacking as a race, it is our ideas of home life," argued Tuskegee's Margaret Murray Washington. Too few African American women knew enough about nutrition, effective childrearing practices, or domestic moral values because under slavery they had been "left to drift and pick up their ideals and ideas by chance." Since both sexes espoused a common goal of advancing the race by inculcating ideals of respectability, home economics was not a contested part of the curriculum at Prairie View.[27]

White women, however, continued to struggle against male resistance as they tried to persuade the University of Texas to authorize a home economics program. The TFWC's Education Committee, which first broached the idea to the board of regents in 1904, was told that no money was available. The clubwomen eventually succeeded through persistence and good connections: Eleanor Brackenridge was a member of the Education Committee and her brother George was a University of Texas regent. George Brackenridge removed the financial impediment by donating the money himself. To direct the new School of Domestic Economy, the university hired Mary Edna Gearing, a Columbia graduate who had designed and administered the domestic science program for the Houston city schools before joining the faculty at New York University. So many coeds signed up for the first courses in January 1912 that the temporary wooden building housing the department had to be enlarged during the summer and two more instructors hired.[28]

Mary Gearing's career at the University of Texas exemplified the productive interaction that early domestic reformers hoped would develop between professional home economists and laywomen. When she returned to Texas, Gearing, who had been a member of the Ladies' Reading Club of Houston, rejoined the TFWC and served in various offices, including chair of the Education Committee. One of her first innovations, launching Home Economics Week as part of the university's extension program, brought clubwomen to campus. Over the years, nationally known speakers as diverse as the president of the New York School of Fine and Applied Art and Florence Kelley of the National Consumers' League (who spoke on child labor in the textile industry) were invited to discuss

Mary Edna Gearing established the School of Domestic Economy at the University of Texas in 1912, eventually becoming the first woman full professor and department chair. Gearing used the university's Extension Department to link home economics with municipal housekeeping, instituting an annual week of lectures and demonstrations that drew clubwomen to campus. (Courtesy of the Prints and Photographs Collection, Center for American History, University of Texas at Austin)

indoor and outdoor housekeeping. Six hundred women and four hundred co-eds attended the first Home Economics Week in 1912, which proved so popular that plans for spinoffs soon formed. In 1915 Fort Worth clubwomen raised the money to finance their own Home Economics Week, with the University of Texas providing the exhibits and speakers; by the following year, women in Dallas and Houston were making inquiries.[29]

Organized women saw Gearing's School of Domestic Economy, like the College of Industrial Arts, as a training ground for social reform.[30] Mary Brown Work, who chaired the TFWC's Committee on Home Economics and was married to the C.I.A.'s president, stressed that the college prepared young women to be socially responsible citizens. "This does not necessarily mean that the school makes suffragettes of its pupils," she emphasized, "but the course in social economics is such as to create enthusiasm and willingness on the part of the girls to enter reform work in their home communities upon leaving school."[31] To Work and her colleagues in voluntary associations, the C.I.A. and Mary Gearing's department at the University of Texas were essential as bases of support for "trained women," and they aspired to make them bases for a new women's public authority as well. The campaign for pure food legislation is a case in point.

The commercial food processing industry furnished abundant proof for Progressive women's contention that modern living had extended the housekeeper's domain far beyond her own four walls. The city wife, who did not churn her own butter, make her own jam, or collect her own eggs, could not be certain what she was serving for breakfast. She had no way of determining if the butter she bought was a "rectified" combination of rancid product churned again with fresh milk. The raspberry jam could be a concoction of apple pulp, dye, flavoring, and grass seeds; the "fresh" eggs might have languished for several weeks in cold storage. The ground coffee could be adulterated with cheap bran. Upton Sinclair's *The Jungle* revealed particularly gruesome possibilities for the sausage: ground up bone and gristle by design, packing house floor sweepings and the carcasses of poisoned rats by accident.

Some preservatives and adulterants merely swindled the consumer; others were potentially dangerous. Dr. Harvey Wiley, the U.S. Department of Agriculture's chief chemist, was systematically identifying these with the help of a "poison squad" of volunteer diners in the basement of the agriculture building in Washington. While muckraking journalists documented in nauseating detail the abuses of the commerical food processers, women's clubs made pure food a priority of their household economics committees. They channeled their concern into an alliance with Dr. Wiley, who was leading the fight for a federal pure food and drug law. By 1904 the GFWC's Household Economics Committee had spun off a standing committee on pure food, which Wiley supplied with adulterated samples for exhibits. The bulletin that he wrote for the committee to distribute, *Some Forms of Food Adulteration and Simple Methods for Their Detection,* included tests that women could do in their kitchens.[32]

In return, women's clubs publicized the problem and flooded Congress with petitions and constituent mail. After the session on Household Economics adjourned at the 1906 GFWC Biennial, the entire assembly—delegates, visitors, officers, and committee members—sent telegrams to their Congressmen urging passage of the pending legislation that became the Pure Food and Drugs Act of 1906.[33]

Through its state chairwomen, the GFWC's Pure Food Committee had already surveyed the existing pure food legislation in the states; it next moved to support the federal law by promoting the need for reciprocal state action. Texas was among those that had no pure food law—for humans. It did have a recent statute forbidding adulterants in commercial livestock feeds, which to women seemed proof that government deliberately ignored domestic welfare. "Pauline Periwinkle" pointed out that women were caught in a double bind: as a disfranchised class they could not vote for pure food laws, and their husbands, who could, stood by indifferently while cities went without food inspectors and babies sickened on contaminated milk. It would hardly have taken a Congress of *mothers* seventeen years to produce the Pure Food Law, she noted tartly, but "men have shut up one eye and squinted so hard at commerical interests with the other, that they see little else. . . . The wonder is that doctors and undertakers and tombstone manufacturers don't join with the grocers in defeating measures bound to injure their trade."[34]

Women expounded variations on this theme throughout the Progressive Era: men were ignoring problems that women had the knowledge and the will to solve, but not the political power. Isadore Callaway's "Periwinkle" columns articulated their frustrations. She printed the USDA instructions for sterilizing milk at home and suggested a novel strategy for drawing male attention to the food problem. While her husband was slathering a fluffy hot biscuit with butter, the wife might innocently read aloud a newspaper account (saved because she knew he would be *so* interested) describing how "stale, rancid, dirty and unsalable butter in various degrees of putrefaction" is "renovated," that is, strained, filtered, churned with sweet milk and sold quickly before the effect wears off and it begins to stink. "And if that doesn't fetch him, tell him about the London chemist who learned to make very good 'commercial' butter out of ordinary city sewage."[35]

The pure food problem drew women into public protest and concerted political action. Callaway's sister members of the Dallas Woman's Forum, a large new club whose nine "departments" included one devoted to home economics

and pure food, pressured the Dallas city council into passing the first municipal pure food ordinance in the state and then took on the grocers' lobby to keep
the effective date from being pushed back. At the same time the TFWC, following the General Federation's directive, began formulating plans to secure a state
pure food law. Dallas-based *Holland's Magazine* helped lay the groundwork
with a series of muckraking articles on the food industry in Texas that began appearing in the fall of 1906 and ran throughout the winter 1907 legislative session.
Holland's discovered formaldehyde in milk samples and meat colored with red
aniline dye and doctored with boric acid and borax, which Dr. Wiley had recommended banning after testing it on his "poison squad." In twenty-three of
thirty-one Texas cities surveyed, meat samples were found to contain such
preservatives and dyes.[36]

The TFWC and the WCTU joined forces in 1906–7 to lobby for a pure food
bill and a state dairy and food commissioner to enforce it. Mary Brown Work,
chair of the TFWC's Committee on Home Economics, took the lead. Bearing in
mind the advice of the General Federation's home economics chairwoman, who
urged state committees to secure enforcement provisions that would insulate
their pure food commissioners from politics, the women's lobby argued against
locating the office in the state health department. Since the department "had
been in the hands of politicians for years," Work contended, clearly, the commissioner's headquarters should be at the female College of Industrial Arts in
Denton. "Imagine politics lifting its head under the close gaze of several hundred pairs of women's eyes!"[37]

Although this was traditional and appealing rhetoric, a good deal more was
at stake than simply fencing off the commissioner from lobbyists and politicians. The same purpose could have been served by locating the office at the
Agricultural and Mechanical College, yet this the women's lobby adamantly opposed. They offered subtly gendered arguments in the guise of simple logic: the
law protecting children's food should be enforced from the women's college,
since the equivalent statute for commercial livestock feed was enforced from
A&M; the girls at the C.I.A. were the state's future cooks, the boys at A&M
merely future eaters. At stake were power and space for women. They hoped that
the office could be informally linked to the college's home economics curriculum, which included coursework in the chemical analysis of foods; it might
serve as an auxiliary laboratory that would help prepare young women for careers as food inspectors.[38] The greatest advantage of all was unspoken: Mary
Work's husband was president of the college, and the TFWC and WCTU between them held three seats on the board of regents.

To succeed, the women needed a strong ally in the legislature, and they found
one in Representative W. L. Blanton of Gainesville, who had tried unsuccessfully

to pass a pure food bill in 1905 and needed supporters himself. After conferring with Mary Work and the Home Economics Committee, Blanton changed his original text to specify that the dairy and food commissioner would operate from the College of Industrial Arts. In return, Work coordinated a massive publicity and lobbying campaign for the bill. Even before the legislature convened in January 1907 she began urging senators and representatives to support the Blanton bill, particularly the provision locating the inspector's office at the C.I.A. Directing all clubs to investigate their community food and sanitation ordinances, Work stressed that she needed their reports "promptly" in order to get the information to the press during the legislative session. She suggested that clubwomen interest their local papers in the issue as well.[39]

Articles by Work and Helen Stoddard appeared in *Holland's Magazine,* along with formal endorsements of the Blanton bill from the officers of the TFWC and WCTU. Members of both organizations circulated the legislative petitions printed in the magazine; Work instructed them to seek signatures from grocers and druggists especially, which would carry more weight with the legislators. "Pauline Periwinkle" championed the Blanton bill in her column, and Mary Work even led a delegation to the National Association of Grocers convention in Dallas to ask for an endorsement. The TFWC's formal lobbying arm, the Outlook Committee, directed clubwomen to send a barrage of telegrams to the capitol as soon as the bill was reported out of committee by the press, and to pressure the male voters in their families to do the same.[40]

It was quickly apparent that securing a law would be relatively easy and that the real issue would be whether the inspector's office should be conceded to the women's college. An amendment to give jurisdiction to the state health department failed, but another transferring the commission to the men's Agricultural and Mechanical College succeeded easily. From the women's point of view, this was even worse; at A&M the commissioner would be completely inaccessible to them. Their allies succeeded in having the unamended bill brought up in the Senate, but it lost decisively there too. On an hour's notice Mary Work caught a train to Austin; while she buttonholed senators, the call went out for female reinforcements. With unremitting effort from the women's lobby, the Pure Food Law of 1907 passed without the A&M amendment.[41]

Winning this political tug-of-war over the commissioner's office brought organized women significant immediate benefits. They secured the appointment of Dallas chemistry teacher J. S. Abbott as dairy and food commissioner, and with his active cooperation set out to make sanitary inspection the province of "trained women." The southern tradition of minimal government and local autonomy, which mitigated against the growth of state bureaucracies, made collaboration with volunteers essential if the law were to have any effect. To compensate for the state's parsimony in allotting the department a budget of only five thousand dollars and no personnel except a stenographer, the TFWC constructed an extra-legal force of female inspectors to serve as unpaid field staff. Without them, Abbott's real influence would hardly have extended beyond Dallas and Fort Worth.[42]

In essence, he and the indefatigable Mary Work arranged for the new Pure Food Law to be enforced through the home economics committees of local women's clubs. Abbott deputized each club's appointee and supplied guidelines and scorecards; the clubwoman collected the food samples, sending nonperishables to him and asking local physicians to analyze perishable specimens. The volunteer donated her time but Abbott's office reimbursed her for the price of the food. Within a year, twenty-six clubs had named volunteer inspectors and four more were studying the idea. It proved so popular that pure food was detached from the TFWC's Committee on Home Economics and given independent committee status—under Mary Work, of course.[43]

The volunteer clubwomen inspectors were particularly attentive to contamination through unsanitary storage and handling practices, which were evident to any woman who had worked through a home economics study syllabus. They reported their findings to boards of health, where such existed; in one case, when this failed to bring results, the clubwomen successfully threatened the offending vendor with a boycott. In smaller communities the pure food committee of the local woman's club substituted for a health department. Women found themselves unexpectedly welcomed by shopkeepers competing for trade who recognized the advantage of the woman's club seal of approval. Club inspectors reported receiving phone calls from vendors who wanted their premises examined and certified as sanitary; the women even went inside meat markets and demonstrated the proper way to clean refrigerators.[44]

Interest, aptitude, and opportunity might have converged to make sanitary inspection the new vocation for women that Ellen Richards envisioned. The College of Industrial Arts was graduating young women with the requisite knowledge of chemistry, and even by traditional definitions food inspection was not difficult to justify as "woman's work." Abbott ingeniously suggested that women inspectors would be more productive than men because "in this as in other things, a woman can make $5 go as far as the average man will make $25 go," an expectation that Mary Work advised clubwomen to meet. But when he recommended that a clubwoman be appointed food sanitation officer in Fort Worth, the city commissioners were predictably dismissive: "It takes a man." Women could be volunteer deputy inspectors in small towns, where the work was unpaid and they were not competing with men for positions. In large cities with municipal health ordinances and paid enforcement officers, "it takes a man" meant that positions involving a salary or political preferment were reserved for men.[45]

In such instances women created their own auxiliary authority, using voluntary associations to gain access to public commercial spaces. The Women's Health Protective Association of Galveston was a notable example. Initially formed to assist survivors of the devastating 1900 hurricane, it stayed together after the emergency because the city health department was run by an "old fossil" with assistants who were "relics of the stone age," as the *Galveston Daily News* said bluntly. The WHPA sent its own inspectors to dairies and markets and filed lawsuits against dairies whose licenses the city had threatened to revoke without following through. In 1915 it pressured the city commissioners into hiring an additional inspector by offering to pay his salary themselves.[46] (The record does not reveal whether there was a female candidate for the job.)

In Houston, the local branch of the Housewives' League, a national, New York-based association founded to extend "higher housekeeping" to every place of business where women shopped for their families, performed a similar function. Organized in 1914 by clubwomen, the Houston Housewives' League soon had fifteen hundred members and instituted a system of bakery and dairy inspections by districts. Its Sanitation Committee accompanied the city health inspector on his regular milk rounds. While he scored the dairies according to the municipal health code—which the Housewives' League was lobbying to strengthen—the committeewomen scored them according to the League's considerably higher standards, which most failed to meet. The Sanitation Committee posted the dairy scores in the exhibit hall at City Auditorium, where the Housewives' League met each week. It advised women not to buy from dairies that scored under 60 percent and checked to make sure that dairies with passing scores were not buying milk from any on the failing list. Businesses that met sanitation and fair price standards were entitled to display the Housewives' League symbol.[47]

Rural women found the empowering potential of household economics much more difficult to realize. Living on isolated farms, they were unlikely to organize into clubs and other voluntary associations that proliferated in towns. Nor did they benefit from the labor-saving appliances displayed at the Columbian Exposition; farm women continued to cook with wood and haul water from wells for decades. As late as 1928–30, a study of five Central Texas counties revealed that less than 9 percent had electricity and nearly half were without a telephone or a daily newspaper. "The isolation of the farm-dwelling woman is marked," concluded the University of Texas labor economist who conducted the investigation. "The man-centered family is less definitely undermined in the rural economic system."[48]

With no separation between home and workplace, the husband-father directed the family labor force and controlled whatever profits resulted. Improving the land and livestock in the hope of producing larger surpluses took priority over increasing domestic comforts, which waited on a series of good crops and "extra" money. For many women, such a time never arrived. President Theodore Roosevelt's Country Life Commission called attention in 1909 to the need for more modern conveniences and household comforts and for organizations that would help relieve women's loneliness and isolation. Four years later a U.S. Department of Agriculture mail survey of fifty-five thousand rural women drew abundant complaints about the hard, monotonous life, especially in the South. A Texas farm wife took time from making catsup and soap to report that she had not been to a lecture, play, or show since her marriage and even neighborly visits were a luxury.[49]

The farm family's "man-centeredness" was strikingly evident during shopping trips to town, which clubwomen observed with a mixture of sympathy (for the wife) and irritation. The farmer had ample space in which to combine business and socializing: he could linger at the cotton gin, the blacksmith shop, the feed and grain store, the bank, the hardware store, and—if he had the inclination and the money—the tavern. His wife, with children in tow, had almost no place to go after making her few necessary purchases. "Pauline Periwinkle" described the farm wives and their broods huddled in the crowded stores, sitting wearily on hot curbs, and wandering the sidewalks toting packages and fretful babies as they waited for "him" to reappear; there was no going home until "he" was ready.[50]

For middle-class town women accustomed to broad personal autonomy such scenes touched a nerve, and clubs in a number of states, including Texas, reacted by fitting up "rest rooms" for country women. Equipped up with a stove, tables, chairs, magazines, and books, rest rooms were sheltered spaces where farm wives could eat lunch, make a cup of tea, nurse babies, and put small children down for naps. The GFWC, noting that the club movement was barely visible in the country, made rural outreach a special concern. By 1913 the TFWC had established a Committee on Rural Life under Mary Gearing, who at the following year's state convention outlined a vision of club-sponsored rest rooms as potential sites of commercial and cultural exchange. Country women could market their fresh eggs and clean butter directly to clubwomen, who in turn would introduce them to club life.[51]

Rural women did not, however, flock to the club movement. They took their own route to self-improvement and social advocacy through the International Congress of Farm Women and its state affiliate, the Texas Farm Women. Led by Benigna G. Kalb, it was subdivided into county and community councils. Like the TFWC the Texas Farm Women restricted membership to white women and a number of its concerns—community improvement, health and sanitation, school quality, and traveling libraries—mirrored those of clubwomen. A Committee on State Colleges and Experiment Stations monitored agricultural research to determine its value to women. The organization's "Declaration of Faith" implicitly criticized the patriarchal dominance of country households, calling for "a fair division of labor and reward in the farm family."[52]

The bridge that joined club and farm women in mutual advocacy was home economics, which unexpectedly set off a battle between the sexes after Congress created the Agricultural Extension Service through the Smith-Lever Act in 1914. Government agriculturalists on demonstration farms had been helping southern farmers battle the boll weevil for more than a decade; the Smith-Lever Act formalized and expanded their role in encouraging scientific farming. Underwritten by federal matching funds, the Extension Service operated from state land grant colleges and divided its programs along gender lines: agriculture for men taught by male agents and home demonstration for women under female agents. State directors had complete authority to decide how funds should be allocated between the agricultural extension and home demonstration sides of the program.

Below the Mason-Dixon line the extension service was further compartmentalized by race, with each state director free to determine what, if any, percentage of Smith-Lever money would be spent on "Negro work." Black home demonstration agents thus worked in isolation from white women in the same positions. At the same time, they experienced more freedom to cross gender boundaries; the Extension Service did not enforce the separation between men's and women's work as rigidly among black agents. In Texas, Mary Evelyn V. Hunter initially carried the entire load of "Negro" home demonstration. Appointed in 1915, Hunter and two black men chosen as extension agents, worked together to launch agricultural extension in the old plantation districts of East Texas.[53]

For Mary Evelyn Hunter, the task of making life easier for rural black women was inseparable from the larger challenge of helping entire families improve their standard of living. Focusing on tenancy as the cause of poverty and rootlessness that kept African American families from educating their children and taking an interest in the community, Hunter initiated an "Own Your Own Home Movement" as the centerpiece of her agenda. After gaining a family's confidence, Hunter would demonstrate how to make whatever she thought the home most needed. "I next had a close talk with the family regarding their financial problems," she recalled, "and then made several recommendations regarding home improvement and farm management. After several visits, I saw a great gain in hope and prosperity."[54] Of necessity, Hunter worked both sides of agricultural extension, advising families on money and farm management, as well as teaching canning, sewing, and homemaking.

Among whites, however, the more rigid separation of the male and female sides of agricultural extension almost immediately generated conflict. Women's organizations accepted the USDA's gender delineations as logical and natural, but they protested second-place status for women's work. As the GFWC's Home Economics Committee and the popular national women's magazine, *The Delineator,* surveyed the states, it quickly became apparent that much more Smith-Lever money was being invested in men's work than in women's. Virtually all states were designating the lion's share of the funds to the agricultural side, teaching farmers to produce better crops and livestock. Home demonstration for farm wives, which could include poultry raising, vegetable gardening, canning and preserving, child care, cooking, sewing—anything that would bring women small sums of personal cash or improve home life—was a lower priority. The percentage of money allotted to the domestic side varied by state, from as little as one-tenth or less up to one-third.[55]

Smith-Lever policy united urban clubwomen and farm women in a defense of home economics that became a national protest over gender inequality. The International Congress of Farm Women and the GFWC insisted that half of the federal money should be allotted to home demonstration, and the GFWC sent a committee to argue the point with Secretary of Agriculture David F. Houston.[56] In Texas, where home demonstration received 24 percent of the state's Smith-Lever money, a standoff soon developed between women's organizations and the director of the Agricultural Extension Service, Clarence Ousley, who administered the funds from his office at the Agricultural and Mechanical College. Encouraged by GFWC president Anna Pennybacker's declaration that "we shall never be satisfied unless fifty percent of the Smith-Lever fund is set aside for women," the Texas Federation of Women's Clubs and Benigna Kalb of the Texas Farm Women demanded an equal division.[57]

Forced to justify his position, Ousley contended that women were not being slighted because the interests of farm couples were inseparable. Increasing productivity and income would benefit the wife as much as her husband; therefore the Extension Service's plan to raise the rural standard of living by demonstrating diversified or "mixed" farming would be a boon to women. "In this southern country of ours," he argued, "we will make the most substantial contribution to the welfare of the rural woman if we can get her out of the cotton patch."[58] Secretary of Agriculture Houston backed Ousley's ruling. Houston was standing fast against the International Congress of Farm Women's demand for a woman's bureau in the Department of Agriculture on the same grounds, although he admitted that farm women's problems had been "somewhat neglected."[59]

Women's organizations unequivocally rejected the Ousley-Houston premise of indivisible interests and persisted in framing the issue in terms of gender. Benigna Kalb cited the cotton culture as proof that farm wives were not equals in decision making. If it had been up to women, farming would have long since been diversified, she contended, for women knew better than anyone that cotton kept children out of school and put no money in the family purse. Deftly inverting Ousley's argument, TFWC Vice President Maggie Barry dryly informed him that his characterization of the farm husband and wife as "a domestic partnership for profit and happiness" was precisely the rationale behind the TFWC's resolution: "it was because they believe so strongly in that very partnership that they were so insistent on that 50 percent."[60]

Women likewise refused to accept Ousley's claim that higher incomes automatically translated into more comforts and advantages for farm wives. The opposite was frequently true; farm wives were full partners in toil, but seldom in profits. The ambitious farmer was more likely to invest in machinery to further increase his yields than in "conveniences" to lessen his wife's labor. Diversified farming demonstrations would not show women how to get a cheap kitchen plumbing system, Benigna Kalb pointed out, nor would instructions to the husband on feeding cattle and hogs help his wife produce healthy and well-nourished children.[61]

The stipulation that Smith-Lever funds be administered through land grant colleges opened a second battlefront in Texas, where the land grant college (A&M) excluded women. The TFWC wanted administrative authority for home demonstration to be vested in women, not in the men who operated the government's "bugologist" stations—as "Pauline Periwinkle" dubbed the Agriculture Experiment Stations. To activist women, experiment stations symbolized government's skewed priorities; it poured millions of dollars into fighting insect pests, while ignoring unchecked infant mortality that ravaged the "baby crop." As Mary Work had earlier pointed out during the pure food campaign, cotton was ranked above babies because men's work was valued over women's. If the men at A&M oversaw home demonstration, it would always have lower priority than boll weevils and hog cholera.[62]

The TFWC pushed the issue to the point of confrontation when it resolved in convention that home demonstration should be administered from the University of Texas, "with the full and hearty cooperation of the College of Industrial Arts." The Smith-Lever Act thus became a struggle over public space and formal authority that replayed the gendered themes of the campaigns for the College of Industrial Arts and the Pure Food Law. Again, voluntary associations were insisting that homemaking was as important and as "scientific" as farming and that women should have jurisdiction over public policy that affected domestic life. In 1907 they had carefully rationalized their demand to have the dairy and food inspector's office located at the C.I.A.; by 1914 they were plain-spoken about the gender issue. The motive behind the TFWC resolution, Maggie Barry frankly told Ousley, was that women did not trust men to look after their interests.[63]

On the jurisdiction issue women had the backing of Secretary of Agriculture Houston, even though he continued to support Ousley on the "meager 24 percent." Nothing in the Smith-Lever Act prevented the land grant colleges from using other state agencies to help administer the program, Houston told Maggie Barry, especially if the land grant college was weak in home economics. He advised Ousley that such cooperative arrangements were in place in South Carolina and Florida and gave permission for Texas to follow suit.[64]

No pressure accompanied the authorization, however, and Houston's distant blessing was no substitute for an alliance with influential men who had their own reasons for lending support, which had helped secure the dairy and food commission for the C.I.A. Ousley refused to surrender any authority over home demonstration, on the grounds that joint administration would be uneconomical and inefficient. Doubtless he anticipated that compromising on location would only encourage clubwomen's determination to secure a fifty-fifty division of the funds. Sharing power with Mary Gearing at the University of Texas was surely an essential if unspoken issue. Without bargaining leverage or interested male allies, the clubwomen's defeat was predictable.

The national and state campaigns to equalize funding between the men's and women's divisions of the Extension Service ultimately failed as well. The U.S. Department of Agriculture was embarrassed by the publicity but determined not to yield any ground. Ousley put his finger on the underlying tension: "sex consciousness." Such a "dangerous potentiality," he warned, "may be developed unawares to the point of antagonism and conflict." Eventually the GFWC gave way and ceased to agitate the issue. Home demonstration in Texas continued to receive only one-quarter of the Smith-Lever funds, although Ousley insisted that in overall benefits "women are receiving directly and indirectly not only an equal share but more than an equal share."[65]

"Sex consciousness," however, shortly resurfaced in a confrontation over Mary Gearing's School of Domestic Economy at the University of Texas. In 1917, when a conservative board of regents in collusion with a governor hostile to the university attempted to fire professors and dictate budgets, Gearing's department became a special target. One of the more prominent regents declared that no woman in the world was worth Gearing's $3,000 annual salary and that his cook, whom he paid $40.00 a month, could fill her position. He demanded—in the end, without success—a 20 percent cut in home economics faculty salaries.

Angry students and women's organizations publicized the issue as "equal pay for women's work and men's work on the basis of merit, not sex" and "the recognition of women at the university."[66] Twenty years after Helen Stoddard first argued for a girls' industrial school, home economics remained a stimulus for protest against gender inequality.

❁

Judged by its long-term effects, home economics was a revolution that failed. In the 1890s and early 1900s clubwomen called their home economics committees Household Economics and Sanitary Science or Household Economics and Pure Food, reflecting the social welfare agenda embedded in the work. As the new century advanced and voluntary associations successfully prodded local governments into assuming a larger role in protecting public health, such committees found themselves with less to do. As their focus narrowed to the unpaid labor women performed at home, their names shrank along with their public influence. Even in its narrower sense, home economics failed to fulfill Ellen Richards's vision. New technologies and labor-saving machinery, rather than freeing women for creative pursuits and public service, led to elevated standards of cooking and cleaning and a comparable investment of time to meet them.[67] Academically, home economics became more rather than less peripheral, a curriculum defined and segregated by gender, and many professional home economists made careers helping market kitchen appliances to female consumers.

But when it was new in the Progressive Era, home economics was a catalyst for women's activism. It encouraged middle-class women to cross boundaries between private and public space and claim new roles without violently offending gender prescriptions. GFWC President Eva Perry Moore reasoned persuasively that since "the individual woman had always been the natural housekeeper," therefore "the collective woman was as naturally the municipal housekeeper."[68] Moreover, home economics brought women male allies in the pure food movement who encouraged them to think of themselves as citizens with public work to do. Health inspectors appeared before city clubs and state conventions to solicit organized women's assistance in lobbying for stronger laws and reporting violators. The enforcement of the state's pure food law lay in women's hands, Dr. E. H. Golaz of the dairy and food commissioner's office told the TFWC convention in 1914.[69]

Seeds of feminist consciousness sprouted from this activity. Women soon came to question why their volunteer policing should not be supplemented with formal power, such as the right to serve on juries. The TFWC investigated and found that excluding women from jury service had no basis in the Texas statutes; after Dr. Golaz's address, the delegates discussed the need for women jurors in court cases involving pure food violations. Clubs stood openly on the principle of equal rights when they demanded an even division of the Smith-Lever money. The defeat was more powerful symbolically because the injustice was so palpable; it was not a case of being excluded from a traditional male privilege like voting, but of being denied what women considered themselves "naturally" entitled to.

In the continuing negotiation between the sexes over public space, home economics supplied motivation and means for challenging male domination and expanding female authority. "If the woman's responsibility as family guardian ceases when the line of her own little circle is reached," asked Mary Work, "who shall assume it on the outside?"[70] Applied to child welfare, the same logic was leading women to form mothers' clubs and extend maternal guardianship to the underfunded and deplorably inadequate public school system.

AT THE SAME TIME that Ellen Richards and her followers were working to establish home economics as an academic discipline, Dr. G. Stanley Hall at Clark University was inventing the field of child psychology and launching the child study movement. His "higher pedagogy and psychology" drew large audiences at a special three-day education congress during the Columbian Exposition. Hall challenged the old view of children as passive beings whose unformed characters absorbed the imprint of a mother's moral guidance like dough shaped to a mold. Linking child development to science, he described an active process in which children recapitulated the evolutionary development of the human race as they progressed from infancy to puberty. At each stage, Hall contended, children manifested special needs and capabilities that mothers needed to recognize to give responsive training and guidance at the appropriate times.[1]

Hall, who lectured widely to women's organizations, encouraged mothers to keep records of their children's development in "life books" and to form study groups in which to share their observations and experiences. As an educational reformer who advocated "natural" learning over rote instruction, he also endorsed the ideas of German kindergarten pioneer Friedrich Froebel, whose concept of structured but spontaneous learning had crossed to America in the 1850s. Froebel assigned the mother, as the young child's first teacher, a crucial role in stimulating mental development; he stressed the importance of "mother-play" with small children and wrote simple learning songs especially for mother and child to sing together. Like Hall, Froebel's disciples stressed that effective motherhood required reading, study, and thoughtful application of new knowledge. "Uncertain instinct" needed to be changed to "unhesitating insight," wrote Elizabeth Harrison, founder of the prestigious Chicago Kindergarten College. Her lectures for mothers, *A Study of Child Nurture from the Kindergarten Standpoint,* which went through fifty editions, credited Froebel with inventing "the science of motherhood."[2]

The child study and kindergarten movements permeated the agendas of women's study clubs and prompted the formation of new groups focused exclusively on child development. Although G. Stanley Hall himself was no fan of the new womanhood, and even maintained that preparation for mothering should be the focus of women's education, "the science of motherhood," like scientific housekeeping, inspired women to social activism. Recollecting how El Paso in 1893 became the first city in Texas to institute a public school kindergarten, clubwoman Olga Kohlberg described the linking of private and public objectives:

> As an outgrowth of our Child Study Circle we had formed a Kindergarten Association, raised money by entertainments and sent for two experienced kindergarteners—Miss Lula H. Jones and Miss Lola B. Smith. Every day they gathered our brood . . . to teach them after Froebel's method. Not satisfied to have just our own children so favored, Mrs. Henry A. True, Mrs. J. E. Townsend and myself bearded the school-board in the State National Bank, and persuaded them to institute a kindergarten in the Central School, offering our equipment, material, and last, not least, our teachers.[3]

Froebel and Hall notwithstanding, "kindergartening," which exploded in popularity in the 1880s and 1890s, was a women's movement. The concept of the educated mother in partnership with the kindergarten teacher, reinforcing at home the guidance of the classroom, appealed strongly to urban middle-class women. Women's voluntary associations raised the money to operate private kindergartens and petitioned male school boards to incorporate them into public school systems. The El Paso women even paid part of the teachers' salary for a year while the board considered whether to make the innovation permanent.

Few boards acquiesced as easily as El Paso's; the overwhelming majority of school trustees regarded kindergartens as frivolous expenditures, childminding services for women who wanted to escape maternal duties. The struggle of the Fort Worth Kindergarten Association was more typical. Organized in 1896 by fifteen women in a mothers' study club, it worked for over a decade to persuade the Fort Worth school trustees to follow El Paso's example.[4]

The Miss Smiths and Miss Joneses who secured jobs as a result of such women's efforts were educated and certified in female-run kindergarten training schools or "colleges." The Fort Worth Kindergarten Training School, opened in 1900, was the state's first, and for a time was affiliated with Elizabeth Harrison's Chicago Kindergarten College. Within a few years kindergarten training schools were also operating in Dallas and in San Antonio; Harrison herself spent a year as visiting director of the latter. After a two-year course, a young woman could graduate as a "kindergartener," self-supporting and independent in a "mother-hearted" profession that could not be criticized as unwomanly. Like domestic science, kindergartening in the 1890s promised to enhance the status of the mother at home and open another career for single women.[5]

Scientific mothering and scientific housekeeping joined forces in the school mothers' clubs that organized along with kindergarten associations in urban areas. The mothers' club of the McKinney Avenue School in Dallas formed in 1895 after a few mothers asked the school board to buy gravel for the playground and were turned down; they gathered a larger group and procured the gravel themselves. The board granted their next request, for a new furnace, but denied a subsequent one for indoor toilets until the mothers went to city hall and petitioned the mayor's office. After the toilets were installed, the women convinced the city to connect the school to the sewer line. In 1905, when the board of education declined to renew the contract of the district's only music teacher, the McKinney mothers joined forces with two other Dallas mothers' clubs to secure a reversal of the decision. The allied clubs then pressured city hall into hiring a truant officer and a sanitary inspector for the school district and adopting new heating and ventilating regulations for the buildings.[6]

El Paso and Dallas were not isolated examples. By 1902 the TFWC's Education Committee was already reporting thirty-five mothers' clubs and twenty-five kindergarten associations in membership, and anticipating that the number would double by the following year.[7] Like household economics, child study afforded middle-class women an opportunity to translate their domestic expertise into a new public role. "Educated mothers" were the allies of the New South's growing cadre of female teachers, graduates of the string of normal and industrial schools founded across the region beginning in the 1880s. As the older tradition of male-taught, harshly disciplined common schools gave way to graded schools and female teachers, school and home drew closer. The maternal teacher in the classroom and the pedagogically aware mother at home were natural collaborators.[8]

In furnishing playgrounds, inspecting buildings, and supplying classroom amenities women's groups sought to impart the comforts and cleanliness of the middle-class home. On a more fundamental level, southern clubwomen's school improvement work embraced the regional crusade to create and fund an adequate public school system. Women's voluntary associations played a role in the South's "educational awakening" that has been scarcely acknowledged, eclipsed in the historical literature by the better-documented efforts of the Conference for Education in the South and the General Education Board's Rockefeller-funded philanthropies.[9]

By the time that northern initiative and money created these two organizations, Texas women had already taken up school improvement and reform through the women's club movement. The state's public school crusade was in essence split by gender. One movement, led and dominated by men, centered on the Conference for Education in Texas during its relatively brief existence from 1907 to 1915. Another, spearheaded by a much larger cast of urban middle-class women, was already underway in the 1890s through groups like the El Paso Kindergarten Association and the McKinney Avenue Mothers' Club and re-mained vigorous after the CET disbanded. Although they intersected at some points, the two movements ran essentially on separate tracks, the men moti-vated by the goal of regional economic progress, the women by the agendas of their study clubs and by their children's experience in local schools.

Texas public schools, like those in the rest of the South, ranked in the bottom quartile for the nation at the beginning of the twentieth century. All shared a common heritage of inadequate funding, short terms, low attendance, and poorly trained teachers. The separate and throughly unequal school system for African Americans was even worse than the substandard white one. Decision making and administrative authority rested with local school trustees, and many states imposed constitutional limitations on the amount of property taxes that could be levied for education. Texas's post-Reconstruction "Redeemer" consti-tution fixed the amount for rural districts at twenty cents per one hundred dol-lars; consequently, the state raised barely more in school taxes than tiny Rhode Island. In 1910 Texas stood thirty-eighth among the states in the overall quality of its public education; fewer than two-thirds of school-age children were en-rolled and they spent on average fifty-six days—not even three months—in class. (In first-ranked Massachusetts, by contrast, the figure was 131 days).[10]

Beginning in 1902, the Conference for Education in the South and its execu-tive arm, the Southern Education Board, spent a decade instigating state-based campaigns to attack illiteracy and poverty by convincing southerners to support universal education and fund an adequate system of public schools. Indepen-dently run and of varying durations and degrees of success, the campaigns were spearheaded by prominent educators and local officials. The CES offered advice and encouragement through annual conferences held in major cities through-out the region.[11] While its reach did not formally extend to Texas, it was the model for the Conference for Education in Texas (CET), organized in 1907. The CET's goals mirrored those of the Southern Education Board: publicizing the inadequacies of the common school system and persuading the public to endorse higher school taxes, longer terms, better facilities, more high schools, and vocational training.

The CET's most visible members were the president, who appointed the seven-member governing board, and the general agent. College and university professors and administrators, influential editors, and the state superintendent of public instruction were prominent in the leadership cadre. The dues-paying membership was recruited from public school teachers and laymen.[12] No women were elected to office, nor were any appointed until after the CET had successfully lobbied the legislature to pass a constitutional amendment raising the school tax limit. It then needed to rally public support for ratification, and the TFWC quickly volunteered the help of thousands of clubwomen. After "Pauline Periwinkle" hinted pointedly that such assistance might not be forthcoming in the future unless one or two women were appointed to the executive board, two influential TFWC past presidents, Anna Pennybacker and Birdie Johnson, were offered seats.[13]

As a propaganda organization dedicated to advancing a cause and shaping public opinion, part of the CET's mission was simply to draw attention to itself in order to make its objectives known. An annual conference and dozens of concise bulletins explaining its purpose and goals helped give it high visibility. Clubwomen, whose educational activism was part of a varied agenda, had a less publicized but longer tradition of working for school improvement. As early as 1896 the GFWC's Education Committee had directed clubs to study their communities' educational facilities, from kindergarten upward, and the 1900 Biennial devoted an entire session to the public schools. The Education Committee reported on the initiatives of affiliated state federations: forming school mothers' clubs, establishing free kindergartens and getting them integrated into the public schools, promoting manual training and domestic science programs, improving the sanitation of buildings and grounds, donating artwork for classrooms.[14]

After 1897 women could also serve the schools through a new federation, the National Congress of Mothers (now the PTA), which arose out of the enthusiasm for child study. Its founding president, Alice McClellan Birney of Washington, D.C., and financial patron, Phoebe Apperson Hearst of California, took their inspiration from the kindergarten movement. Birney invoked the memory of "the great and good Froebel" in her opening address to the organizational meeting, and G. Stanley Hall gave the first of many speeches that he would make to the assembly over the years. Two thousand delegates convened in Washington for the first meeting, and by 1915 the organization had grown to sixty thousand members.[15]

The National Congress of Mothers helped popularize the new theories of child guidance, urging "educated mothers" to use their expertise to promote child welfare in their communities. As Molly Ladd-Taylor has observed, these "sentimental maternalists" also idealized motherhood as a woman's highest calling, a view encouraged by Hall and other male supporters such as Theodore Roosevelt, who sat on the advisory board. (One of Roosevelt's more controversial speeches to the organization denounced modern women whose preference for small families was causing Anglo-American "race suicide.") Yet despite its sentimental rhetoric the NCM gradually developed an activist agenda. It put special stress on developing closer ties between home and school through mothers' clubs; by 1908 the school connection had become so prominent that the organization changed its name to the National Congress of Parents and Teacher Associations.[16]

That same year a representative was appointed to search out an African American woman who could organize a "colored" association. Although a group was formed, the National Congress of Colored Parents and Teachers was not formally organized until two decades later. By contrast with the rigid exclusionary policy of the GFWC, however, the NCM's stance was moderate and more closely resembled the WCTU's. Prominent African American women from time to time addressed the national conventions, and the records of the NCM's Texas affiliate show that delegates from the white convention at least once carried an official greeting to the black one and accepted the African American mothers' invitation to address their meeting. By southern standards in the 1910s, it was generous exchange.[17]

Like the GFWC the National Congress of Mothers drew its membership from middle- and upper-class married women, but state branches formed as a result of contacts initiated by national headquarters, not spontaneously from alliances of local groups. In 1899 the NCM began appointing state extension workers to sit on the board of managers until states could form their own organizations and send delegates to the annual convention. Organizers were subsequently designated for six states, including Texas, where the responsibility was assigned to Dallas clubwoman Ella Caruthers Porter.[18] Porter, who had been a delegate to the NCM's national organizing convention, spent nearly a decade preparing the ground for a state Congress of Mothers. In the process, she incurred the private displeasure of some leaders in the Texas Federation of Women's Clubs, who considered the Congress of Mothers to be infringing on work that the women's club movement was already doing through designated committees.

Although many women, like Porter, belonged to both the GWFC and the NCM, a quiet rivalry for members and influence developed at the higher echelons.[19] The resulting competition had beneficial consequences in Texas: ever larger numbers of women were pulled into the child study movement, swelling the ranks of women working for local school improvement. The TFWC leadership responded to Ella Porter's initiative by creating a special Extension Committee to work intensively with its district presidents in organizing more school mothers' clubs. It even hired a field worker to assist the Extension Committee chairwoman and convinced the University of Texas Extension Division to pay half of her salary and supply literature.[20]

Ella Caruthers Porter began public work by organizing a Department of Mothers' Meetings in the Texas Woman's Christian Temperance Union in 1892. In 1909 she became the founder and first president of the Texas Congress of Mothers (subsequently the PTA) and a year later presided over the state's first child welfare conference. (From *Who's Who of the Womanhood of Texas*, vol. 1, 1923–24 [N.p.: Texas Federation of Women's Clubs, 1924])

By the time Ella Porter formally organized a Texas Congress of Mothers in Dallas in 1909 countless mothers' clubs had formed throughout the state. While the TCM was never as large as the TFWC it grew rapidly, reporting 8,800 members in 162 full membership clubs and 106 affiliates in less than two years.[21] Each organization erected a formal structure to advance its work in the schools. The TFWC, in addition to the special Extension Committee, had long maintained standing education and kindergarten committees, and the civics committee included school buildings and grounds in its mandate. The new TCM quickly created standing committees on education, school improvement, and kindergartens.[22]

The network of women's clubs, kindergarten associations, and mothers' clubs dispersed across the state marked an essential difference between the Conference for Education in Texas and the women's organizations. Only the latter had grassroots networks working for change at the local level. The TCM organized its urban clubs into city-wide federations called mothers' councils: in 1910 it reported mothers' councils with twenty-three affiliated clubs in San Antonio, eighteen in Houston, fifteen in Fort Worth, and fourteen in Dallas.[23] Each city's federation of women's clubs counted additional mothers' clubs in membership (the TFWC did not provide numerical breakdowns) and the larger women's clubs, such as the Dallas Woman's Forum, incorporated child study and school improvement as departments of work.

Multiple layers of organization enabled the TCM and TFWC to accomplish more in concrete terms than the CET had the reach and resources to attempt. The campaign to increase public education revenues is a case in point. The CET's first successful project was persuading the legislature to pass a constitutional amendment raising the limit on school taxes from twenty to fifty cents per $100 of property valuation. The process of actually securing more money for the schools, however, required two additional steps: ratification of the amendment in the general election, followed by individual bond issue campaigns to increase local taxes.

Organized women, with years of experience in working for social change through campaigns of public education, were central to the success of these second and third stages. The TFWC made the 1908 school levy referendum an official project. State President Ella Dibrell directed local clubs to hold at least one public meeting featuring a thorough discussion of the school tax amendment, to secure supportive resolutions, and to make certain that the resolutions appeared in the newspaper. Following Dibrell's instructions, clubwomen offered to assist local and county school superintendents with publicity and asked their ministers to preach on education. "Pauline Periwinkle" promoted the levy in her column, reminding readers that the state ranked thirty-seventh in per capita spending on education. In some districts, she asserted, the barns were in better shape than the school houses.[24]

Thanks in part to the TFWC's efforts, the school tax amendment was ratified by a huge margin. The local clubs then took up the challenge of persuading the men in their communities to raise their own taxes. Voters in Austin had already turned down several attempts to increase the levy when the school board asked for a $175,000 bond issue in 1910. By that time all eight of the city's white public schools had mothers' clubs, and they made the bond issue a priority. "In a quiet way we worked on this every morning for thirty days," a correspondent reported to *Texas Motherhood Magazine.* One tactic was to secure endorsements from prominent business and professional men to use as newspaper publicity; this time the bond issue succeeded. Small-town clubs reported similar efforts in progress: $25,000 for a new high school building in Texarkana, $30,000 for a brick building in Floresville. There is simply no way of calculating in how many school districts the influence of women's and mothers' clubs may have helped bond issues to succeed.[25]

Year after year, the TFWC and TCM steadily and without fanfare committed their own funds to school improvement. Mothers' clubs raised money that provided what the backward and underfunded public education system did not: laboratory equipment, library books, pictures and maps, pianos for music instruction, gravel and shade trees for playgrounds. Over the course of a few years an individual club could furnish hundreds of dollars to its local school, and the aggregate of such efforts amounted to significant sums. Between 1908 and 1910 the white mothers' clubs of Houston contributed more than $21,000 to the city schools "for things which probably would not have been secured had they been left to the public money," the superintendent reported. Four of the Houston clubs spent over one thousand dollars each on equipment to institute domestic science and manual training courses, while a fifth shouldered half the cost.[26]

During the same period, the African American mothers' clubs of Houston raised $477, including the salary of a sewing teacher. Documentation is sparse for black schools, but clubs that sent reports to the TACWC were plainly working on a parallel track. In Waco the Mothers' Progressive Club goal for 1913 was to build a membership of forty, with each member attempting to raise five dollars during the summer; the East Waco Mothers' Club worked at landscaping. The emergency room at the Colored High School in Houston owed its furnishings to the city federation of African American clubs. The black clubwomen of Beaumont bought a lot and secured the school board's promise to erect a manual training building on it.[27]

In some villages and small towns white schools no less than black were indebted to mothers' clubs for basic necessities. The Goliad school trustees apparently provided little more than the building: the mothers' club paid for teachers' desks, lamps, water coolers, trash baskets, reference books, and even a cistern pump. Mothers' club reports indicate that women raised money for everything from bare essentials such as a cement floor for a basement to auditorium lights and piped-in water. Club money even financed urban curriculum enrichment. The Waco mothers' clubs introduced music instruction by buying pianos and hiring their own music teacher until the school board agreed to authorize a position.[28]

The ability to improvise local remedies while they lobbied in Austin for substantive change distinguished organized women's path to school reform from that of the Conference for Education in Texas. The CET maintained a lobbying presence in Austin, but at the local level it could only distribute brochures and offer encouragement. The structure of women's organizations enabled them to approach the problem from both directions. While the TCM's legislative committee promoted a bill to outlaw the common drinking cup and towel (without success), local clubs rooted out the germ-infested bucket and dipper in their own districts. Some supplied individual drinking cups; those with more abundant resources paid to have sanitary drinking fountains installed. The most impressive single effort may have been in Denton, where the Woman's Shakespeare Club spent five years raising eight hundred dollars to provide every school in town with a drinking fountain.[29]

The same dual-fronted approach characterized the TFWC's effort on behalf of public school kindergartens. By 1904 clubwomen were funding fifty-eight free public kindergartens, and the following year the Fort Worth Kindergarten Association drafted a bill specifically authorizing school districts to support kindergartens with public funds. Sixteen kindergarten associations sent delegations to Austin to lobby for the bill. It failed the first time, but succeeded at the next session in 1907 when the TFWC made it a legislative priority. Within two years the Fort Worth school system had incorporated five kindergartens, but few other districts followed its example. Finally the TFWC's legislative chairwoman collaborated with the state superintendent of public instruction to draft a bill *requiring* schools to establish kindergartens upon petition by twenty-five or more parents with children below scholastic age. When it passed in 1917, the TFWC Kindergarten Committee helped get the word out by distributing hundreds of copies of the law through the clubs.[30]

In light of the financial resources and human energy that organized women commanded, the CET might have been expected to seek a close working relationship with the TFWC and TCM. North Carolina offered a model of such cooperation in the Women's Association for the Betterment of Public Schools, organized by Charles McIver, a member of the Southern Education Board and president of North Carolina Normal and Industrial College for Women at Greensboro. The WABPS was pursuing essentially the same agenda as school mothers' clubs in Texas (and in 1919 it merged with the newly established North Carolina Congress of Mothers and Parent-Teacher Associations). Active since 1902, the WABPS was partly funded by the state campaign committee of the Conference for Education in the South and the Southern Education Board.[31]

No similar relationship developed in Texas. The cooperation between the TFWC and the CET during the 1908 school levy referendum proved to be the only educational initiative on which female and male reformers genuinely worked in concert. There was always an abundant display of public goodwill on both sides. The presidents of the TFWC and TCM were invited to address the CET annual conventions, and its general agent spoke at theirs. He sought their endorsements, included their membership rosters on the CET's mailing list, and supplied Isadore Callaway with CET literature to use in her "Pauline Periwinkle" columns.[32] But however much women were welcomed as foot soldiers, they were excluded from the officer corps. After the TCM formed in 1909 and asked for equal recognition with the TFWC on the CET executive board, it became apparent that the women would never have more than two token slots. The TCM's request was not granted until one of the TFWC representatives resigned late in 1912 for personal reasons. Even after the organization revised its constitution in 1913, expanding the executive committee from nine to fifteen members, no additional women were appointed.[33]

Clearly women could accomplish more through their separate organizations than in the CET, where they were shut out of leadership positions. But ideological divergence also separated the TFWC and TCM from the CET; men and women tended to view education reform from gendered perspectives. CET spokesmen framed their arguments in terms of economic progress for the New South that aspired to be economically and industrially competitive with the North. The organization's literature elaborated variations of the theme that "Texas is not doing for her schools what other new States of less means and fewer people are doing for theirs." Public education was not charity but a "paying investment" argued Dr. Alexander Caswell Ellis of the University of Texas in a CET bulletin. A resource-poor region like New England produced more wealth than richly endowed Texas because a state like Massachusetts annually invested thirty dollars per child in its public schools and made attendance compulsory, while Texas spent only thirteen dollars and allowed parents to do as they pleased.[34]

Since the CET's goal was to persuade the male electorate to raise taxes and spend money, it pitched education as a business investment certain to yield profitable dividends for the state. Organized women's perspective, on the opposite hand, was noticeably more child-centered, a result of long involvement in the child study movement and direct observation through school mothers' clubs. Men were more likely to stress what the state lost by not educating its children, women to emphasize what children lost by not being educated. Consequently, women's voluntary associations and the CET envisioned fundamentally different solutions to the public school problem.

The men of the CET focused on building more secondary schools and instituting vocational training curricula to teach industrial skills and scientific agriculture. This was a common preoccupation of state campaigns inspired by the Southern Education Board and addressed the South's real need to diversify its agriculture and develop an industrial base. After the school tax campaign, the CET's other notable achievement was a constitutional amendment permitting school districts to extend across county lines, thus allowing adjoining counties to cooperate in building high schools in districts otherwise unable to afford them. A few years of schooling for basic literacy would not meet the needs of students or the state in the twentieth century, CET literature warned; Texas needed to produce high school graduates who could be productive farmers and skilled workers.[35]

Organized women approached school reform from the opposite direction, the lower grades. While the CET pushed for rural high schools, the TFWC championed urban kindergartens. Having studied the theories of Froebel and Hall, clubwomen insisted that graded schools beginning at age seven missed the most important years in children's mental and moral development. They promoted kindergartens with the same passion that educators half a century later would invest in Head Start programs. With more conviction than evidence, middle-class women claimed that "kindergarten training" could accomplish everything from enhancing intelligence to preventing juvenile delinquency. "The kindergarten product will not be found deserting the school room to put in a period of street loafing," Isadore Callaway, who was a member of the Dallas Free Kindergarten Association, asserted via "Pauline Periwinkle." "The industrious habits taught in the kindergarten will become second nature."[36]

Such rhetoric—and there was plenty of it—has left the kindergarteners, like progressive school reformers generally, vulnerable to criticism that their true motives were social control and disciplining working-class and immigrant children to be cogs in industrial society.[37] Undeniably, they considered a strong infusion of middle-class culture to be the best preventative for social disorder. The Dallas Free Kindergarten Association stressed "a need for the rousing of industrial ambition" in the parents of children who suffered from "wretched homes, [and] lack of parental care." Kindergartens reached out to "the poor 'tenter,' the cotton mill worker, the foreign so-called 'Bohemian' element,"

"Pauline Periwinkle" explained, teaching "the dignity of manual labor" and inculcating the "spirit of self-respect and self-help."[38]

This attitude of paternalism and noblesse oblige motivated women such as Johanna Runge, who established the state's first charity kindergarten. The wife of one of the directors of the Galveston Cotton Mill, Runge was so distressed over the "unkempt and dirty" factory district children that she finally decided to take the worst cases home with her, two or three at a time. "The nurse gladly bathed and combed these poor children," she reported to the TFWC, "and after dinner the house girl took them home again. But those clothes that they had shed were not to be touched with human hands. We wrapped them up and returned them, so that they could have them washed and in that way have a change." Sympathizing with the mill women who worked all day and came home exhausted at night, Runge reported that after the children had been washed and given fresh clothing, "the good mothers took heart" and tried to keep their offspring presentable; they had only wanted cheering on.[39]

The equally likely possibility that the mill mothers might have been embarrassed and determined not to have their children singled out again apparently did not occur to Joanna Runge. She likewise seemed unaware that the problem was rooted in the low wages that her husband and other mill owners paid, forcing entire families to work for subsistence. Her husband, Julius, who bought the fuel for the Runge Free Kindergarten and donated two cottages when it outgrew its first headquarters in a church, may indeed have wanted to instill good habits in the tots who would become part of his labor force.[40] But however naive her assumption that mill mothers who lacked nursemaids and house girls needed only encouragement and example in order to be "better" parents, Runge showed genuine concern for the children. Other elite women expressed the same impulse. "Surely in the crowded streets of a great City it is a blessed work to gather the ragged little ones into the kindergarten, wash and clothe them, feed them and smile upon them, and in a hundred ways give them a glimpse of a better life," pleaded an officer of the Dallas Free Kindergarten Association.[41]

Without recognizing such conviction, it is difficult to explain why clubwomen devoted so much time and energy to raising money for public kindergartens; they invested more of themselves than simple self-interest can account for. A "free" kindergarten was an expensive proposition for the women who ran it. Johanna Runge and seven other women raised the $1,300 in start-up costs for Galveston's kindergarten, assumed the continuing responsibility for meeting operating expenses, and served as an unpaid board of directors. Fundraising was not entirely a matter of planning profitable parties. To open its first public kindergarten in 1899, the Dallas Free Kindergarten Association raised seed money with genteel entertainments such as ice cream festivals, "musicales," and teas. Four years later when it was supporting three, at an annual cost of nearly eight thousand dollars, the membership dues, entertainment receipts, and contributions could not cover expenses. The women then opened the Kindergarten Lunch Room in a downtown department store, "earning our living by the sweat of the brow and the blistering of the hand by serving dinner six days a week to the public."[42]

Class and racial prejudices notwithstanding, a strong emphasis on democratic inclusiveness infused clubwomen's passion for kindergartens. Olga Kohlberg and Johanna Runge left statements indicating that their motivation came from observing how much their own children benefited from attending private kindergartens, and they were surely not the only elite women so moved. "Not satisfied to have just our own children so favored," in Kolhberg's words, they insisted that the opportunity should be widely extended. Pointing out that kindergarten was the connecting step between home and school, Margaret Grabill, chair of the TCM's Kindergarten Department, asserted that "we are learning that *we have no right to deprive any child of that step,* thereby leaving out many important stones in the foundation on which he will build his future life and character" (emphasis added).[43]

This commitment to what is now called "early intervention," was one of the most important differences between female and male education reformers. The CET approached the issue of introducing vocationalism into the curriculum, for example, from the perspective of producing a class of skilled high school graduates. The TFWC and TCM viewed it in terms of extending as much benefit as possible to as many children as possible.[44] Clubwomen who had studied John Dewey's new theory of learning by doing stressed the need to begin "manual training" in the lower grades. They repeatedly pointed out that high schools with vocational training programs would benefit only a small segment of the scholastic population; 90 percent of children never advanced to high school. Manual training, they hoped, would lower the dropout rate by engaging the interest of those working-class boys who preferred activity to dull book drills. And those compelled by economic necessity to leave before finishing grade school would have developed at least some rudimentary skills.[45]

Clubwomen's democratic vision was not colorblind. When they spoke of "all children," they meant all white children; "public schools" meant the white public schools. "Colored" schools endured the poorest facilities, the most overcrowded classes, and the shortest terms. A Dallas newspaper in 1890 pronounced three of the city's four black schools unfit for use; Colored School Building No. 1 was marooned on a railroad embankment so high that the teacher had to pull the smallest children up the twelve-foot incline at the end of a rope. None of the black schools had libraries ("on account of their insecurity," the Dallas school board rationalized), and African American parents protested the board's failure to provide playgrounds and connections to the sewer line. In Houston, as late as 1928, an Urban League investigator discovered that African American schools lacked kindergartens and music instruction and that the value of white school property was sixty times greater than black.[46]

Hispanic youngsters suffered the double discrimination of race and language. Segregated by custom rather than by law, they were even less likely than black children to acquire more than basic literacy and numeracy. In El Paso only those who already spoke English were admitted to the "Mexican" schools, and most left between the fourth and sixth grades to work. When these children were the subject, white middle-class women tended to abandon maternalist rhetoric for class- and race-based arguments. The El Paso Women's Civic League proposed establishing a secondary school for Hispanics using the same return-on-investment arguments that characterized male discourse. A "Mexican" vocational school would be a service for the city: training would make the Mexican population more productive and would benefit "American" families by increasing the supply of "house girls" with desirable cooking and sewing skills.[47]

Clubwomen also vigorously supported the poll tax amendment passed in 1901 for the combined purpose of raising money for the public schools and reducing the number of black and Hispanic voters. The TFWC executive board authorized a special Committee on Constitutional Amendments to promote ratification "in the cause of education." Anna Pennybacker, who was state president at the time, issued a public endorsement letter urging each woman to do her duty to the schools by advocating the tax. Reminders appeared in the "Woman's Century" page of the Dallas and Galveston *News*, where "Pauline Periwinkle" asserted that men who owned no taxable property ("many are colored") but sent their children to the public schools did not deserve to vote if they were unwilling—and the issue was always framed as one of willingness rather than ability—to pay a $1.50 poll tax. Although clubwomen consistently stressed the school revenue aspect of the tax, they usually mentioned "purifying the ballot" as a secondary benefit; they were well aware that its underlying purpose was black disfranchisement.[48]

Standing shoulder to shoulder with men on the issue of white supremacy, the women who promoted the poll tax with "the quiet dignity characteristic of Southern womanhood" (in Pennybacker's words) might have been expected to champion the South's other traditional values, limited government and local autonomy. But here again organized women parted ideological company with organized men. They were early and vocal supporters of strengthening the state's power to compel school attendance. Middle-class women's conception of democracy inverted the traditional southern emphasis on the right to be left alone; in their view it was undemocratic that only *some* children were getting the benefit of an education. Lacking real understanding of the tangled social and economic roots of southern poverty, clubwomen tended to define the school attendance problem partly in terms of willful neglect by working-class and rural men. The TFWC went on record for compulsory education in 1902, when it first began investigating child labor. Within two years after its founding, the TCM was also passing annual resolutions in favor of compulsory education.[49]

By contrast, the CET stressed voluntary action at the community level. Its primary goal was removing the artificial constraints, such as tax and boundary restrictions, that had kept school districts from raising adequate revenue and cooperating to extend limited resources. Not until 1913 did it finally endorse compulsory education. The leadership argued, not illogically, that the state simply did not have enough schools to accommodate the entire scholastic population; the time to press for a law would be after more buildings were erected and the school term lengthened. Women, however, condemned the "crime" of permitting children to be victimized by the state's indifference and the "outrage against childhood" committed by parents who asserted their "right" to their youngsters' labor.[50]

Confronting deeply entrenched cultural values of independence and individualism, organized women had a hard fight to secure even a relatively moderate compulsory education law. The CET issued a bulletin explaining the need for it, but clubwomen seem to have done most of the legislative lobbying. After failing on the first try in 1913, the TFWC Education Committee immediately began to prepare for the next biennial session. In 1914 it placed promotional "facts and data" in sixty newspapers across the state and printed three thousand leaflets and postcards, reserving half for a promotional blitz timed to coincide with the opening of the legislative session the following winter.[51]

The TFWC designated compulsory education its sole legislative objective in 1915. President Florence Fall called on every clubwoman to write her state legislators, and the Education Committee oversaw mass mailings. Fall and Anna Pennybacker, by that time in her second term as GFWC president, testified together before the Senate Committee on Educational Affairs. (Pennybacker was armed with a folder of information and arguments that the Alabama Federation of Women's Clubs was using in its own compulsory education campaign; clubwomen were "networking" long before there was a term for it.) Their opponents countered with a week-long filibuster. The bill that finally passed required children between the ages of eight and fourteen to attend school for a minimum of sixty days (three months) in 1916, eighty days the following year, and one hundred days (five months) by 1919.[52]

When the compulsory education act passed without any provision for an attendance officer to enforce it, male and female reformers reacted consistently
with their different philosophies. The CET considered its mission accomplished
and disbanded, leaving the local districts to comply voluntarily—or not. Clubwomen, as they had earlier done with the pure food act, went to work to fill the
void. The TFWC Education Committee, while attempting to convince state authorities to appoint an attendance officer, mobilized the clubs' help to police
their own communities. It directed the education chairwomen for the five districts of the state federation to appoint a sub-chairwoman and committee in
every school district to visit the superintendents, county school trustees, and local school boards and volunteer their assistance as truant officers.[53] As always,
organized women turned to their own grassroots strength for local remedies,
without relaxing their uphill battle to expand the power of the state.

❀

Extensive involvement with their children's schools inevitably led some middle-
class women to conclude that the men in charge of public education were making a poor job of it. "We have only one thing in town worse than the school
buildings," a Laredo club woman lamented, "and that is the politician who has
charge of the schools and who never spent a day in the school-room in his life
since his school days, and they were very few." After Isadore Callaway toured
fourteen Dallas schools with a mothers' club representative in 1907, "Pauline
Periwinkle" demanded to know why students and teachers still had to huddle
around area stoves and use outdoor privies (situated, at one school, at an angle
that allowed the wind to blow the stench into the classrooms). The school
trustees did not tolerate such primitive and unhealthy conditions in their own
businesses, she pointed out; offices, stores, and even factories were equipped
with modern heating systems and indoor washrooms and toilets.[54]

Callaway saw gender at the heart of the matter. Part of the problem was obviously the reluctance of male voters to authorize sufficient taxes. But the
underlying difficulty was that male trustees could not spare the time and attention from their business careers to do a proper job of school administration,
while women, who did have the time and the expertise, were excluded by custom. (Despite being disfranchised, women were legally eligible under the state
constitution to hold most public offices.) Over the next several years Callaway
returned again and again to the theme that women should be encouraged to
serve on school boards and allowed to vote in school elections. Popular opinion
to the contrary, she argued, the idea was not "foreign to Southern conceptions
of woman's 'sphere' "; Kentucky had been the first state to grant school suffrage,
and neighboring Louisiana allowed taxpaying women the same privilege.[55]

Even in Texas, it was hardly a new idea; the state WCTU had endorsed women school trustees in 1888, along with woman suffrage.[56] At that time it was primarily a symbolic declaration; the WCTU seems not to have promoted the idea. Twenty years later the concept of women school trustees was still radical but no longer outrageous: from school mothers' clubs to mothers on the school board was not a great ideological leap. A mother's responsibility followed her children out the front door, organized women argued; the school, the place where children spent the most hours outside her supervision, therefore should be considered an extension of the home. This conviction underlay the first campaigns to elect women to the Dallas and San Antonio school boards in 1908 and 1909, respectively. In both cities the candidates were selected and promoted by the women's and mothers' clubs.

The willingness of some progressive men to accept women as the embodiment of efficiency, expertise, and disinterested virtue helped elect clubwomen Adella Kelsey Turner and Ella Isabelle Tucker in Dallas and Anna Hertzberg and Jeanette Noyes-Evans in San Antonio, even though the presidents of both school boards were strongly opposed. All four women were prominent in their city federations and notable examples of educated motherhood. In Dallas one of the incumbent board members—a judge—who had planned to run for reelection declared that Turner, a former TFWC president, was the best qualified candidate in the district and withdrew in her favor. Equally important were the candidates' maternal and "womanly" images. Turner stressed that women had no desire to take over the board; they merely wanted to use their influence with the male members for the children's benefit, just as they did at home with their own children's fathers.[57]

Running as mothers was essential to the legitimacy of the clubwomen's campaigns. Isadore Callaway even declined to be nominated in Dallas on the grounds that she was childless (although she was rearing two nieces), perhaps a rationalization to cover her more serious liability of outspoken feminism. A Callaway candidacy would also have forced "Pauline Periwinkle" into modest silence, depriving the campaign of a useful publicist. What father would claim to know his children as well as his wife did, she asked in a column that stressed the similarities between running a household and overseeing a school. And maintaining school buildings hardly differed from a wife's responsibility for furnishing and maintaining a home. By virtue of training and experience, "Periwinkle" argued, women were better prepared to make good decisions about sanitation, lighting, decoration, and the like.[58] Such reasoning, which engaged the progressive enthusiasm for professional expertise and efficient management without overtly threatening male supremacy, targeted men likely to vote for "good government."

Most important, women had the time to devote to school matters that busy men lacked. As Mary Work pointed out, the school board member who had the leisure to study "sociology, educational economy, or even simple school house-keeping," as clubwomen did, was a "rare exception." Many women, like Work herself, were not only mothers but former teachers, who could bring the benefits of both perspectives to school management. It would simply be efficient and cost effective to have women board members. "Pauline Periwinkle" reasoned creatively that such service would not actually bring women into politics because education should never be a partisan issue. The fact that men did their best to make it one by using school boards as stepping stones to higher office was all the more reason to elect women.[59]

In both San Antonio and Dallas clubwomen avidly promoted the female candidates. One of the vice presidents of the Woman's Club of San Antonio served as campaign manager for Hertzberg and Noyes-Evans. The Dallas Federation of Women's Clubs endorsed the candidacies of Turner and Tucker, appropriated the money to print ten thousand cards elaborating the two women's qualifications, and distributed them in ward by ward canvasses. Isadore Callaway, who was DFWC president that year, reported having "thoroughly worked" the factory district, as well as handing out cards in drug stores, grocery stores, and "spots wherever men were assembled." Turner and Tucker did not speak on their own behalf—male supporters handled that most "public" aspect of the campaign—but their sister clubwomen lauded them in the press.[60]

Turner, who was one of the preeminent activist women in Dallas, won easily and Tucker by a small margin; both served their terms without incident. The victories of Hertzberg and Noyes-Evans in San Antonio, however, were short-lived. They were elected while a new charter for the city school district was pending before the state legislature in 1909, and local opponents of female school trustees succeeded in having a provision inserted that required trustees to be "qualified voters." The governor signed it despite a flood of protest petitions from club-women (drafted by the San Antonio Federation and distributed to every club in the state for signatures), thereby invalidating the election results.[61]

Once elected, the women pursued issues already familiar through mothers' club work. As a member of the Dallas board, Adella Kelsey Turner served on a committee, created at her request, to investigate the cost of installing sanitary drinking fountains. She chaired the committee on rules for janitors, drafting a detailed report that the board adopted on a motion by Ella Tucker. With women on the board, petitioning mothers' clubs like the McKinney Avenue group (which had become the William B. Travis Mothers' Club when their school was rechristened) found receptive listeners. When they asked that the school janitors be prevented from selling candy and chili to the children, Turner and Tucker constituted themselves a committee of investigation and subsequently recommended that soup, hot rolls, and hot chocolate be made available instead.[62]

Despite the fact that their names had appeared on a ballot and women's clubs functioning like ward committees had run their campaigns, Turner and Tucker were essentially doing what they had done for years through their clubs—working for school improvement. More significant than the fact that they and a few other women actually won school board seats was the newly manifest desire among clubwomen for "one woman on every school board."[63] Involvement in school reform was one of the most common and direct ways that middle-class white women were drawn into politics and public advocacy. Beginning with the domestic side of school needs, the housekeeping details of buildings and grounds, they refashioned the Victorian concept of gender to accommodate a new image of motherhood. "Educated mothers" had public work to do.

San Antonio women demonstrated their determination when the city charter was revised again in 1913, after the legislature granted cities home rule. The president of the San Antonio Council of Mothers, several members of the Woman's Club, and two male supporters formed themselves into a committee and successfully sponsored an amendment requiring that three of the nine school trustees be women. The *San Antonio Light* editorialized in favor of the new provision and, in a burst of liberalism, declared that women should have the right to vote in school elections as well. A women's meeting selected three candidates—Anna Hertzberg, Mrs. Atlee B. Ayers, and Mrs. Milton J. Bliem—who were unanimously approved when their names were put forward at the men's nominating meeting and won their races easily. Hertzberg, at the time in her second term as TFWC president, was subsequently elected vice president of the board.[64] Thereafter, women school trustees were a fixture in San Antonio. The objections, observed the superintendent of schools, arose "mainly from those who want janitors' jobs for themselves and their friends" and expected women to be less susceptible to informal influence.[65]

The image of women as apolitical and civic-minded was a strong aspect of their appeal as candidates, but the competition between the TFWC and TCM for the three allotted slots in San Antonio revealed them to be anything but politically naive. After the new city charter was approved, the president of the Woman's Club issued a call for representatives of all city clubs to attend an open nominating meeting for women candidates. The president of the Council of Mothers then moved to strengthen her own organization's position by scheduling a caucus immediately before the nominating meeting. The mothers' club women selected Mrs. Ayers as their candidate and adjourned directly to the general meeting to place her name in nomination. Four women's club members were also put forward, but the Council of Mothers remained firmly pledged to

Ayers and ensured that she was among the three top vote getters who won the nominations. The reporter covering the meeting noted that the women were "fairly accomplished politicians" and the competition "just a bit tense."[66] If the clubwomen retained misgivings about mixing in politics, they refrained from expressing any.

❁

Women's public culture helped structure the better schools movement and was in turn expanded and shaped by it. For many women, school mothers' clubs may have opened the most direct and "natural" path to public activism. Concerned for their own children and inspired by the authorities on child development and progressive education, middle-class women began working for better schools earlier than the Conference for Education in Texas. And they persevered longer, through a well-established network of voluntary associations with the ability to pursue school reform at both the local and legislative levels.

Women's and mothers' clubs imprinted a female perspective on education reform, one that held kindergartens as necessary as high schools and child welfare as important as regional development. Exclusion from the high echelons of school administration as well as from electoral politics gave them more freedom than male school reformers to advocate radical change. The leaders of the CET were constrained by the need to appease local school committees and to tread lightly on the southern tradition of minimalist government; voluntarist women did not hesitate to press for higher school levies, curriculum enrichment, and a proactive state with coercive power. Within a remarkably short time they reached for power of their own, the right to serve as school trustees.

There was no functioning state suffrage association in Texas while clubwomen were seeking school board seats, and the women did not at first suggest that they should be able to *vote* in school elections. But by 1912 TFWC President Anna Hertzberg and TCM President Ella Porter were openly pondering the idea. Hertzberg and Porter used their invitations to address the CET in 1912 to point out that excluding women from school governance was neither efficient nor logical. If women were fit to organize the state into mothers' clubs and qualified to heed the call every time men requested their assistance to promote bond issues, they were surely capable of being school trustees, and even, Hertzberg frankly suggested, of voting on school issues. Porter, who was also a WCTU suffragist, posed a telling question: considering organized women's long tradition of educational activism, "and how indirectly their work must be accomplished, the question is naturally forced upon the understanding, 'what would they *not* accomplish if theirs were the power?' "[67]

The school board campaigns helped organized women formulate the rationale that they would use to justify asking for suffrage a few years later. The stress on sexual difference rather than equality, on women's special qualifications as mothers and housekeepers, and on the benefits to society (as opposed to themselves) would be the foundation of the suffragists' house in the 1910s. In the years when suffrage activity was dormant, the effort to elect female school trustees kept alive the idea of women as voters and officeholders. As the new women school trustees in San Antonio celebrated their victory, Ella Porter's question— What would women *not* accomplish if they had the power?—hung tantalizingly in the air.

THE EDUCATED mothers and scientific housekeepers who founded free kindergartens, labored to improve their children's schools, and inspected their neighborhood markets and dairies, marked a new departure in the female invasion of the public sphere. As Glenna Matthews has pointed out, women have seldom enjoyed access to public space on the same terms as men; much public space has been sex-segregated or proscribed to "respectable" women. The equating of respectability with the private sphere and unrespectablity with the public—the term "public woman" itself signifying a prostitute—restricted women's access to public roles and even to public facilities. As New South cities like Dallas and Fort Worth more than doubled in population during the first decade of the twentieth century, increasing numbers of women claimed rights to the expanding public domain.[1]

Women's clubs, as they moved out of domestic parlors and took up residence downtown, enabled middle-class women to assert modest and defensible claims to public space for their own sake rather than on behalf of others. "Department" clubs with citywide membership, which began appearing in Texas at the turn of the century, quickly grew to the point of requiring public gathering places. Within half a dozen years of its founding in 1906 the Dallas Woman's Forum had enrolled 160 members and bought a lot on which to erect a clubhouse. Other groups acquired their own clubhouses by renting or renovating existing structures. As the female counterpart of the gentleman's club, where men had traditionally enjoyed themselves without the constraining presence of women, the increasingly common clubhouses became "homes" in public.[2]

Clubs also extended their space in the built environment by founding public libraries. Many a community library evolved from the collections of books and periodicals that clubwomen amassed to prepare literary papers and began opening to the public one or two afternoons a week. Other women acted with deliberate purpose. Olga Kohlberg and five colleagues from the El Paso Woman's Club, one of whom was a teacher with a large book collection, formed themselves into the El Paso Library Association. They installed the books in a downtown office building and offered part-time lending service to the community. The Woman's Club met in the same room. The El Paso Library Association and its books subsequently moved to larger quarters in city hall and eventually into its own library building.[3]

In Houston, the Ladies' Reading Club politely but insistently challenged the Houston Lyceum, a predominately male private literary organization, for control of library space. In 1894 the club asked the men to allow nonmembers to borrow its books and to move the collection from Market House to a location more accessible to Houston women. The clubwomen were granted permission to use the book collection, but it remained at Market House for another three years, until the women themselves paid to have it relocated. The Ladies' Reading Club built up the new facility by donating its own magazine files and books and earmarking five dollars a month for acquisitions. It became a public reading room after they persuaded the Houston City Council to contribute two hundred dollars a month, despite the objections of an alderman who grumbled that if women were properly attending to their domestic responsibilities they would have no time for books.

The city flatly refused the club's appeals to construct a library building, however, prompting two members to write to Andrew Carnegie, who agreed to finance a building if the city provided a site. Consequently, in 1900 the Ladies' Reading Club and four other women's clubs united as the Houston Federation of Women's Clubs to pursue the goal; they worked with the Lyceum to raise money to purchase a downtown lot.[4] The same process was already winding to a successful conclusion in Dallas, where the Pierian Club's collection of five hundred books constituted a circulating library. The Pierians and five other clubs joined forces to raise money toward securing a Carnegie Library; by 1898 they had formally united as the Dallas Federation of Women's Clubs in order to see the project to completion.[5]

Although the rationale behind library construction was community improvement, the buildings were female-dominated public spaces. Public libraries provided meeting rooms for women's clubs and boards of directors on which women could serve alongside men and in equivalent numbers. Club leaders such as May Dickson Exall in Dallas and Olga Kohlberg in El Paso served as library board presidents. Each new public library also provided paid professional work for women, who held directorships even in cities as large as Dallas, Houston, and Fort Worth. Houston's Julia Ideson, a graduate of the first library

training class at the University of Texas, was an outstanding example. Ideson became director of the Houston Lyceum and Carnegie Library in 1903, and in the
course of a long career helped secure four branch libraries while participating
actively in the club and suffrage movements.[6]

At the same time, clubwomen's study of "social economics," the underlying
economic causes of society's ills, supplied a different motivation for incursions
into the public domain. The Progressive Era marked a new departure in
women's claim to public authority. Genteel Victorian women had claimed rights
in the public domain by turning their prescribed role as society's moral
guardians to their own purposes. Motivated by a conviction of religious duty,
small groups of women had established and maintained orphanages, homes for
indigent elderly women, and shelters for "ruined" girls and "fallen" women. Institutions such as the Woman's Home in Fort Worth, the Sheltering Arms in
Dallas, and the Lasker Home for Children and the Bethesda Door of Hope
in Galveston, represented benevolent women's attempts to create female-
dominated refuges in morally dangerous urban environments.[7]

The WCTU continued to use moral authority, to more dramatic effect and
with appropriate symbolism, in staging street protests. Local option elections,
which polled the (male) electorate on the question of banning saloons, brought
out WCTU members in pubic demonstrations. Symbolically and literally, they
went from the church to the fray, like the temperance women in the Panhandle
town of Canadian, who gathered in the Presbyterian Church for a prayer meeting on election morning. "The ladies with school children carrying banners and
mottoes, preceded by the Canadian band, then marched down Main Street
singing, 'The Whiskey Shops Must Go' . . . ," the WCTU secretary recorded.
Sherman, near the Oklahoma border, voted dry after the eloquent state WCTU
president mounted the bandstand. According to the *Texas White Ribbon*, "The
children threw over her head the snow-white banner of prohibition, with its rib-
bons floating in the breeze, and she urged the people to vote 'for God and home
and native land.' "[8]

Through benevolence and moral reform women had claimed significant but
limited social space in the nineteenth century. The WCTU's visibility often
waned after a successful local option campaign; state reports always noted revived and reorganized chapters among the membership "gains." In Texas the organization was never large and prosperous enough to erect a headquarters
building or other notable structures. By and large temperance women continued to meet in the churches; only one local chapter owned a meeting house.
Benevolent women made more of a mark on the built environment, but their institutions, which depended on private funding, could "rescue" only a worthy minority and create new roles for the few elite women who became lady managers.

After the turn of the century, however, the effects of industrial development and urban growth opened new opportunities for voluntarism that enabled women to expand their public influence dramatically and claim social space. By 1910 Texas counted four of the South's dozen largest metropolitan areas—San Antonio, Houston, Dallas, and Fort Worth—and was experiencing the dislocations that attended urban living. While benevolent societies and the WCTU continued their efforts to protect the endangered, rapidly multiplying clubs and civic associations motivated by "social economics" attempted to reshape the urban environment. Neither philanthropy nor moral reform, they had come to believe, could solve social problems rooted in poverty and labor conditions.

White middle-class women's attempts to cross class lines began in Texas with social settlements.[9] They had no equivalents of Hull House or Henry Street and their female luminaries; most southern settlements were small and centered around kindergartens and home missions.[10] Yet for precisely those reasons they were important in enabling women, who overwhelmingly dominated both fields, to claim public space in southern cities. This was clear to a contemporary, who described the movement as extensive, listing participating institutions— "churches, missionary societies, federations of women's clubs, kindergarten associations, the Council of Jewish Women, nurses, sororities"—that unmistakably bespoke female influence. Nationally, women comprised an estimated 60 percent of settlement residents. Although their total numbers in the South were much lower, the percentage was considerably higher; in the nine former Confederate states surveyed in the *Handbook of Settlements* (1911), women made up 83 percent of the residents and volunteers. For the seven Texas settlements listed, thirty-five of the thirty-eight residents and volunteers (92 percent) were women.[11]

These settlements were women's space in a double sense: cooperative homes for the unmarried resident workers and social space for the network of married clubwomen who helped sustain them. The Neighborhood Houses in Dallas (1903) and Fort Worth (1908) and Rusk Settlement in Houston (1909), were inspired by northern models but shaped by local clubwomen and their allies to their own circumstances and agendas. Neighborhood House in Dallas, the state's first social settlement, was planned partly to solve the housing dilemma plaguing the Dallas Free Kindergarten Association's teachers, who had been unable to find "suitable" boarding places in the surrounding neighborhood of immigrant families. It was a voluntary association project from the outset, the creation of the Free Kindergarten Association and the Dallas Federation of Women's Clubs, to which the Kindergarten Association belonged.[12]

Kindergartens were the nuclei of Neighborhood House of Dallas and of its smaller counterpart in Fort Worth, which was established a few years later by the Fort Worth Kindergarten and Social Settlement Association. In addition to its "mother" free kindergarten on site, Neighborhood House in Dallas established branch kindergartens on the city's east side and in the south side cotton mill district, where the association also maintained a day nursery for the mill women's children. The Dallas house also set up a teacher training program with a faculty of eight. The young female students studied music, art, storytelling, child nature, "the psychology of play," and a variety of handicrafts under instructors like Edith O'Grady of the Pestalozzi-Froebel Training School and the Chicago Commons. They went on to complete a second year at kindergarten colleges in Chicago, New York, Louisville, or Grand Rapids, Michigan. By 1911 the Dallas settlement had fourteen residents; Fort Worth's had three residents and four volunteers. All were women.[13]

These seem insignificant numbers when measured against Hull House, which occupied an entire Chicago city block and housed fifty-one residents, or Lillian Wald's Henry Street nurses' settlement in New York, with forty-six. But the importance of the southern settlements as women's space is more truly measured by the extensive female voluntarist networks that nurtured and financed them. Most of the operating expenses of Hull House, for example, were underwritten by a few large donors. In a New South city such as Dallas, where millionaire industrialists and monied women were not in abundant supply, funds were raised publicly by the many instead of privately by the few. To help raise the money to open Neighborhood House, for example, the Kindergarten Association and the Dallas Federation of Women's Clubs joined with the Elks (which probably included a number of club husbands) to sponsor a three-day festival of nations billed as "Columbia's Reception."[14]

The women also filled their coffers through Tag Days, a fundraising strategy that thrust proper ladies into the public in a bold and unorthodox way. Scores of women stationed themselves downtown and solicited money from passersby, who were "tagged" in return for donations and thus protected from being accosted again. Soliciting money from men on the streets, an activity previously associated with "public women" of a different kind, would have shocked their mothers and grandmothers. By the new century, however, women were supporting many more social and civic projects than parlor entertainments and sewing circles could finance. The next level, fairs and festivals like Columbia's Reception, required an enormous investment of time and energy for uncertain return. Tag Days were a more efficient deployment of womanpower and the money collected was pure profit. They became annual events and an indispensable source of revenue for voluntary association projects.

After Neighborhood House became a reality, the clubwomen of the kindergarten association (expanded and renamed the Dallas Free Kindergarten and

Industrial Association) served as its financial managers and board of directors. They organized the settlement house on club principles, with the kindergarten and industrial departments each entitled to representation in the Dallas Federation of Women's Clubs. Vice presidents were designated for each of the three kindergartens and for the settlement's individual departments of work. Separate committees oversaw the building, looked after the training class students and helped place them after graduation, and raised the annual operating budget, which by 1907 was sixty-five thousand dollars.[15]

That same year, in Houston, plans were launched for Rusk Settlement. A dozen women formed the Houston Settlement Association to expand the work that the Woman's Club and several teachers at Rusk School, led by Sybil Campbell, had begun a few years earlier. Campbell had been appalled to discover an unsupervised preschool sibling of one of her students sleeping on the schoolhouse steps one day, and had persuaded the Woman's Club to build a free kindergarten and day nursery for the children of working mothers. After hours, Campbell and several other teachers had been conducting sewing classes for older girls and young mothers in the kindergarten cottage, which was adjacent to the school grounds. When the groups outgrew the kindergarten rooms, the women decided to organize on a larger scale. The Houston Settlement Association quickly grew to nearly two hundred members; all of its officers and directors were women.[16]

Through settlement houses professional women and club volunteers demonstrated their faith that scientific homemaking and mothering could alleviate the poverty and high rates of infant mortality in working-class communities. The kindergarten was the opening wedge into the neighborhood. The "kindergarteners" combined the roles of teacher and home visitor, encouraging working-class mothers to sample the settlement's programs. Neighborhood House in Dallas organized a mothers' club whose meetings concluded with a scientific cooking demonstration. Public health nurses there and at Rusk showed mothers how to sterilize milk and prepare infant food. Settlement services and activities—domestic science classes, playgrounds, branch libraries, and boys' and girls' clubs—bespoke the influence of the women's club agenda. Only Rusk had a men's club, probably because it imported a Chicago-trained man as its first head resident; he was later succeeded by Sybil Campbell.

While club and college women used secular settlements to claim new territory as childsavers and municipal housekeepers, evangelical women combined social economics with the older tradition of religious duty. Through mission settlements they attempted not only to rescue individuals but to modify the environments that put individuals at risk. Evangelia Settlement (1906) in Waco originated as a combination of church and charity. It began with the efforts of two young women who set up a day nursery next to the woolen mills for the workers' children and grew into a full-fledged settlement administered by a board of twenty women representing all of Waco's Protestant denominations.[17]

Nondenominational mission settlements were the exception, however. The urban mission effort was overwhelmingly dominated by Methodist women, who moved from building parsonages to erecting settlement houses. The Woman's Board of Home Missions of the Methodist Episcopal Church, South, and the city mission boards that the Methodist General Conference authorized in 1894 worked cooperatively in this endeavor. Called Wesley Houses, the mission settlements combined social services and evangelism, or in churchwomen's words, "Americanizing and Christianizing." Local boards, comprised of representatives from the Woman's Home Mission Society auxiliaries of each Methodist Church in the metropolis, raised 90 percent of the operating budget for each Wesley House. The city mission boards functioned as the religious equivalent of the city federation of women's clubs, and they stood in the same relation to religious settlements that clubwomen did to secular ones.[18]

Like the secular settlement houses, Wesley Houses were staffed by professionals, widowed and single women who made careers in church work. Many of these resident deaconesses were educated at Scarritt Bible and Training School in Kansas City, which had been founded by Methodist women to train home and foreign missionaries. After the city mission movement was launched Scarritt added a department of "Christian Sociology" to prepare women for settlement service. The Dallas Woman's Board of City Missions opened the first Wesley House in Texas in 1903, and others followed quickly in Galveston (1906), Houston (1907), Fort Worth (1911), and San Antonio (1913).[19] The Houston board acquired its house by remodeling an old hotel, noting with pride how the "male" rooms were transformed for "female" purposes: "A SALOON . . . was torn away and converted into a large Kindergarten and Day Nursery; a BILLIARD Hall . . . gave place to a very well equipped clinic and dispensary with . . . trained nurse in charge; and the Hotel sign replaced by Wesley House."[20]

Wesley Houses combined a full complement of social services with mission work, and in Texas they especially targeted Mexican immigrants, the poorest of all the working classes. Far more isolated from the dominant white culture than their counterparts in the African American community, Hispanic women at the turn of the century had no equivalent voluntary association tradition or self-help network; their activities focused around family and the parish church. Lacking benevolent societies, clubs, and civic groups, they were without a corresponding tradition of social activism and a female public culture.

It was these women and their children whom the Methodist deaconesses especially sought to draw. The state's only Wesley House without a "Mexican mission" was in Galveston, which had no appreciable Hispanic community. Even in

Fort Worth's polyglot packing house district, which the deaconesses considered "almost a foreign town" with immigrants of eighteen nationalities, the Wesley House stressed outreach to Mexican and Mexican American families. In each city a volunteer Mexican American minister conducted regular services in Spanish, while the deaconesses enrolled the youngest children in the settlement kindergarten to learn English.

The effect of the deaconesses' proselytizing is unknown. It is possible that a good many who attended the Spanish services were already Protestant. Historian Vicki Ruiz has speculated that such was the case in El Paso's Segundo Barrio, where the Rose Gregory Houchen Settlement (1912) metamorphosed over time into a community center. Interviewing families in the neighborhood in the 1970s, Ruiz found that the predominantly female Hispanic clientele saw the settlement as "not a beacon of salvation but a medical and social service center run by Methodists." The Hispanic women set the terms of interaction, using the clinic for health care and allowing their children to play on the playground but admonishing them not to go inside for cookies and story hour.[21]

Although there are no corroborating records for the Wesley Houses, it is likely that their clinics, too, were more popular than the Protestant preaching in Spanish. In San Antonio the Wesley House provided free health services and operated the only free dental clinic in the city. It persuaded doctors to donate their services to the dispensary and secured the cooperation of the city health department in providing staff nurses. In effect, the Wesley House deaconesses erected female-run medical and social service centers in barrio neighborhoods, saving bodies as they sought souls.[22]

❀

The most vigorously contested public spaces were the "vice" or "reservation" districts that were as much a part of early twentieth-century cities as shopping blocks. Some were legally sanctioned and others unofficially tolerated for the fees and fines that prostitution generated for city governments and law enforcement officers. Texas's most famous one was Fort Worth's legendary Hell's Half Acre, where Butch Cassidy and the Wild Bunch sat for an outlaw family portrait at the turn of the century. Waco, the site of Baylor University, maintained by the Baptist General Convention, was also home to the state's oldest licensed reservation district. Houston, Austin, Dallas, San Antonio, El Paso, and numerous smaller cities had flourishing red-light districts. The deaconesses of Dallas's Wesley House counted forty houses of prostitution (and thirty saloons) within the six blocks surrounding their first mission. The vice district was encroaching so rapidly on the neighborhood that the Woman's Board of City Missions was reluctant to have the deaconesses stay in residence.[23]

Rapid urbanization and the influx of young white women into the labor market generated anxiety over working-class women's sexuality and inspired a social purity movement in which evangelical women figured prominently. Emphasizing the ease with which such "unprotected" females could supposedly be lured into prostitution by "white slavers," purity reformers crusaded to raise age of consent laws, the age at which a girl was deemed old enough to consent to sexual intercourse. Most states set this at age ten or twelve, which female purity reformers denounced as blatantly anti-woman and protection only for male license. In 1885 the national WCTU made social purity a department of work and began petitioning and lobbying to raise the age to eighteen in every state and territory. In Texas the WCTU succeeded in raising the age from ten to twelve in 1891 and to fifteen in 1895.[24]

Purity reformers shaped their appeal around Victorian culture's belief that women were inherently pure and passionless; they portrayed men as sexual predators and women as prey. The arguments of Texas lawmakers against raising the age of consent to eighteen reinforced the perception, exposing the assumed sexual right to women of subordinate status and race. Working girls, it was claimed in the legislature, would use the law to blackmail their employers into marriage. Worse yet, the "colored" girl would be protected along with the white. White southern women were generally reluctant to acknowledge the sexual vulnerability of black females, but WCTU president Helen Stoddard confronted the objection squarely. The number of mulatto children visible on the streets suggested that the colored girl *needed* protection, she countered.[25]

Following the evangelical tradition of rescue and reform, social purity feminists like Stoddard sought to safeguard women as individuals with the armor of the law and to urge men as individuals to renounce the sexual double standard. After the turn of the century, women's groups focused on policing and prohibiting the dangerous public space itself, especially parks and dance halls that attracted working-class youth. They asked that municipalities add police matrons to their all-male law forces, a demand for formal, female authority in public that men resented and resisted. The petitioning women were often forced to raise the necessary money themselves, as did the clubwomen of Dallas, who engaged and paid the city's first policewoman.[26] The police matron specialized in "protective work" for young working-class women at risk of becoming sexually active, and consequently, it was widely believed, taking the first step down the road toward prostitution.

The police matron represented a new approach to public vice and prostitution, the progressives' faith in solving problems by giving charge to an acknowledged authority. While the WCTU continued to confront prostitution as a moral evil, clubwomen embraced and promoted the physician-led social hygiene movement that displaced social purity in the early twentieth century. A widespread public perception that venereal disease had increased to epidemic proportions—some sources claimed that at least 75 percent of all men were infected—sparked a nationwide campaign to shut down brothel districts. There are only fragmentary statistical data for venereal disease during this period; the actual male infection rate may have been anywhere between 10 to 50 percent. Unlike the white slavery scare, however, the danger was real even if the magnitude was exaggerated. Medical remedies were of limited effect; syphilis remained incurable until the invention of penicillin in the 1940s.[27]

Social hygiene redefined prostitution as a public health problem and identified a new victim of vice, the virtuous wife and mother. Dr. Prince Morrow's *Social Diseases and Marriage,* published in 1904, explained what medical research had discovered about venereal pathology and became the manifesto of the social hygiene movement. Morrow made dozens of speeches stressing the sexual danger that prostitution posed to the middle-class; young men contracted venereal disease in brothels and passed it on to innocent, unsuspecting brides when they married. The results were birth defects caused by syphilis, babies blinded from gonorrheal contamination as they passed through the birth canal, and wives rendered sterile from internal scarring.[28]

Dr. Rachelle Yarros, resident physician at Hull House and a founder of the American Social Hygiene Association, constructed a typical narrative in "The Secret Plague," which appeared in *Texas Club Woman* and other women's magazines. Yarros described the plight of wives who were puzzled at their chronic ill-health after marriage, discovering only when they had to go under the surgeon's knife that the family physician had kept the husband's "medical secret." Pointing out that "the cause is woman's," the TFWC president urged Texas clubwomen to investigate the vice traffic and bring pressure upon the authorities who allowed red-light districts to exist.[29]

Convinced that public ignorance about the transmission of venereal disease sustained the epidemic, social hygienists demanded an end to the "conspiracy of silence" that suppressed discussion of sexual matters. As a corrective, they pushed to have "sex hygiene" introduced into the public school curriculum. Their goal, a single standard of morality for men as well as women, differed little from that of the Victorian purity reformers, but the approach was scientific and rational. The innovation, which provoked sharp opposition from traditionalists, was endorsed by no less an authority than G. Stanley Hall, himself a social hygienist.[30]

The medical and educational approach to combatting prostitution thus opened the way for genteel women to take part in the new public conversation on sexual matters. Once the subject was connected to safeguarding the middle-class family and to the curriculum of the public schools it ceased to be unfit for ladies to know and talk about and became municipal housekeeping. A Chicago vice reformer addressed the 1910 GFWC Biennial, and in New York City John D. Rockefeller Jr. was overruled when he protested the unseemliness of appointing women to the Committee of Fourteen that investigated the city's prostitution problem. Three representatives from the Congress of Mothers served on the board of the Texas Social Hygiene Association and its president, Dr. Malone Duggan, spoke often to TCM conventions.[31]

Reconceptualizing prostitution as one more public health problem in need of a solution moved it beyond the purview of evangelical reformers and onto the woman's club agenda. The GFWC created a social hygiene committee, chaired by Rachelle Yarros, within its Department of Public Health, and a subcommittee on social hygiene in the normal schools chaired by Maggie Barry of Texas. In her enthusiasm, Barry even suggested that clubs in every community should cooperate to organize a social hygiene committee that could arrange for free public talks on the subject. "Women Will Not Hush Up" proclaimed an article in *American Club Woman* in 1914.[32] A GFWC member acknowledged that her mother would have been "terribly shocked" at such discussion and that in the 1890s she herself could not have mentioned the subject in mixed company without blushing. By the 1910s she had concluded "It is as much our duty to try to suppress the social evil as it is to promote education or secure a living wage for women in employment."[33]

In that sense, women's anti-vice work was not unlike their campaigns for municipal sanitation or pure water; it was an issue of pollution that breached the boundaries of the private home. To organized women who had learned "that effectively to 'swat the fly' they must swat its nest," as Mary Beard wrote, attacking the problem at its source meant eliminating vice districts. The Texas Congress of Mothers freely discussed strategies "to save the home from devastation from the *Great Black Plague*" and appointed a special committee for social hygiene. The organization's vice chairwoman for legislation called for a state red-light abatement law, quoting a Texas State Board of Health physician who attributed 90 percent of gynocological surgery and 80 percent of blindness in newborns to venereal transmission from husbands.[34]

Although no law was passed, several cities closed or constricted their reservation districts. The Beaumont Council of Mothers forced the city to act by presenting evidence that high school students were cutting through the reservation on their way home from school. In Houston, women's organizations and school trustees protested when "Happy Hollow" began to overflow into the Rusk School district; the district attorney forced the houses to relocate. The Austin City Council shut down "Guy Town," where an anti-vice reformer claimed to have counted as many as a hundred University of Texas students in one evening, in 1913, and Dallas did the same with its "Frogtown" district.[35]

The reformers, whose view of female sexuality precluded them from understanding prostitutes in any capacity other than victims, thought of themselves, however naively, as liberators. Before the Dallas County attorney served notices on 129 landladies and 211 inmates, all were visited by a committee of women who offered to help them find new homes and employment. The reformers were disappointed and disillusioned when only five accepted; few prostitutes wanted to be "rescued" into the hardship and low pay of domestic service or the restrictive supervision of a shelter for fallen women.[36] Evicted from "homes" in female-run brothels, prostitutes were forced into walking the streets under the control of pimps, the unintended consequence of middle-class women's desire to protect and purify.

❀

Like shuttering of brothel districts, extending the legal reach of segregation into new parts of the public domain increased female access to public space at the expense of groups considered "dangerous" or disreputable. Ironically, vice districts, which organized women of both races deplored, were an arena of permeable racial boundaries. In Houston's relocated reservation white and black women shared houses until 1909, when the justice of the peace ordered them to separate. Twenty-six black women who refused were arrested as vagrants and took their case as far as the state supreme court without success.

By the time they lost their last appeal in 1911, the census showed that almost no black women were living in brothels headed by white women. A significant percentage of those headed by black and mulatto women, however, continued to be racially mixed. What went on in black-headed houses, suggests historian Thomas Mackey, was probably a matter of indifference to white Houston. The real aim of the Jim Crow directive may have been to minimize racial conflict by keeping black men from patronizing white-run brothels.[37]

Edward L. Ayers has likewise pointed out that segregation, or the absence of it, was linked to gender. White women and black domestics shared the kitchen and nursery in private homes, while white and black males mingled freely in "bars, race tracks, and boxing rings" that were "often barely segregated at all."[38] Enlarging public space for respectable white women was inseparable from constricting that of the African American male; segregation made socially dangerous spaces "safe" for the New South's new women. The late nineteenth century saw laws mandating segregation in public transportation and accommodations added to southern statute books, although it is not entirely clear whether this marked a turn away from more flexible policies or merely formalized established custom.[39]

Beginning in 1891 Texas law required racial separation on passenger trains, and after the turn of the century city ordinances extended it to streetcars. In 1903 Houston and San Antonio instituted Jim Crow cars, prompting African American boycotts that lasted until 1905.[40] When Austin passed a restrictive ordinance in 1906, the newspaper was amused by domestic servants' threats to quit their jobs rather than take segregated street cars to their employers' homes. City council members would be in trouble at the polls, it announced jocularly, if both the "colored gentry" and the "indignant housewife" influencing her husband's ballot joined forces to turn them out. Predictably, white women supported the color line. Segregated transportation gave them the freedom of their growing cities, substituting the force of law for the protection of a male escort. The following year the state legislature amended the 1891 law to include streetcars and interurban railways, imposing lasting hardship and public humiliation on black women.[41]

White women accepted and perpetuated the Jim Crow system, voluntarily segregating their community building projects. The public libraries that clubwomen established were restricted to white users. Houston acquired its "colored" branch through the efforts of the African American community, and a Carnegie grant for a permanent building required the intervention of Booker T. Washington. White charities practiced various levels of racial discrimination. The director of the Sheltering Arms in Houston, who said she had "never been interested in colored organizations," summed up the prevailing sentiment. The Dallas Infants' Welfare and Milk Association required black mothers to enter its milk station by the side door and tolerated them on the condition that they did not come "in such numbers" as to be "objectionable to white people." The Industrial Day Home in Houston adopted a simpler policy: "We do not take colored children or Mexicans."[42]

Settlement houses seldom reached out to African Americans either, a situation nearly as prevalent in the North as in the South. Houston, which had the state's largest concentration of urban blacks (30 percent in 1910) finally established a neighborhood center for them late in 1917. Bethlehem Settlement, initiated under the auspices of the Social Service Bureau of the Texas Conference of Charities and Correction (which had absorbed the Houston Settlement Association), was administered by a board made up of equal numbers of whites and blacks. Located between the city dump and the vice district, the house stood at the end of a "steep rough road" that inevitably became known as the Road to

Bethlehem. The clubs it sponsored had names like Little Housekeepers (for young girls) and Self-Improvement (for older ones), reflecting the tendency of whites to blame the economic and social problems of the black community on disorganized home lives—and the determination of middle-class black women to overcome the stereotype.[43]

The social geography of race hid from most whites the parallel women's culture in the African American community. With a small and unevenly dispersed population upon which to draw, the state's federation of black clubwomen, founded in 1905, grew less quickly and uniformly than the white one. City federations formed later, and there were fewer of them. NACW records show that Paris, a railroad center in North Texas, reported an African American federation of clubs as early as 1908, uniting the Women's Home Progressive Circle, American Sewing Circle, Christian Home Talent Club, White Swan Social Club, Ladies Reading Circle, and the 1906 Art Club. San Antonio formed a city federation in 1913, but Dallas apparently had no federated black clubs at all until the Priscilla Art Club organized in 1911.[44]

Although the Texas Association of Colored Women's Clubs remained one of the smallest southern federations in the NACW, it expanded in membership and focus under the administration of Mary Alphin (1910–16). The wife of a Waco minister, Alphin also headed the NACW's Department of Relgious Work for most of her tenure as TACWC president, bringing deep conviction to both positions. When she assumed the TACWC presidency in 1910 federated club-work was "at a low ebb"; only eleven clubs were represented at the state convention. The following year, after Margaret Murray Washington visited the state and spoke in several cities, thirty-one clubs sent delegates. Revenue of more than $180 in 1911, up from less than $30 in 1910, encouraged the TACWC to commit itself to its first social welfare project, "a charitable institution for our boys who are unfortunate in life."[45]

Middle-class white women who willingly undertook the work of "uplifting" immigrants and working-class women of their own race, left to this tiny African American middle class the overwhelming task of saving the black masses. The name and membership criteria of Houston's Married Ladies Social, Art, and Charity Club, restricted to "respectable married women living with their husbands," eloquently expressed the dilemma of African American clubwomen. They had to raise their image in white eyes, struggling against prejudice and stereotype that branded black women as amoral, sexually promiscuous members of a "degraded race." At the same time, they could not isolate themselves from the enormously needy black underclass; self-culture and racial uplift—art and charity—were interwoven. "We watched closely the aim set forth in every club report," the TACWC's corresponding secretary wrote of the 1915 convention, "and thank God, not one read that the aim was for self-pleasure—the sentiment of every report being 'non mihi, sed alis'—not myself, but for others."[46]

Because African Americans were largely denied access to public services, the work of black clubwomen in providing for the needy and improving living standards represented community development as well as charity. They invested money not in clubhouses for themselves but structures for the community. The Colored Woman's Progressive Club organized in Galveston in 1913 "to disburse charity, to improve social and civic conditions, and to work for the uplift of juvenile offenders" within two years began discussing fundraising for a home for elderly women. The Heart's Ease Circle of the King's Daughters already had a similar project underway in Austin; it was raising one hundred dollars a month to maintain six women in a rented cottage and planning to purchase a permanent residence. The TACWC reported at mid-decade that clubwomen were "buying parks for children's playgrounds, equipping schools with swings and gymnasiums, doing settlement work" and other projects demonstrating "that there are a few women on Texas soil who have their eyes open to the needs of our people."[47]

Racism forced black women to rely on their own resources and networks. On occasion, however, women's groups might cooperate across the racial divide to accomplish a specific purpose. Christia Adair, an African American church activist, was affronted at the existence of a protected gambling house on the edge of the black district in Kingsville. Knowing that the corrupt sheriff would ignore black women's protests, Adair approached the president of a white mothers' club and pointed out their mutual interest in shutting down a vice lure for adolescents. With the white women's advice and support, Adair organized a mothers' club in the black community and called on the district attorney, who investigated and forced the house to close.[48]

❀

The women who most dramatically engaged popular attention as they invaded public space were the new "working girls." In Houston women workers early demonstrated a public labor presence. In 1900 fourteen of Southwestern Telephone and Telegraph's "young lady operators," having learned from some linemen in their boarding house of the sickness and death benefits available through the International Brotherhood of Electrical Workers, joined Local No. 66. Two were immediately fired and the others threatened with dismissal. Forty more operators then joined the union and all of them, along with thirty men from the line and ground crews, went on strike. "It has come to a pretty pass when the officials of a corporation shall dictate to a poorly paid, hard working, honest class of girls what they shall and shall not belong to," one of the striking operators told the *Houston Post*. Southwestern Telephone's attempt to break the strike with new operators provoked a crowd action outside the building, and after six days the company relented and rehired the striking workers.[49]

Later that year some of the telephone girls walked out again, this time in sympathy with San Antonio operators, who wanted their eleven- and thirteen-hour shifts reduced. This strike was less successful, but it spread to Dallas, Fort Worth, Galveston, Waco, and several smaller cities with relay stations before dissolving. By 1915, however, local chapters of the Telephone Operators Union had been established in Port Arthur and Denison. The Port Arthur operators struck the following year when the Texas Long Lines Company refused to recognize the union or raise wages, which began at eighteen dollars a month after an unpaid training period of two to four months. Despite support from the town's trade unions and guidance from the International Brotherhood of Electrical Workers, the Port Arthur strike failed; the operators did not have the financial resources to survive a prolonged walkout.[50]

The unprecedented numbers of young women who entered wage labor between 1890 and 1910 initiated a women's politics based on labor activism and a new kind of female public presence. Nationally, the number of wage-earning women had been growing almost twice as fast as the adult female population since 1880; 28 percent of urban women were employed by 1900. Houston—where women could already be identified in thirty different occupations as early as 1890—showed a figure of 27 percent. Dallas counted 26 percent and the younger city of Fort Worth 22 percent, just one point below Chicago. Black women who toiled as domestic servants and laundresses accounted for part of these figures, but the new jobs opening up in factories, stores, and offices were filled by a cohort of young white women or "working girls."[51]

Unlike the daughters of poor, black, and immigrant families, who had always been a visible but unremarked part of the labor force, the new female workers attracted attention because they were native-born, white, and "respectable." A great many were farm girls drawn to the labor-hungry cities. Segregated into low-paid "female" jobs, they were a plentiful supply of cheap labor for the late nineteenth century's dramatic business and industrial expansion and a source of moral anxiety to middle-class observers. "Never before in civilization have such numbers of girls been suddenly released from the protection of the home and permitted to walk unattended upon city streets and to work under alien roofs," worried Jane Addams.[52]

The vast majority of such women did not earn enough for subsistence. In Houston at the turn of the century, the Southwestern Telephone and Telegraph

Exchange operators took home $3.50 a week—assuming they had not missed any days because of illness or been docked for any tolls the company had been unable to collect. Saleswomen at the new department stores, Foley's, Levy's, and Meyer and Gimbel, began at about the same minimum. Less refined employment at one of the overall factories, the Oriental Textile Mills, or Texas Bag and Fiber paid a living wage (estimated at eight dollars a week in 1914) if there were no seasonal layoffs or slow downs, as there nearly always were.[53]

At the turn of the century, one such urban working woman in five was estimated to be dwelling apart from family or employer. While self-supporting young men living in boarding or rooming houses or as lodgers in poor working-class households were perceived as resourceful and independent, society viewed their female counterparts as "adrift," unanchored to the supervision of a patriarchal family. The working girl's precarious economic status and unwonted freedom seemed to court sexual danger, especially as rising food and labor costs encouraged boardinghouse keepers to convert to the more profitable and impersonal practice of simply letting out rooms. Rooming houses lacked the familial atmosphere created by communal dining and socializing in a common parlor, and there was no place for women to receive male guests except in their bedrooms.[54]

Consequently, middle-class women sought to create affordable and morally safe living spaces for young working women through subsidized boarding homes and cooperative residences. The U.S. Department of Labor tallied some ninety such establishments in forty-five cities by 1898, and after the turn of the century they became part of the urban landscape in Texas. The Young Women's Co-operative Home in Houston began as a project of the Woman's Board of City Missions, first in a small rented house in 1907, later as part of the Wesley House, and finally in 1912 in its own building. Board was charged on a sliding scale, according to income, while laundry and sewing facilities enabled the young women to save the additional cost of outside services. To the mission society, however, the building's great appeal was its resemblence to a bourgeois home presided over by motherly deaconesses. The report dwelt on the wholesome domestic comforts: the library, current magazines, the social hall equipped with grand piano and victrola. Most important, "there are parlors, porch, and lawn where one's friends may be entertained—a very essential element in a program of protection for girls."[55]

The Young Women's Christian Association, which was already forty years old in the North, reached the state at the same time. The YWCA held its first Texas convention in 1906 and built the first city "Y" in Houston the following year, charging $2.50 to $3.75 a week for board. By 1910 YWCAs had been erected in Dallas, Fort Worth, San Antonio, and El Paso. The smaller cities of Austin,

Beaumont, and Galveston followed by 1916, and the state's first black YWCA, Houston's Blue Triangle Branch, was built in 1918 (see chapter 6). YWCAs of- fered Bible classes, mission study classes, and Sunday vespers to address spiritual needs, while "social evenings," entertainments, and self-governing clubs ap- pealed to secular ones. Girls could improve their bodies in the gymnasium, their minds in the reading room, and their vocational and domestic skills through classes in modern languages, office procedures, dressmaking, millinery, and cooking.[56]

With its chaperoned social gatherings and requirement that male guests be re- ceived only in formal parlors during designated hours, the YWCA upheld the conventions that had long secluded middle-class daughters and safeguarded their reputations. Working-class girls accustomed to less domestic privacy and a social life centered around the neighborhood and front stoop chafed at such restrictions and displayed more enthusiasm for the attractions of the new het- erosocial culture of commercialized leisure. The crowds of unchaperoned young women who mingled with strangers in movie houses, dance halls, and other "cheap amusements" were claiming urban space after their own dramatic fash- ion.[57] Cultural elites, worried over what appeared to them as declining moral standards, responded with attempts to censor movies and regulate dance halls.

Young working women's general preference for mixed company and com- mercial amusements over the YWCA's emphasis on sex-segregation and sister- hood has been well noted.[58] Resisting the restrictions of genteel culture, they pioneered new freedoms in the anonymity of urban life that inevitably spread to their middle-class sisters. In one respect in which the YWCAs did fill an un- met need, however, they were popular and well-patronized. Young working women used them to claim public privileges similar to those that their male counterparts enjoyed through traditional saloon culture, to which women had only restricted access.

The urban saloon was the laboring man's club and its ubiquitous "free" lunch with the purchase of a five-cent beer supplied many a workingman's chief day- time nourishment. "Working girls," especially those in the white-collar office and retail sectors, used the YWCA for equivalent purposes. The most popular draw was the inexpensive cafeteria, the working girl's equivalent of the saloon free lunch. For poorly paid women who ordinarily ate little or nothing at noon, the lunchrooms were an affordable alternative. In the 1910s the Texas YWCAs calculated the average price of their meals at sixteen to seventeen cents and re- ported lunchtime crowds as high as 150 to 200 daily. Cafeteria statistics were the most impressive numbers in the annual reports: more than 51,000 meals served in Fort Worth in 1908; 53,630 in Houston in 1912; 72,000 in Galveston in 1915. Also popular at noontime were rest rooms furnished with couches where women could lie down and put their feet up, and reading rooms supplied with newspapers and magazines.[59]

Through the formal agency of middle-class women, "working girls" also found some of the social supports that saloonkeepers extended informally to working men: information on employment opportunities and charitable relief in emergencies. The YWCA employment bureau listed job openings and kept files of women who applied for work. Those new to the city applied to the Y to get their bearings. "They come to us to tell them a good place to board, or a good bank in which to place their money, or help in securing positions," the Dallas chapter reported. The Houston chapter referred five hundred women to acceptable boarding houses in 1910. It was not unusual for women in dire straits to be accommodated for free at the local Y while they got on their feet again; San Antonio's indicated that "many girls have been helped who were out of money and employment."[60]

The YWCA also posted travelers' aid secretaries at railroad stations to exert female guardianship over unsophisticated country girls (in popular imagination the potential victims of seducers and "white slavers") seeking city jobs. The general secretary of the Fort Worth Y advised that this was a job for the *"best trained, most consecrated worker."* She drew a verbal picture of the "innocent young girls who are lonely and frightened, and who are very willing to trust strangers," the naive "young women coming into the cities to hunt for work, 'without money and without price,' and not knowing where to lay their heads at night." The travelers' aid secretary directed them to reputable hotels and boarding houses, or to the Y, or helped them locate friends and relatives. Houston's secretary reported assisting nearly three hundred women in one month in 1910.[61]

At the same time that the YWCA provided protected social space for wage-earning women it opened public opportunities for the middle-class women who ran each branch. Elite local women sat on the city boards, while younger women in search of a profession found full-time work as administrators or "secretaries." The YWCA National Training School in New York City offered social service training to young college women like Helen Knox, who took the course after graduating from the University of Texas and returned to Austin to serve as state secretary. Every city Y required a staff of paid secretaries that included a general administrator and directors in charge of specific phases of the work, such as membership, travelers' aid, physical culture, lunchroom, and boarding home. And each chapter enrolled hundreds of members, quickly becoming its city's largest woman's organization. By the early 1910s the Dallas and Fort Worth YWCAs each counted some eight hundred members. Houston had fourteen hundred, San Antonio nearly nineteen hundred, and Galveston two thousand.[62]

Through the YWCA church and club women cooperated to support the labor activism of working-class daughters. In 1911 the National Y formally committed itself to an education campaign that stressed the need for a living wage for women and to promoting legislation to regulate wages and hours. Since Texas had no branch of the Woman's Trade Union League (which did not reach the South until the 1920s), the Y was the only cross-class women's organization working to improve conditions for wage-earning women. Religious outreach work at local factories, where Y workers held noontime meetings, allowed them to see working conditions firsthand. In 1915 secretaries from the Austin and Houston YWCAs testified before the state legislature that some young women in their boarding homes were paid as little as three to five dollars a week and urged the legislators to enact a minimum wage bill.[63]

Labor activism enabled working-class women to assume a public role that middle-class women had already perfected, legislative lobbying. An organized attempt to reduce hours for women workers in Texas depended heavily upon the public presence of Eva Goldsmith, the energetic and articulate president of the Texas District Council of the United Garment Workers. Goldsmith was one of Houston's "women adrift" securely domiciled in the Young Women's Cooperative Home. Like untold numbers of other farm girls, she had come to the city in search of better prospects and more money. She worked at various factory jobs and eventually became a mainstay of United Garment Workers Local No. 31 and a labor spokeswoman.[64]

Eva Goldsmith was the Texas State Federation of Labor's star lobbyist in 1913 as it pressed for a bill restricting working women's hours to a maximum of fifty-four a week. Arguing against a coalition of employers from the cotton mills, commercial laundries, telegraph, and telephone companies, Goldsmith was represented in the labor press as a public heroine. The *Houston Labor Journal* compared her to Sam Houston defending the Texas Republic from the Mexican army. Although the businessmen succeeded in mutilating the bill almost beyond recognition, Goldsmith's eloquence and the petition of other labor women resulted in her appointment as the first woman member of the TSFL's Legislative Committee. She was back in Austin at the next biennial session in 1915 to get the Fifty-four Hour Law expanded and strengthened and to lobby for a minimum wage law for women. The YWCA, Woman's Christian Temperance Union, and Texas Federation of Women's Clubs turned out in support.[65] The women were only partially successful—the minimum wage bill failed—but a cross-class coalition had been formed, and it would continue to press for additional reforms.

❀

By the 1910s women had made irrevocable inroads into the public domain. Working-class women claimed new roles in employment and discovered a voice as labor activists. Middle-class women reached the apotheosis of their voluntarist politics predicated on morality and domesticity and sought connection with their working-class counterparts through social settlements and YWCAs. Through the social hygiene crusade against urban prostitution, they fatally undermined the tradition that safeguarding female purity required keeping women ignorant of vice and opened a door once closed against their full participation in public forums. As women gained public access, the argument that they would be morally compromised by entering politics and voting lost credibility.

Women's new visibility and outspokenness did not necessarily signify an emerging feminist consciousness; female public activity is not feminist unless it challenges male domination.[66] But women such as Eva Goldsmith had already committed themselves to suffrage. As chair of an ad hoc committee of the Houston Woman's Political Union, she spent the summer of 1916 campaigning against local candidates for the legislature who opposed woman suffrage. The WPU was weak and the legislative district large, and although Goldsmith was not optimistic about the suffragists' chances of success, she vowed "to work till I die if necessary."[67]

As Glenna Matthews has stressed, "feminism could never have been formulated until a wide array of women had felt some security in staking out their claims to a wide variety of public roles."[68] In the two decades between 1890 and 1910 women did claim such public social and cultural roles in Texas. Like Eva Goldsmith, the most outspoken of these "public women" had begun to formulate a feminist demand for equal legal and political rights and were prepared to fight a hard battle against long odds.

"I Wish My Mother Had a Vote"   5

BY THE TIME a sustained and successful suffrage movement took root in Texas in the 1910s, two previous attempts had expired in failure. The Texas Equal Rights Association (TERA), organized by the National American Woman Suffrage Association in the spring of 1893, lasted only until 1896. A few years later in Houston Annette Finnigan and her two sisters organized the Texas Woman Suffrage Association, which functioned, with only nominal growth in membership, from 1903 until the Finnigans moved to New York in 1905. A lecture tour by NAWSA President Anna Howard Shaw in 1908 prompted a society to form in Austin, and for the next four years it was the only active suffrage association in the state.

The rebirth that followed was due in large part to the influence of Eleanor Brackenridge, who brought the San Antonio Equal Franchise Society into being in 1912. A year later she revived the state organization. Brackenridge was by then seventy-five years old, with an extensive record of progressive activism. Yet despite her long sympathy with woman's rights, she had taken no part in the two earlier organizing efforts. The time had not been right then, she later explained; the public was not ready for suffrage.[1]

By 1912–13 the time was obviously right. As Anna Howard Shaw and organizers from NAWSA toured the state in 1912, urban women responded by forming suffrage societies whose membership expanded rapidly. San Antonio's began with 75 members in February. The number increased to 144 by the end of March, and to nearly 400 by November; by April 1913 membership stood at 575. Galveston, which organized with 81 women, counted 300 members by 1915. Forty-three Dallas women formed a suffrage society in 1913 whose membership more than tripled within a month and continued to climb.[2]

For the first time, local growth was vigorous enough to sustain a strong state organization. Within two years the Texas Woman Suffrage Association had 2,500 members in 21 local societies; by 1916 the number of locals had risen to 80 and membership was estimated at 9,500. The suffragists of the 1890s had held their meetings in hotel parlors and private homes; those of the 1910s moved into the parks and streets for open air rallies and parades. The Dallas ESA regularly set up a banner-draped booth at the State Fair; at the first one in 1913 the organization handed out more than forty thousand leaflets and gave away copies of the *Woman's Journal.* In the years that followed the members publicized "Suffrage Day" by staging an automobile parade to the fairgrounds, decorating the cars with the suffrage colors of yellow and white.[3]

A similar pattern was repeating itself across the South. Suffrage associations that had been founded in the 1890s, only to disintegrate or go dormant within a few years, were revived and revitalized. Nationally, the movement was emerging from the "doldrums," a fourteen-year stretch of failed state referenda that broke when Washington enfranchised women in 1910. California followed in 1911, and Oregon, Kansas, and Arizona in 1912. As suffrage became a mass movement in the 1910s the South, at last, was part of it. Although southern suffragists were unable to secure full voting rights in any state, they pried partial concessions from stubborn legislatures: primary suffrage in Arkansas (1917) and Texas (1918) and presidential suffrage in Tennessee (1919) and Kentucky (1920).

Unlike the first southern suffrage movement of the 1890s, which was small and short-lived, the second one of the 1910s was broad-based and enduring. Its successes were limited by the region's political conservatism and racial polarization, but its leaders were dedicated workers with unimpeachable credentials as southern ladies. A decade earlier suffrage had stirred little response in such women. What then prompted the rise of a second generation of southern suffragists, why did they succeed where the first generation had failed, and how did they negotiate the rocky terrain of racial politics?

When the Texas Equal Rights Association quietly expired in 1896 the idea of a state suffrage society seemed decisively discredited. The TERA began with forty-eight charter members in 1893 and never thereafter reported membership figures, but it apparently increased very little. Only nine local chapters were founded, most of them in the towns where the officers resided. Insufficient funds forced it to abandon the office of state organizer in 1894, and in 1895 the press superintendent announced that there was not enough money to publicize the work. That year the treasurer reported revenues of $13.50 and just three new memberships.[4]

The stigma of radical feminism kept the TERA small and struggling throughout its brief existence. Its most outspoken members openly criticized the clergy and declared their disdain for female subordination as decreed by St. Paul. Elizabeth Turner Fry, the wife of a prominent San Antonio merchant, had contributed heavily to the erection of the city's Missionary Christian Church and organized its Sunday School, but she clashed with her pastor on the issue of female emancipation. The suffragist goal of making women self-reliant individualists "should be presented weekly from the pulpit," Fry argued, suggesting that ministers who kept silent were no better than those who preached against women's rights. Dr. Grace Danforth, who had become a suffrage convert during her medical student days in Chicago, after hearing Lucy Stone speak, frankly declared that the church was woman's worst oppressor. President Rebecca Henry Hayes agreed, pointing out that whenever women asked for the use of a church they invariably were told to meet in the basement.[5]

In the 1890s, the TERA's vision of equality was simply too radical to attract broad support. Grace Danforth's announcement that "we in this day and generation do not propose to be hampered by either Moses and the prophets or Blackstone" offended women who had been brought up on the Bible. And Blackstone meant nothing to those who had not personally confronted gender discrimination in the legal system, or studied it, as clubwomen would in the new century. The plan of work adopted for the local level, compiling lists of women taxpayers and identifying court cases in which judges had handed down sex-based judgments against women to use as "campaign documents," had little appeal for women who were not already committed feminists.[6]

Political abstractions did not move many either. The TERA's lofty Jeffersonian motto, "Governments derive their just powers from the consent of the governed," lacked resonance for wives and mothers engrossed in domestic responsibilities. When Rebecca Henry Hayes patterned her 1894 presidential address on the radical 1848 Seneca Falls "Declaration of Sentiments," she was preaching to the converted.[7] Her quotations from the Declaration of Independence and recitation of the injustices to which Texas women had been subjected failed to stir privileged women who asserted that they had all the rights they wanted.

The TERA suffragists pitched their argument to justice because they as yet had no other vision. Nor could most women yet imagine what they might actually do with the vote other than perhaps abolish saloons; significantly, the TERA's core membership came from the WCTU. Eight of the eleven women who signed the call to organize and nine of the ten officers subsequently elected are known to have been temperance workers. Such women had experience as social activists and belonged to a national organization that had endorsed woman suffrage. They had rejected keeping silence in the churches and committed themselves to, in Elizabeth Fry's words, "advanc[ing] God's kingdom beyond the home."[8]

By 1913, when a statewide suffrage movement finally took hold, thousands of women had learned how they could use the vote. The new voluntary associations founded in the decade and a half following the TERA's demise had shown them, even though none had been founded to advance women's rights. The Texas Federation of Women's Clubs, Young Women's Christian Association, and Texas Congress of Mothers had not yet endorsed suffrage, but women from these organizations swelled the second generation of suffragists. Most shunned the emerging new concept, "feminism," which the *Houston Post* denounced as "abhorrent to the Southern idea of home and society," but still they doubted that men could represent women's interests at the polls.[9]

Especially among women of middle age or older, support for suffrage was linked to membership in voluntary associations. In Galveston, for example, twenty-one of the twenty-four Equal Suffrage Association officers had extensive records of volunteer activism in a total of nineteen other clubs and societies. Half of the Galveston ESA officers also held offices in from one to three other clubs; nine served in leadership positions in four or more.[10] In San Antonio, Eleanor Brackenridge assumed the presidency of the Equal Franchise Society after a long career in voluntary associations. She was a member of the WCTU and YWCA, founding president of the San Antonio Woman's Club, a vice president of the TFWC, and served on the education committees of both the TFWC and GFWC. Brackenridge had helped found at least three school mothers' clubs in San Antonio; organized the San Antonio Council of Mothers and served as its first president; and held the offices of legislative chair and honorary president in the Texas Congress of Mothers.[11]

As Brackenridge discerned, an important difference between the "wrong" and the "right" time for suffrage was the existence of this web of associations, an essential precondition for the emergence of suffrage as a mass movement. So greatly did the multiplication of voluntary associations alter the social landscape for women that in Texas the suffragists of the 1890s and those of the 1910s quite literally lived in different worlds. In Houston, for example, the city directory for 1887–88 counted eighteen women's church and missionary societies, a WCTU chapter, the Ladies' Reading Club, and a kindergarten association. By 1913 the directory listed ten additional fine arts and literary clubs, with a total of more than 250 members. There was a huge Civic Club reporting 400 "earnest, active women," while the downtown Woman's Club and the Houston Heights Woman's Club (which had its own clubhouse) together counted 133. Seventeen school mothers' clubs, most founded between 1907 and 1909, totaled nearly 700 members.

The women's clubs had united to form the Houston Federation of Women's Clubs, and the mothers' clubs had joined together as the Houston Council of Mothers and Parent-Teacher Associations. The city by then had a YWCA (900 members), a Woman's Protective Association, and an eighty-five-member local union of the United Garment Workers of America. The Houston Lyceum and

Carnegie Library Association and the Houston Settlement Association operated under all-female boards. Together these organizations constituted a vast pool of potential members for a city-wide suffrage society that counted members by the hundreds instead of by tens. When Annette Finnigan revived the Houston Woman's Political Union, which had failed to thrive a decade earlier, two hundred women came forward at once. Mrs. Harris Masterson of the YWCA filled the vice presidency, Julia Ideson of the Library Association served as treasurer, and Eva Goldsmith of the garment workers' union gave speeches.[12]

Discovering civic activism on behalf of goals such as health and sanitation, education, and child welfare enabled women to evaluate suffrage in a new context. In the 1890s the arguments of Ellen Lawson Dabbs and Grace Danforth that women should vote on school issues brought no answering response except from the WCTU, which was already on record for it.[13] Over the next two decades, however, members of women's and mothers' clubs bent on improving their children's schools confronted the frustrations of importuning local school boards for change. In Dallas and San Antonio clubwomen backed by their city federations successfully put themselves forward for board seats. School suffrage had been only a political abstraction in the 1890s; by the 1910s the mothers' movement and the better schools campaign had made it real and desirable.

Married women's property rights became a personal issue in the same fashion; clubwomen backed into it through their concern over laws regulating the labor of women and children. In Texas the influence of Spanish civil law had modified the English common law doctrine of coverture, which entitled a husband to his wife's property and earnings and sole guardianship of their children. But while the state's community property statute recognized a married woman's right to own property, it denied her control of it. The husband had the sole right to manage his wife's share of the community property *and* her separate property—that which she owned before marriage or received afterward by gift. Only the husband could dispose of community property, and the wife's share could be seized in payment of his debts. The TERA had earlier tried to dramatize the problem by assigning Alice McAnulty to compile a report on the legal status of women. The project proved more than McAnulty could carry out alone in the 1890s. She ended up consulting a judge who flatly, and not entirely accurately, informed her that "under the laws of Texas women had no legal status," and the effort went no further.[14]

A decade later, women's clubs began to explore married women's legal disabilities. Through Isadore Callaway, the Dallas Free Kindergarten and Industrial Association persuaded journalist Lawrence Neff to compile a digest of state laws, *The Legal Status of Women in Texas* (1905), which it sold to raise revenue for the kindergarten association. Clubwomen who used it as a study text—one club required members to answer roll call with a quotation from the statutes—learned that they did not have all the rights they needed after all. A delegate to the TFWC's 1906 convention provoked appreciative laughter by relating how she discovered that if her husband died intestate she would be legally barred from drawing the funeral expenses from his bank account; when she showed him the passage, he immediately transferred the account to her name.[15]

Clubwomen, beginning without TERA's feminist conviction, made a success of the issue because what they had instead—large membership and financial resources—mattered more in the long run. In 1907 the TFWC suggested that each club devote at least one meeting to women's disabilities under the law, and Eleanor Brackenridge assisted by funding a printing of *The Legal Status of Women in Texas* for free distribution. The Texas Congress of Mothers got its information through its vice chair (under Brackenridge) for legislation, Hortense Ward. The first woman in Texas to pass the bar examination and a partner with her husband in the Houston firm of Ward and Ward, she explained coverture in an article for the *Houston Chronicle* that was subsequently reprinted as a pamphlet.[16]

Working separately, the TFWC and the TCM in 1913 mobilized Texas women to demand a married women's property law, the means by which state legislatures had been eroding coverture in various degrees since the 1830s. Susan B. Anthony and Elizabeth Cady Stanton had argued for New York's statute more than half a century earlier in the feminist language of natural rights, denouncing coverture as "a condition of servitude most bitter and absolute." Clubwomen cast their own arguments in maternalist rhetoric: security for the working-class wife whose children went without necessities if she had an improvident or drunken husband who appropriated her wages, and for the middle-class wife whose individual property could be seized by creditors if her husband's business failed.[17]

The 1910 GFWC Biennial authorized the appointment of a special committee to survey women's legal rights and restrictions across the country, and two years later it was ready to act. A popular women's magazine, *The Delineator,* had also begun to investigate the issue after muckraking journalist William Hard took over the magazine's social policy column in October 1911. Prompted by a letter from a reader in San Antonio describing Texas law, Hard instigated a series exploring the legal status of wives and mothers. He also spoke in 1912 at the National Congress of Mothers convention and the GFWC Biennial, which resolved unanimously in favor of equal child guardianship rights for mothers and married women's property laws "for the greater honor and greater stability of the home."[18]

The *Delineator* invited clubwomen and women everywhere to pursue this goal by joining the magazine's new "Home League." Members received digests of the relevant laws for their own states—for Texas it was Hortense Ward's "Legal Status of Married Women"—and notification of pending legislation so that they could initiate grassroots publicity and exert constituent pressure on their legislative representatives. The campaign reached huge numbers of women. The GFWC alone counted more than three-quarters of a million members, and *The Delineator*, published by the Butterick Company, whose name was synonymous with home sewing patterns, was the nation's third largest women's magazine; it had a million subscribers. Through William Hard's series they learned that, the tradition of Stanton and Anthony notwithstanding, asking for equal standing before the law was neither radical nor unwomanly.

Since neither the GFWC nor the Congress of Mothers had endorsed suffrage, Hard (who personally favored it) carefully separated the two issues, assuring readers that the Home League was not agitating for "any political right whatsoever." It sought only "the complete protection of wifehood and motherhood." Delicate line drawings of attractive young mothers with children at their knees or babies in their arms illustrated Hard's articles. "*It is not at all necessary that we should be in favor of suffrage in order to be in favor of the increase of women's powers in their homes,*" he emphasized.[19]

These arguments lined up the TFWC, TCM, and WCTU, as well as the United Daughters of the Confederacy, Daughters of the American Revolution, and Daughters of the Republic of Texas behind the effort to secure a married women's property law in 1913. The photographs of their presidents accompanied Hard's article, "Will Texas Do Better by Its Married Women?"[20] Both the TWFC and the TCM made married women's property rights the sole focus of their legislative work that year. The bill they secured gave a married woman control of her separate personal property and excluded her personal earnings and income from her rental property and stocks and bonds from her husband's management. The wife's separate property and the portion of the community property that she managed was exempted from seizure for the husband's debts.[21]

The parallels between legal coverture and its political equivalent, disfranchisement, were obvious though unspoken. If a woman was entitled to control her own property, why should she not be released from political coverture to cast her own ballot? Coverture at law assumed that the interests of husband and wife were the same and that the husband would manage his wife's property judiciously. The same rationale underlay female disfranchisement; a man supposedly represented the family's interests at the polls. Both conditions forced women to depend on the wisdom and goodwill of men, who frequently disappointed them. Because the legal and political coverture justified as "protecting" women so frequently did the reverse, women were able to turn the rationale to their own advantage. They could argue the need for married women's property law, and a vote, to defend their interests and those of their children. Reconceptualized and de-radicalized by an infusion of Progressive-Era maternalism, both demands gained popularity.

Hortense Ward's argument for the married women's property law, "a legal slave, though the chains be of rose leaves, does not make the highest type of mother," required only slight semantic modification to become a suffrage motto. A woman deprived of the ballot did not make the highest type of mother, either. The theme of mainstream suffrage activism in the 1910s would be Jane Addams's question, "May we not fairly say that American women need this implement in order to preserve the home?" A modern woman could not fulfill her responsibilities as mother and housekeeper by her own efforts alone, Addams reasoned, "because she is utterly dependent upon the city administration for the conditions which render decent living possible." Galveston's Perle Penfield, the TWSA's first organizer, began her work in 1914 by stressing the same theme: "It is no more than right that the mother should have a voice in stating what should be done to protect her home, her family's food, and her family's surroundings."[22]

Some form of this argument was on the lips of nearly every mainstream suffragist after 1912, and its popularity suggests a need to reevaluate the "doldrums" between 1896 and 1910. Sara Hunter Graham has contended that these years were actually a time of renewal during which the leaders of NAWSA reshaped the movement's image; they distanced it from nineteenth-century radicalism and pursued a "society plan" to win converts among wealthy women. The mushrooming of local suffrage societies in Texas after 1912 indicates a parallel transformation at the grassroots: during the so-called doldrums the expansive growth of voluntary associations produced the women who would become the rank and file of a mass suffrage movement. The social reform agenda that middle-class women had developed through their voluntarist politics became part of the "new" NAWSA. By the mid-1910s its journal, *The Woman Citizen*, periodically featured a "Wheel of Progress" tracking state advances in implementing ten social justice and municipal housekeeping reforms directed at the welfare of women and children.[23]

In Texas and the nation the ubiquitous municipal housekeeping rationale, stressing the differences rather than the similarities between the sexes, marked the emergence of the progressive New Suffragist of the 1910s. While a radical minority of suffragists broke away from NAWSA to form the National Woman's Party and picket the White House, the moderate majority increasingly emphasized the social utility of a female ballot. Aileen Kraditor, in her seminal analysis, identified a shift in emphasis from justice to expediency in suffrage arguments between the nineteenth and twentieth centuries. Focusing on rhetorical strategy, however, obscures the underlying social metamorphosis. Suffrage ideology changed because the composition of the movement itself altered; in the 1910s thousands of "domestic feminists" who had acquired their convictions through women's clubs and civic organizations joined the suffrage ranks.[24]

These women brought their causes into the suffrage movement, reshaping its rhetoric accordingly. The infant welfare movement furnishes a notable example. The National Congress of Mothers and *The Delineator* had begun cooperating in a campaign to educate mothers about infant and child health in 1909, and by 1912 the GFWC was planning one as well. Beginning in 1913 organized women in hundreds of communities across the nation staged "Better Babies" contests, instigated by clubs and the *Woman's Home Companion* to help mothers identify developmental problems such as insufficient weight gain or the symptoms of vitamin deficiency. Local competitions in Texas in 1914 culminated in a grand contest at the State Fair. That year also saw the beginning of "Baby Weeks" in major cities such as New York, Chicago, and Dallas to publicize the problem of infant mortality. By 1916 Baby Week was being observed in small towns—at least 150 Texas communities participated that year—and rural areas, wherever the GFWC's network of clubs penetrated.[25]

By the mid-1910s the link between babies, mothers, and ballots was prominently featured in the literature the NAWSA distributed through state suffrage associations. Broadsides such as "Women in the Home," "Twelve Reasons Why Mothers Should Have the Vote," and "Better Babies" stressed the potential power of enfranchised women to safeguard child health. The progressives' passion for science and statistics infused the message, "proving" a connection between woman suffrage and low infant mortality. Much was made of the fact that New Zealand, where women had voted longest, had the lowest infant death rate in the world; in the United States the West Coast suffrage states stood out. The sharply contrasting rates for Spokane, Washington (55 deaths per thousand), and San Antonio (245 per thousand) in NAWSA's "Better Babies" broadside led easily (if not accurately) to the desired conclusion.[26]

Suffragists did not abandon the equality argument by any means; the letterhead of the San Antonio Equal Franchise Society proclaimed "Justice Under the Law for All" and "Citizenship for Women." By the 1910s, however, some of the worst forms of discrimination that had once kept women out of universities and the professions and under coverture had been mitigated. At the same time, voluntarist politics had refined women's belief in the value of a female perspective. The TWSA, which changed its name to Texas Equal Suffrage Association

(TESA) in 1916, drew up guidelines for local speakers that included a reminder to "by all means touch on the need of Mothers for the ballot for the protection of home and children." The San Antonio Equal Franchise Society went so far as to ask the city's clergy to preach "Votes for Mothers" sermons on Mother's Day. Dallas ESA members wrote a series of testimonials for the *Times-Herald* under titles such as "The Political Dominance of Men is an Evil to the Mothers," "There is Need of the Mother Heart in Legislation," and "Women in Home Should Have Voice in Government."[27]

Here at last was a broadly appealing rationale. Combining arguments for difference and sameness, for duties as well as rights, enabled suffrage to become a mass movement. When Elizabeth Fry asserted in 1889 that "to individualize woman, to render her self-reliant, to endow her with full responsibilities of thought and action is the constant aim of suffragists," she defined suffrage in terms that contradicted the cultural definition of womanliness. By contrast, Isadore Callaway, an equally passionate feminist who would have endorsed every word of Fry's statement, offered via "Pauline Periwinkle" a rationale for Everywoman: "As no mother can be sure that she is protecting her own home unless she see that all other homes are protected, the duties and responsibilities of the domestic woman have arrived at such a pass that she needs suffrage in self-defense."[28] Fry's suffragist emphasized what the vote would do for her, Callaway's stressed the good she could do for others. Fry's sought independence, Callaway's embraced maternal duty and responsibility. The New Suffragist, as a "domestic woman," was appropriately focused on home and family.

In itself, this was hardly a new concept; the WCTU had been advocating a "home protection" ballot since the 1880s. But twentieth-century suffragists changed the focus from weakness to strength. Frances Willard and the WCTU had exploited "the feminism of fear," in Suzanne Marilley's phrase, to rally women who felt physically and economically vulnerable. Progressive suffragists turned the home protection concept upside down: women themselves became the protectors, municipal housekeepers whose expertise in matters of germs and sanitation could be translated via the ballot into laws that would safeguard their homes and guarantee their children's health. NAWSA's "Better Babies" broadside summed it up with one of Rose O'Neill's popular Kewpie doll drawings, a cherubic toddler worriedly eyeing a horde of multi-legged microbes advancing from under the street door toward her fallen pacifier. Like the Kewpie baby, the caption was irresistible: "I wish my mother had a vote—to keep the germs away."[29]

When Isadore Callaway and other suffragists spoke of needing the ballot in self-defense, they described it less as a shield than as a weapon. Sleeves rolled up and broom in hand, the New Suffragist patrolled her children's environment. NAWSA's "Woman in the Home" broadside blamed men—government officials and the male voters who elected them—for consigning children to live in unclean, unsafe homes, eat unwholesome food, breathe tuberculosis germs, and be tempted by "immoral influences of the street." The solution was to let women "have a hand in the city's housekeeping" since "women are, by nature and training, housekeepers."

Emphasizing feminine expertise effectively undercut the traditional objection that women could exercise power equally well through indirect influence. "Men cannot understand the need of many things that are plain enough to any woman," Perle Penfield asserted. "Therefore it is right and proper that woman should have a voice where her discernment is keener than a man's."[30] To hundreds of thousands of women in federated women's and mothers' clubs who had studied scientific housekeeping, imbibed the gospel of "better babies," and labored in school improvement campaigns, this was persuasive logic. Men could not represent women's interests at the polls because they lacked women's special knowledge.

As more and more women developed suffrage convictions, they pressed their organizations to endorse the ballot formally. Although Anna Pennybacker managed to keep suffrage from becoming an issue in her successful campaign for the GFWC presidency in 1912, it was obvious that the prosuffrage faction would soon have sufficient strength to force the question. A Houston delegate had issued a warning that could hardly be ignored: "If the federation does not endorse women's suffrage at this convention, there are thousands of women in Texas who will ask this delegation why." One of Pennybacker's first acts as president was privately to commission Olga Kohlberg, and Kohlberg's daughter, Elsie, to collect state-by-state data on suffrage sentiment. By 1914 it was clear that she would either have to support endorsement or risk nomination from the floor of a prosuffrage opposition candidate.[31]

Suffrage dominated the 1914 Biennial in Chicago, where NAWSA President Carrie Chapman Catt was among the invited speakers. Early reports indicated that seventeen state delegations had already endorsed it and prosuffragists were working to secure more. A thousand delegates, twice the number anticipated, bought tickets for the banquet sponsored by the Illinois Equal Suffrage Association. On opening night delegates cheered Jane Addams's reminder that without the ballot women were "shut out of the game" being played by statesmen "attempting to translate the new social sympathy into action." The following morning Pennybacker preempted divisive debate and assured her reelection with a surprise announcement that a suffrage resolution would be submitted to committee and put to a vote. The prosuffragists praised her loudly, and the resolution passed two days later with no speeches in opposition.[32]

In Texas, it was not quite so easy. At the TFWC convention that fall President Florence Fall and Mary Terrell, the latter dismayed and angry at Pennybacker's concession in Chicago, were able to prevent the state federation from coming out for suffrage.[33] Early in 1915 the prosuffrage element within the TFWC began laying plans to force the question at the five district conventions in the spring. The Fifth District secretary, who was also an officer in the San Antonio Equal Franchise Society, vowed that "we are going to endorse woman's suffrage here if we have to break up the meeting." They accomplished it with only one dissenting vote. The Second District also went on record for suffrage, and although President Fall was able to cut off a similar coup in the Third District, the majority of clubwomen were ready to declare themselves. Endorsement at the state convention in the fall of 1915 was a foregone conclusion.[34]

Through the efforts of Eleanor Brackenridge, the Texas Congress of Mothers had endorsed suffrage in 1914 over the president's opposition, and even though the National Congress was not on record for the ballot. As the district conventions approached in 1915 a number of TCM women agreed with their extension chairwoman, who told outgoing TWSA President Annette Finnigan, "the time has come when I feel I *must* work for equal suffrage, for after all, everything else depends on it." After the Fifth District TCM meeting adjourned a number of the prosuffrage delegates stayed on and called a special meeting to distribute literature and discuss organizing local suffrage clubs. In spite of the fact that the National Congress never did endorse the ballot, the TCM counted increasing numbers of suffragists in the ranks, women like Dallas Council of Mothers President Lala Fay Watts, who summed up her rationale in 1917: "When I became a mother, I became a suffragist." After the state convention that year the TCM president noted approvingly that it seemed every speaker had made a suffrage speech.[35]

Criticism of clubwomen's late endorsement obscures the important role that the federated club movement played in nurturing suffrage sentiment. Nonsuffragists did not join suffrage societies, but many suffragists did join clubs, which provided a forum in which the issue could be discussed and debated. Prosuffrage members saw to it that noted suffragists appeared on club programs; Isadore Callaway, in her capacity as president of the Dallas Federation of Women's Clubs, made sure that Anna Howard Shaw addressed the district club convention when she visited the state in 1908. Women like Anna Pennybacker changed their views under the influence of prosuffrage colleagues and through self-study courses on political science designed to educate them on the workings of government. The GFWC's political science department supplied clubs that requested suffrage information with a persuasive pamphlet, "A Mother's Sphere," by noted Kentucky suffragist and NAWSA board member Madeline McDowell Breckinridge.[36]

At the same time, club-directed social and civic activism provided an unanticipated political education. Elizabeth Ring of Houston, who joined the Ladies' Reading Club in 1888 but not the TERA in 1893, summed up the change of heart she had undergone by the 1910s: "After 30 years of working for clean towns and homes and pure foods and decent school buildings and public parks and good roads, and kindergartens and compulsory education, I have at last realized we could do all this work much better and quicker and with less loss of time and dignity and self respect by casting our vote as full fledged citizens."[37]

Federation endorsements did not, of course, turn all clubwomen into suffragists, but the clubs' embrace of suffrage played a vital role in making it a mass movement. A city federation that committed itself to the cause had the requisite numbers, resources, and organizational structure for effective work. By 1916 the president of the San Antonio City Federation had promised Eleanor Brackenridge to appoint a suffrage committee for each district in the city, and plans were underway for reaching country women through the public schools. Each of the federation's twenty-eight clubs was assigned a rural school to visit and offer assistance in organizing a mothers' club, starting a library, planting a school garden, or any other improvement project. While stimulating the women's interest in their children's schools was the overt goal, Brackenridge anticipated that "incidentaly [sic] suffrage will of course come in."[38] It had become inextricably part of progressive women's agenda.

❀

Although the New Suffragist readily crossed the Mason-Dixon line, women in Texas and other southern states found their efforts complicated and frustrated by the prejudices of a racially polarized society. Southern suffragists have been shadowed by a reputation for racism since Aileen Kraditor asserted in 1965 that their primary argument was an expedient one: giving the vote to white women, who outnumbered African Americans of both sexes combined, would make white supremacy permanent and invincible. Marjorie Spruill Wheeler has shown that this "statistical argument" held sway only in the 1890s, but she offers unequivocal evidence that the first southern suffrage movement was purposely timed to take advantage of rising sentiment against black voting.[39]

Closer examination of southern suffrage at the state level suggests that generalizations based on the region's small leadership cadre need further refining.[40] Southern suffragists did not speak with one voice, and the arguments of prominent women preoccupied with political strategy did not necessarily reflect local sentiments. In Texas race was not the "principal argument" of the movement in either the 1890s or the 1910s; it was not even a minor one. Texas women asked for the vote on the same grounds that northern women did: equal justice in the 1890s and municipal housekeeping and motherhood in the 1910s.

This is not to argue that Texas suffragists held enlightened racial views or to absolve them from complicity in the casual and pervasive racism of their era. Like most southern whites—and a good many northern ones—they were elitists who were willing to limit the ballot to the white, native-born, and educated. They openly expressed resentment that "the most ignorant, degraded negro ha[s] the right to vote, but a woman is denied that right, no matter how much taxes she pays."[41] Even Eleanor Brackenridge, who personally funded an African American kindergarten in San Antonio, supported the poll tax that disfranchised blacks as a means of curbing vote buying and election fraud. The distinction between racial attitudes and racially motivated action needs to be carefully held in mind, however. Personal sentiments did not necessarily dictate political strategy. Racially conservative Texas women made the colorblind argument for the vote as a natural right, while veteran Massachusetts abolitionist Henry Blackwell originated and promoted the "statistical argument" for enfranchising white women.

Kentucky's Laura Clay, the most prominent southern suffragist in the 1890s, embraced Blackwell's strategy after it received a serious hearing before the Mississippi constitutional convention of 1890. The convention ultimately adopted the infamous "Mississippi Plan" for disfranchising blacks, but Clay was convinced that the statistical argument might have succeeded if there had been a suffrage association in Mississippi to promote it. She persuaded NAWSA in 1892 to authorize a special committee to begin work in the South. Over the next decade money from Clay's Southern Committee helped organize state suffrage associations below the Mason-Dixon line, including the Texas Equal Rights Association in 1893. Just four made appeals to their legislatures, however, and the only success occurred in Louisiana, which in 1898 granted taxpaying women the right to vote on tax questions.[42]

Despite the circumstances of its founding, the TERA seems never to have advocated the statistical, white supremacist argument. Instead, its language echoed the 1848 woman's rights convention at Seneca Falls that launched the suffrage movement. In speeches, newspaper articles, convention reports, and statements to curious journalists, the Texas suffragists focused on equal justice and natural rights. It was a travesty of justice, Dr. Grace Danforth declared at the TERA organizing convention, that women were taxed without representation and disfranchised under a government claiming to rest on the consent of the governed. Elizabeth Turner Fry asserted that "suffrage will come upon us like the emancipation of the slaves," and contended at the Texas Women's Con-

gress that woman's "inherent right in creation" entitled her to equal rights and privileges with men.[43]

Ironically, it was the determination of some TERA members *not* to be perceived as race-obsessed and reactionary that helped bring the organization to grief. As part of its southern strategy, NAWSA proposed to send Susan B. Anthony and Anna Howard Shaw on a speaking tour late in 1894 and for the first time chose a southern venue, Atlanta, as the site for the 1895 convention. When the TERA discussed the cost of bringing the Anthony tour to Texas, the northern-born president, Rebecca Henry Hayes of Galveston, objected. A former abolitionist like Anthony should not appear in Texas or any other southern state, Hayes argued, until after the Atlanta convention, where northern women would be able to meet southern suffragists and "obtain a true insight into the situation." Afterward northern women could work in the South "with a full understanding of southern character and southern womanhood." The sole male delegate backed Hayes's position, implying that Anthony might meet hostile, and even unruly, audiences in Texas.[44]

Other delegates leaped to their feet and indignantly denied that southern womanhood was backward and bigoted. The convention voted to contact Anthony about her schedule and fees and the executive committee subsequently decided to issue a formal invitation. Hayes promised to report the decision, but warned that in her capacity as a NAWSA vice president she would vote against the southern tour. (It was subsequently approved but Anthony did not visit Texas.) Thereupon the pro-Anthony faction, led by Grace Danforth and Elizabeth Fry, declared that Hayes had forfeited the presidency by opposing the executive committee and installed Fry as president. Both sides poured out their grievances to Laura Clay. Hayes's insinuation of southern intolerance infuriated native daughter Danforth: "How dare she misrepresent us so before the world!" Although the NAWSA ultimately upheld Hayes as president, the schism helped kill the TERA, which held only one more convention.[45]

Twenty-one years later, in 1917, seventy-four-year-old Mary Kittrell Craig recalled the cultural opposition that suffrage faced in the nineteenth-century South: "I was taught to believe that Susan B. Anthony, Julia Ward Howe, and their contemporary workers were only powerful influences for evil." Active in the club movement since the early 1890s, Craig had remained aloof from the decade's short-lived suffrage agitation. That era was finished and the times greatly changed, she concluded, when she decided to become a charter member of the Dallas Equal Suffrage Association in 1913. While fewer than five hundred Texas women affiliated with the National Woman's Party, whose Washington picketing and protests were widely disapproved, nearly twenty thousand joined Mary Craig in embracing the moderate NAWSA.[46]

Like their northern counterparts, the majority of southern suffragists endorsed the federal or Susan B. Anthony amendment, rejecting the intransigence of the states' rights minority led by Kate Gordon and Laura Clay. They accepted, albeit regretfully, NAWSA President Carrie Chapman Catt's 1916 directive against expending any more time and money on campaigns for state constitutional amendments in the unpromising South, where all efforts had failed. Catt's "Winning Plan" required southern women to concentrate on building support for the federal amendment, even though the overwhelming majority of their congressmen and senators opposed it.[47]

None worked harder at prying loose those essential votes than Minnie Fisher Cunningham, who headed the TESA after 1915 and was appointed secretary of NAWSA's congressional lobby in 1918. At every turn Cunningham and other southern suffragists confronted the question put by Texas's old-line Democratic senator, Charles Culberson, who asked how TESA "expected to take care of the negro vote." Carefully and precisely, TESA members explained that the federal amendment would not negate the poll tax and white primary laws and would not confer suffrage on anyone; it merely specified that sex could not be used as a disqualifier. Southern suffragists endlessly reiterated this argument. The "negro problem," they insisted was a trumped up issue, since few blacks could meet the requirements for voting. Such rational rejoinders had little impact in a race-polarized society. The debate was shaped by antisuffragists like former Texas governor Oscar Colquitt, who declared that "when you give the ballot to women, you give it to all women, regardless of color. . . . you abandon your state's rights and you make it possible for negro equality such as you suffered in the carpet bag days after the Civil War to be forced on you again."[48]

It is within this context that the decision of the TESA leaders to deny membership to an African American women's group in 1918 must be evaluated. In remote El Paso, where the black population was small and whites considered themselves burdened with a "Mexican problem" instead, the Equal Suffrage League and the Colored Women's Club had established cordial relations. Several of the white suffragists had spoken at the black clubwomen's programs, and one of them described the president, Mrs. Edward Sampson, as "a well-educated woman" and "desirous of recognition from the white people." She suggested that the Colored Women's Club affiliate with NAWSA, apparently without realizing that direct group memberships had been eliminated and clubs could join only through their state suffrage organizations. Thus when Mrs. Sampson inquired about membership, her two-sentence note precipitated a sheaf of anxious correspondence between TESA and NAWSA headquarters.[49] After weeks of worried consultation, the white suffragists denied the club's application.

Minnie Fisher Cunningham helped organize Galveston's equal suffrage league in 1912 and became president of the Texas Woman Suffrage Association in 1915. She spearheaded one of the South's few successful suffrage movements, shrewdly exploiting a rift in the Democratic party to pry partial suffrage from reluctant state legislators in 1918. (Courtesy of the Austin History Center, Austin Public Library, Austin, Tex.)

As Suzanne Lebsock has perceptively argued, historians need to examine such racially motivated action through two lenses, one sensitive to present-day egalitarianism and a second that focuses on the realities of southern politics at the time.[50] The first lens magnifies the injustice to the black women, whose feelings readily can be imagined. Without the second lens, it is less easy to recapture the context of the white suffragists' action. TESA President Minnie Fisher Cunningham, born and raised in a black-majority county in East Texas where her parents had once been slaveholders, might have been predicted to echo the blunt racism of Louisiana's Kate Gordon and Mississippi's Belle Kearney. She did not, and nowhere in the exchange of letters did the Texas suffragists voice any personal objection to admitting black women; their concern was the devastating political ammunition that they would be handing their opponents.

They might also have rejected the application immediately, without two months of consultation. At its 1903 convention on Kate Gordon's turf in New Orleans, NAWSA had courted southern support by adopting a states' rights policy that permitted southern women to participate on their own terms; consequently the TESA leaders could have turned down the Colored Women's Club on their own initiative. Instead Cunningham sought Carrie Chapman Catt's counsel and followed her advice to tell the black women "that you will be able to get the vote for women more easily if they do not embarrass you by asking for membership." Undeniably, Cunningham chose the expedient solution, but it was identical to the policy that NAWSA pursued in the North. The following year, when the Northeastern Federation of Women's Clubs, an African American organization, applied for cooperating membership, NAWSA asked them to withdraw the request. When the black federation persisted, the NAWSA executive council voted to deny affiliation.[51]

The antisuffragists' deliberate and often flagrantly dishonest manipulation of the racial issue left the TESA and other mainstream southern suffragists cornered and defensive. An antisuffrage broadside circulated widely in the South and preserved in the Texas suffrage papers vividly captures their dilemma. Reproducing an illustration taken from the NAACP periodical, *The Crisis,* it depicted a black woman with children clinging to her skirts swinging a club representing the Constitution against vultures labeled Segregation, Jim Crow Law, and Grandfather Clause. The caption proclaimed "What Votes for Women under the Susan B. Anthony Amendment means for the South," and on the other side the sender scrawled a bitter personal note: "May this be scorched upon your soul." The relentless racism of their opponents left Texas suffragists with the same uncompromising alternatives that Lebsock has identified for their counterparts in Virginia: "they could deny that white supremacy was in danger, or they could hush up and go home."[52]

Faced with hard choices, Texas suffragists consistently chose moderate responses, and they refrained from venting their frustration on African American women. Minnie Fisher Cunningham informed Mrs. Sampson that since the Colored Women's Club application was unprecedented it would require a convention vote. The next convention would not meet until the spring of 1919, by which time, she added, they hoped the federal amendment enfranchising all women would have passed. Although her strategy was politically calculated, Cunningham's sentiments were genuine. No TESA suffragist expressed any objection to including black women in the electorate, and Cunningham opposed de facto literacy tests, such as requiring a woman to fill out her registration form in her own hand.[53]

Neither the TESA literature nor the correspondence of the members reveals any evidence that they argued for suffrage on racial grounds. Cunningham rejected out of hand Kate Gordon's suggestion in 1917 that southern suffrage presidents petition their legislatures to cease holding white women politically inferior to black men. Gordon and Clay's states' rights minority never grasped what Cunningham pointed out in her reply: southern suffragists' chances of success depended upon race *not* becoming an issue. Bigotry and fear being nearly impervious to logic and statistics, race was the antisuffragists' best weapon, and they used it ruthlessly to inflame anxieties that went much deeper than voting.[54]

Clearly some politicians, particularly those in Deep South black belt regions, believed that woman suffrage posed a potential threat to white supremacy. In states that refused to ratify the Nineteenth Amendment, such as Alabama and North Carolina, legislators from black-majority counties voted overwhelmingly in the negative.[55] Texas, however, shows no such pattern. A breakdown of the 29 Senate votes cast in 1919 reveals that 63 percent of those who voted yes and 70 percent of those who voted no came from counties where African Americans were only one-quarter or less of the population. Senators from counties that were one-quarter to one-half black voted yes twice as often as those who voted no, and the only senator who lived in a county more than 50 percent black voted yes.[56] (This one, Walker County, was also the one Minnie Fisher Cunningham called home, despite her years of residence in Galveston.)

The pattern that does emerge reveals that the issue linked to suffrage was not race but prohibition. Twenty of the twenty-nine senators who voted on ratifying the Nineteenth Amendment had also sat in the previous legislature, which ratified the Eighteenth Amendment imposing national prohibition. Eight of the ten antisuffragists voted against it; nine of the ten prosuffragists voted for it.[57] This is consistent with what Texas suffragists had always claimed; they counted potential votes in the legislature according to whether the men were wet or dry, not the racial composition of their districts. Jane Y. McCallum, TESA's publicist and Cunningham's lieutenant in Austin, disgustedly rattled off the names of five antiprohibitionists in the lower house who led the opposition to the suffrage bill that failed in 1917. All of them, she recorded angrily in her diary, were "*hired, bought & paid for.*"[58]

The evidence was not in doubt; a successful antitrust suit against seven Texas breweries in 1915 had revealed that they had been funneling large sums, raised by an assessment of sixty cents per barrel sold, into legislative races for years. The brewing interests, afraid that enfranchised women would vote in prohibition, were so politically powerful that NAWSA leaders dubbed them the "invisible enemy." Liquor money funded organizations like the Texas Business Men's Association, which distributed antisuffrage and antiprohibition boilerplate to hundreds of county newspapers. Other interests such as cotton textile manufacturers, who feared women's potential votes for child labor legislation, appear to have played a similar role elsewhere in the South.[59]

Special interest politics and racial politics were so intertwined that they are difficult to untangle, but in Texas all of the prominent race-baiting antisuffrage politicians were also staunch opponents of liquor regulation, the political issue that overshadowed all others in the state during the Progressive Era. As a strategy, however, special interest politics had the disadvantage of dividing white voters into sharply feuding factions. Racial politics was all embracing, bringing together voters who disagreed about liquor or child labor to uphold a cultural tradition that had universal support and deep emotional resonance. It would prove an insurmountable obstacle for Texas suffragists until 1918, when a split in the state Democratic party unexpectedly gave the women legislative allies with expedient reasons for supporting a female ballot.

❀

As prohibition came to dominate the Progressive political agenda in Texas, and the emphasis in suffrage rhetoric shifted from justice to motherhood, a paradox emerged. The second generation of suffragists only marginally included the WCTU, the organization most deeply committed to outlawing alcohol, the first to endorse suffrage, and the originator of "mother-heartedness" as a rationale for activism. In the 1890s the majority of TERA officers were WCTU members. In the 1910s almost none of the TESA officers were, even though most suffragists favored prohibition and the organization formally endorsed it after the country entered World War I. The temperance organization never renounced the commitment to suffrage that it had first made in 1888, but its participation in the second suffrage movement was largely rhetorical. In the 1910s the Texas WCTU lacked outspoken advocates of women's rights in the tradition of Grace

Danforth, Elizabeth Fry, and Rebecca Henry Hayes. The ranks did not grow; membership in 1914 was only 2,600 and the number of unions—125—was smaller than a decade earlier.[60]

By the 1910s the WCTU, a far-sighted social reform organization in the late nineteenth century, had largely reverted to its original focus on liquor suppression and moral reform. Some of its passions appeared eccentric and cranky. State president Nannie Webb Curtis (1909–20) expended time and ink atempting to have the battleship *Texas* christened with water instead of wine. Local unions were urged to pressure telegraph companies not to hire boys who smoked. In Texas and throughout the country, unions began to emphasize the organization's past glory and to hold special services commemorating the date of Frances Willard's death or "heavenly birthday."[61] The WCTU's nineteenth-century image had little appeal for the new generation of progressive women, who instead sorted themselves into organizations less constrained by the lingering religious and moral intensity of Victorian women's culture.

Demographically and culturally, the TESA and the WCTU were more dissimilar than alike. WCTU members tended to be religious activists and most of their leaders were well past middle age; state president Nannie Webb Curtis had been born in 1861. The mother of three grown sons, Curtis was a Methodist minister's daughter with a talent for public speaking and evangelism that she developed into a vocation after her second widowing by taking a course in oratory at North Texas Female College. Thereafter, Curtis earned her living by lecturing on prohibition and woman suffrage for the national WCTU and on the Chautauqua and lyceum circuits. A old-fashioned pulpit orator, she declaimed against the spiritual corruption of a "liquor-soaked society" and kept the WCTU focused on moral crusading.[62]

By contrast, TESA women were decidedly secular and the leadership was more likely to have been born in the 1870s and 1880s. (Eleanor Brackenridge, who was the oldest of all and almost sui generis because of her wealth and influence, spanned both traditions.) College-educated New Women like TESA President Annette Finnigan (1914–15) and Minnie Fisher Cunningham (1915–20) were in nearly every respect the opposite of Curtis's cohort. Finnigan graduated from Wellesley in 1894, and rejected a leisured "society" life in favor of doing settlement work and helping her father manage the New York branch of his mercantile office. Cunningham was one of the first women to earn a pharmacy degree from the University of Texas Medical Branch (in 1901) and was a self-supporting professional woman until she married two years later. Afterward she participated in Galveston's female voluntary association culture through the Woman's Wednesday Club and the Women's Health Protective Association.[63]

As progressives, such women endorsed prohibition as part of a broad reform agenda. But in their eyes, the villain was not Demon Rum but the "Liquor Trust," a political octopus with tentacles that reached out to buy influence and corrupt the democratic process. Suppressing it was one of many uses that suffragists envisioned for the ballot, while the evangelistic WCTU women emphasized a dry society as their primary goal. In the early 1890s the WCTU's support for suffrage had attracted women's rights advocates who had no other organizations through which to protest the status quo. In the words of Grace Danforth, it was "the first organization looking to the emancipation of women." By the 1910s, however, women could pursue self-discovery and social reform through a plethora of organizations, and the WCTU was increasingly displaying a tendency that had irritated Danforth two decades earlier: "resolv[ing] itself into a prayer meeting."[64]

Drawing its membership heavily from an older cohort of women active in church societies, the WCTU was linked only marginally to the second generation of suffragists. When the state suffrage organization was revived in April 1913, Nannie Webb Curtis appeared only as a guest speaker, not a delegate. Presiding over the WCTU's annual convention a month later, Curtis did not even mention the suffrage convention (which only one of the WCTU delegates had attended) or include suffrage in her formal recommendations.

Instead, the temperance women, who were assembled as usual in a church, staged the kind of public display that had stirred such a powerful response among Victorian women but now struck a younger generation as anachronistic. They held evangelistic street meetings to "let our enemies know we are here" and punctuated the three-day convention with devotionals, hymns, and choir music. Demonstration Evening featured tableaux of downfall and salvation reminiscent of nineteenth-century melodramas. A scene entitled "Life's Pilgrim" portrayed a young man taking the first drink that led to his ruin. While his mother pleaded in the background, an unseen chorus sang the sentimental Victorian standard that the WCTU had turned into its theme song, "Where is My Wandering Boy Tonight?"[65]

By the time a second generation of suffragists took up the cause in Texas, the WCTU had already made—indirectly—its most significant contribution to securing votes for women. Through temperance women's tireless work in local option elections, county after county voted to exclude alcohol within its boundaries. It was not uncommon for WCTU chapters to orchestrate an all-day vigil at the polls, singing, exhorting, and praying. Inverting the male tradition of treating the voters, WCTU women fed them, passing out sandwiches, pie, and coffee as they appealed for votes. When statewide prohibition finally passed in 1918, most of the state had already gone dry through local option. Liquor-free election days, the resulting indirect benefit, were a boon to the suffragists' cause. Drying up the polling places, in conjunction with the poll tax and the white primary, helped make this public space potentially "safe" for white women. Neither the prohibitionists nor the disfranchisers had such a goal in mind, of course, but wherever the electorate was mostly white and entirely sober, the antisuffragist argument that women risked insult or moral injury by voting lost conviction.

The WCTU's highly visible role in local option campaigns temporarily mobilized many women who never formally joined the WCTU's "white ribbon army." In and around the small town of Bryan, for example, 840 women responded to the WCTU's call to make their voices heard in the 1903 local option election. Their petition, published as a newspaper supplement, displayed seven full columns of names, calling on husbands and fathers to "*Save our boys! . . . Kill the enemy of your homes, your women, your children.*" When the issue was on their own doorstep, the shared bonds of motherhood could rally hundreds of women willing to work for the short term in a WCTU-led campaign to protect the family by closing saloons. The collaboration was so common that after 1910 unions were authorized to enroll half-way or "campaign" members who were exempted from the other duties of membership.[66]

The exhilaration of carrying local option elections helped push some previously uncommitted women into the suffrage ranks. "The ladies and children won the day," a woman from Conroe, near Houston, wrote triumphantly to her cousin in 1915. "I have never cared to vote except for Prohibition but now I am open to conviction for suffrage!"[67] At the same time, however, the WCTU was a victim of its own success. In safely dry counties the organization's appeal was limited. "Campaign members," who were only temporarily allied, might go back to their homes or on to civic activism through the more diversified women's and mothers' clubs. As the United States was drawn into the Great War already raging in Europe, organized women would find their greatest opportunities of the decade.

"These Piping Times of Victory" 6

IN JUNE 1918 a week-long conference billed as the "War College for Women" drew nearly one hundred participants to the University of Texas. As leaders of women's organizations, the conferees were already veterans of war on the homefront. They came in dual roles, as members of the voluntary associations in which they had been working for years and as state and local officials of the new organizations created to help wage a world war: the U.S. Food Administration, the Woman's Liberty Loan Committee, the National League for Women's Service, the Woman's Committee of the Council of National Defense, and the Commission on Training Camp Activities. Representatives from the Washington, D.C., headquarters of these agencies shared the speakers' platform with the Texas directors, whose names on the program read like a who's who of the state's voluntary association officers.

Chaired by Mary Gearing, then in her sixth year as head of the School of Domestic Economy at the university, the War College covered every aspect of women's war service: conserving food, monitoring child welfare, improving the working conditions of women in industry, selling bonds, and providing wholesome recreation for the soldiers and airmen in military training camps. Nearly a third of the speakers were men, and the governor gave one of the keynote addresses. On the day allotted to the Woman's Division of the Council of National Defense (CND), the delegates moved downtown to the Capitol and convened in the Senate Chamber, where formerly they had been admitted only as special pleaders. Symbolically at least, they were sharing the seat of government power.[1]

Women's organizations threw themselves enthusiastically into winning the war on the homefront without siphoning energy from the social reforms that they had been pursuing for two decades. Paradoxically, World War I helped advance their agenda. It focused government attention on issues for which women had long sought support, such as home economics training, infant welfare, child labor restriction, and the suppression of prostitution. The federal government's cooperation—and in some cases, pressure—helped raise the status of home economics and home demonstration programs, implement child welfare reforms, bring on prohibition, and eliminate vice districts. War provided white suffragists with new arguments for the vote and black women with the opportunity to begin YWCA work in Texas. New roles and added responsibilities enlarged women's public culture and challenged the boundaries of gender and race.

Equally important, war gave organized women a new ally in the federal government and new opportunities, through service on government war commissions, to pursue public work and progressive objectives. The names on the Women's War College program represented some of the most prominent women in the women's club, mothers' club, and suffrage movements. The women's war agencies, set up to "assist" parallel male bodies, looked and operated much like women's own federated voluntary associations. The Woman's Committee of the CND was even created specifically to coordinate the activities of the various women's voluntary associations and prevent duplication of effort. It was organized in a format familiar to every federated clubwoman: headquarters in Washington, D.C., oversaw state organizations subdivided into county and community units that worked through ten (later twelve) departments dealing with such matters as food production and conservation, child welfare, women in industry, and relief.[2]

Bringing long experience in voluntarism to the new committees and commissions, organized women could tap their established grassroots networks to tackle county-wide projects in support of the war. In this, they had an advantage over their male counterparts. The chairwoman of the Woman's Liberty Loan Committee in Shelby County was appalled to discover that the chairman was planning to send out blank pledge cards for the Fourth Liberty Loan canvass without doing the record keeping requested by the government: filling in the address and school district and checking the tax rolls for each individual's assessment. He rationalized that "it was such a big job they could not get it done." The chairwoman replied that *she* could; she divided the work into segments and put a subcommittee in charge of each task. The Woman's Liberty Loan Committee chairwoman in Bowie County was similarly undaunted. As president of the Texarkana Mothers' Council and of her church missionary society, and an active member of the Civic League, the Wednesday Music Club, the Daughters of the American Revolution, and the United Daughters of the Confederacy, she had seven hundred female volunteers in place and was impatient at having to "wait for the men."[3]

Perhaps the most immediate and visible manifestation of the new working relationship between government agencies and organized women was the food conservation effort. The drive to preserve garden and orchard produce and the need to plan "wheatless" and "meatless" meals focused more attention on home economics than its proponents in Texas had been able to attract in twenty years of proselytizing. With General Chairwoman Anna Pennybacker presiding, the Texas Division of the Army Food Service met in Dallas in April 1917 to discuss how women's organizations could cooperate with the federal Department of Agriculture in conserving food.

One of the principal speakers was Clarence Ousley, director of the state Agricultural Extension Service, who only two years earlier had refused the demand of Pennybacker and the GFWC for an equal share of federal funds to promote home demonstration work. Now, carrying out the Extension Service's new wartime mandate, "Feed Yourself at Home," Ousley proposed to mobilize college students with home economics backgrounds to spend their summers demonstrating how to can and dry food. That summer 371 young women at five colleges and universities were trained as volunteer demonstrators and dispersed across the state; the program proved successful enough to repeat in 1918.[4]

Mary Gearing, publicity chair of the conference, put her School of Domestic Economy at the University of Texas to work on the food supply problem. As early as 1914 she had begun experimenting with cottonseed meal flour as a partial substitute for wheat flour in baking bread; now the research was extended to the possibilities of peanut meal and rice flour as ingredients in "war bread." Gearing became one of the most visible women in the state, serving as Texas director of home economics for the federal Food Administration, and as state chair of both the urban food conservation program and of the Home Economics and Food Conservation Department of the Women's Committee of the CND. In 1918 she took a leave of absence from the university to work with Herbert Hoover, director of the U.S. Food Administration, in Washington.[5]

The food conservation effort also forced the state to acknowledge the importance of professional home demonstration agents. Until 1917 Texas county governments had contributed nothing toward funding these positions. A female agent could be hired only if local businesses and clubs raised money privately to meet the county's share of her salary. Prompted by the war emergency, the state legislature authorized the county commissioners' courts to pay salaries for "canning demonstration agents," who were no longer seen as peripheral but essential. Canning became a public and patriotic activity. Adapting military rhetoric, one county chair of the Women's Commission of the U.S. Food Administration vowed to "wage a thorough canning demonstration campaign." The Women's Commission set up "victory kitchens" in the public schools, where women learned to can the surplus of their backyard victory gardens. In Houston, eight victory kitchens, each directed by ten "trained women" had preserved fifteen thousand cans of vegetables by June of 1918.[6]

The eagerness to encourage food production and conservation even promoted a degree of rapprochement across the racial divide. The suggestion that Texas take up "colored work" as part of the effort to grow more food was made gingerly from Washington in July 1918. The state food administrator was assured that the organizer from Tuskegee Institute was traveling in the South "purely in an advisory capacity," and that if Texas chose not to avail itself of his services, "all concerned will understand." Texas did choose, however; that summer it established a Colored Section of the U.S. Food Administration. Mary Evelyn V. Hunter of the Cooperative Extension Service at Prairie View State Normal and Industrial College for Negroes became the state director of Colored Women's Work. Her report in November showed four field agents at work in East Texas, where the black population was concentrated. Nearly five thousand African American women and girls were by then enrolled in "regular" canning clubs, with an additional "emergency enrollment" of almost three thousand.[7]

By that time, however, black women and white ones from the Women's Commission of the Food Administration had been meeting in the kitchen for many months. Houston's white chairwoman reported in June 1918 that "the same work is done with the negroes, all making good assistants." In San Antonio, at a community center for African Americans funded by Eleanor Brackenridge, the Women's Commission gave weekly canning demonstrations that attracted as many as sixty women at a time. The canned goods were then displayed in the neighborhood drugstores and "hundreds of colored women became interested in the work of canning," the chairwoman reported. A white aide told of doing her best work there: five weeks of demonstrations, during which she trained and certified two "colored" assistants to take over. They in turn gave a series of demonstrations at an African American school.[8] The glowing reports from both cities were presented at the Women's War College by the white chairwomen. No African American women were present; wartime exigency expanded their roles, but their "place" remained fixed.

❀

American entry into World War I at last focused government attention seriously on the country's infant mortality rate, one of the highest in the industrialized world, and on organized women's demand to conserve the "baby crop." After years of pressure from women's groups and social reformers, Congress had created the U.S. Children's Bureau in 1912, but with a budget and staff so small as to suggest that the lawmakers intended a symbolic gesture rather than significant action. But the Great War, as Mary Gearing pointed out, was encouraging the government to stand behind mothers; child welfare measures that women had been advocating for a quarter of a century were suddenly on Uncle Sam's agenda as war measures. Statistics had more impact when presented in the war context: babies died at seven times the rate of soldiers on the battlefield, and almost 30 percent of draftees were rejected as medically unfit, the majority because of the effects of childhood diseases.[9]

Since the inception of the Children's Bureau, its politically astute director, Julia Lathrop, had been working in conjunction with women's organizations to make the agency an effective force in improving child health and welfare. Lathrop had an especially close relationship with the GFWC, one of the groups that had lobbied hard for the bureau. In one of her first acts as director, Lathrop appeared before the 1912 GFWC Biennial to explain how the small, underfunded new agency and the huge federation of clubwomen could cooperate to realize their shared child welfare goals. An investigation begun in 1913 to check the comprehensiveness of local birth registrations (a prerequisite for compiling accurate infant mortality statistics) was the first joint project. The Children's Bureau prepared the forms and other materials; clubwomen gathered the data.[10]

The same principle guided their joint sponsorship of National Baby Week in 1916. The Children's Bureau supplied the exhibits, literature, and press publicity for clubs that orchestrated the local observances. The outbreak of war redirected the GFWC's work for children through the Department of Child Welfare of the Woman's Committee, CND. The president of the GFWC was appointed chair of the Child Welfare Department, and she at once invited Julia Lathrop to serve as executive chair. Lathrop quickly outlined a wartime childsaving program that the Woman's Committee adopted as the Child Welfare Department's official agenda. Known as Children's Year, it was formally launched on April 6, 1918, the anniversary of the nation's declaration of war. President Woodrow Wilson announced the government's new pronatalist policy in a widely publicized letter declaring that protecting children was a "patriotic duty" second only to supporting soldiers at the front.[11]

The goals of Children's Year—to reduce child mortality and establish "irreducible minimum standards for health, education, and work"—united all the Progressive-Era childsaving themes from years of separate campaigns. It brought together programs for the poor and the middle class, for babies and school children, and targeted the previously overlooked preschool group. Government authority and patriotic ardor created momentum for projects that child welfare reformers had so long advocated: infant welfare stations, Baby Weeks, medical inspection of school children, and child labor restriction.

Children's Year mobilized vast numbers of women into volunteer government service. Its success derived from the enthusiastic cooperation of the GFWC and the NCM, with their extensive networks of state and local affiliates. Texas alone had a corps of seven hundred district, county, and local chairwomen for Children's Year, women who were active in the TFWC and TCM. Dora Hartzell Fleming, the immediate past president of the TFWC and state chair of the CND Woman's Committee, assigned the Child Welfare Department to Mrs. E. A. Watters, president of the TCM. Such unprecedented cooperation between the two organizations was probably motivated by pragmatism; the TCM already had a grassroots network of mothers' clubs and PTAs in place to take up the work. Fleming instructed her county chairwomen to appoint TCM women to oversee child welfare work wherever these groups were already functioning in the school districts. With founding president Ella Porter rendering influential assistance to Watters through the post of executive chair, Children's Year dominated the TCM's agenda for 1918.[12]

The primary purpose of the campaign was to save 100,000 young lives nationwide, 5,000 of them in Texas, where 4,747 babies had died in 1917. The Baby Week observances of previous years had been structured like patriotic celebrations, complete with parades and flags. With the country now at war, Children's Year projects could make explicit the connection between children's welfare and the nation's. The government furnished bales of promotional posters, nine thousand in Texas alone, and supplied blue "Save the Children" emblems that women sold on the streets for a nickel minimum to raise money for infants' milk. It was a new variation of the familiar "tag day" fundraising, at which organized women had long since proved their expertise. Watters and Porter asked the governor to proclaim "Children's Day" on July 3, the eve of Independence Day, and cooperating women's organizations across the state took to the streets, collecting more than eight thousand dollars.[13]

The most ambitious project of Children's Year was a weighing and measuring campaign of enormous scale. The concept was familiar from Better Baby Contests and Baby Weeks, but now all children under age five were included and a systematic effort was made to locate as many as possible. Local CND Woman's Committee units set up the weighing and measuring centers in neighborhood schools, recruited volunteer doctors and nurses to staff them, and canvassed house to house distributing appointment cards designed by Watters and Porter. The Children's Bureau supplied two-part record cards (fifty thousand in Texas, six million nationally) on which to record the examination data. After the examination the parent was given one half of the record card and the second half was mailed to the Bureau, which used the cards to compile national child health statistics.[14]

Watters and Porter also directed their chairwomen to print and fill out Permanent Record Cards for each child to be used in follow-up work. The weighing and measuring tests supplied abundant proof of the need. Statewide, 20 percent of the children examined were discovered to be underweight and 30 percent of the births had not been registered. Local variations could be considerably higher: in Fort Worth, for example, almost 32 percent of the 2,437 children examined were underweight, and nearly half the births unregistered. On race and ethnicity, the statistics are nearly silent. The instructions Watters and Porter issued said nothing about including or excluding minority children, and the decision seems to have been left to the local workers. The Fort Worth Woman's Committe collected the only surviving data on African American children, and the racial disparity revealed in the numbers was probably not atypical. Nearly 54 percent of the more than three hundred black children examined were underweight, and not one of the births had been registered.[15]

Some physicians performed complete physicals on the children they examined. The revelations of swollen tonsils, weak eyes, and decayed teeth in preschoolers bolstered the long-standing demand of the TCM and TFWC for school nurses and regular medical examinations of school children. Houston, Austin, Galveston, and El Paso had already initiated medical exams, but Fort Worth and Dallas did not act until compelled by war and assisted by military officials at the new training camps. The officers at Camp Bowie carried out Fort Worth's school health inspection. Children's Year forced the Dallas school board to institute medical inspections, which were planned in consultation with the sanitation officer at Camp Dick. Lala Fay Watts, president of the Dallas Council of Mothers and chair of Children's Year for the city, declared that women were "elated" that the federal government had forced the issue. The school board was not, but as one reluctant member conceded, "if the Government wants us to have inspection, why there will be nothing else to do but comply."[16]

Draped for the first time in the mantle of federal authority, Watts and her counterparts throughout the state seized the wartime opportunity to expand the voluntarist projects they had long advocated. The Children's Year Committee of the Dallas Council of Mothers hired a public health nurse for each of the city's two poorest school districts. After demonstrating their effectiveness, the committee turned the nurses over to the city's Infant Welfare and Milk Association, while it repeated the project at new locations. Watts inaugurated a home survey to identify working mothers who needed child care so that the Mothers' Council, operating under Children's Year auspices, could set up day nurseries. In San Antonio the Children's Year Committee equipped two new community health centers and laid plans for a special facility for children.[17]

Organized women found in Children's Year an ideal opportunity to mount a public awareness campaign on behalf of the existing child welfare laws. Lala Fay Watts led a delegation to Austin that reviewed the relevant legislation and met with state officials, and the TCM's legislative chairwoman mailed out more than 3,500 copies of statutes covering health, labor, and education. Even the kindergarten crusade begun in the nineteenth century was fitted into the new mandate for children: the 1917 kindergarten law received special publicity, and establishing a kindergarten in every community was made an official Children's Year goal in Texas.[18]

Organized women also used the Children's Year mandate to demand that a special child welfare inspector position be created in the state's understaffed Bureau of Labor Statistics. The Texas Commissioner of Labor reported that under the pressure of wartime labor shortages the child labor law "has almost been set aside in some places"; the war emergency provided "a thinly veiled excuse for profiteering and exploitation." Mrs. E. A. Watters, in her joint capacity as president of the TCM and state chair of the Child Welfare Department of the CND Woman's Committee, formally requested action from the governor. When he hestiated, Lala Fay Watts went to Austin to do some personal lobbying. In what was perhaps the crowning achievement of Children's Year in Texas, Watts herself was appointed to fill the new position. She left Dallas to take up her official duties firmly resolved that "our children must not fight this war."[19]

❀

In quite a different sense the war *was* being fought by these women's children: young enlisted men, many still in their teens and each one "some mother's boy." A quarter of a million recruits went through basic training in Texas, which had boot camps at San Antonio, Houston, Fort Worth, and Waco. There were numerous officer training schools and military airfields as well; nearly every major city acquired some sort of military presence during the war.[20]

None of the cantonments were places to which middle-class mothers could send their sons without misgiving. The camp towns along the Texas-Mexican border, where federal troops had been mobilized against Pancho Villa's raids since 1916, were already so notorious that they had been investigated under War Department auspices. The appalling details appeared in the journal *Social Hygiene* just as the United States entered the war. With few other diversions, soldiers spent their off-duty hours drinking and visiting prostitution "cribs" where they contracted venereal diseases at alarmingly high rates. In some camps several hundred men daily reported to the medical officers for prophylaxis after sexual contact. Reports of vice and debauchery were on the minds of many women as young men were called up in 1917; one Austin mother wept for days when her son was sent to the border.[21]

The Secretary of War, Newton D. Baker, and the noted social investigator Raymond B. Fosdick, who had reported to him on the Texas border posts, were determined to ensure that the new training camps did not pose a threat to the recruits' health or morals. Fosdick was appointed to head a new war agency, the Commission on Training Camp Activities (CTCA), charged with suppressing liquor and prostitution near military encampments and supplying recreation on base for the soldiers. To provide recreational alternatives outside the camps, the CTCA requested the Playground and Recreation Association of America to create the War Camp Community Service (WCCS); its function was to encourage communities to open social clubs and sponsor special events for soldiers.[22] Although both agencies were directed and staffed by men, they relied in part on women's voluntary associations to help meet their objectives. The YWCA and the GFWC, which had created special War Work Councils when the conflict broke out, enthusiastically grasped the opportunity to become active protectors of the boys in uniform.

The YWCA enjoyed the status of an official CTCA affiliate. Through its War Work Council the "Y" moved onto military bases, establishing Hostess Houses where servicemen could pass their free time reading books and magazines, listening to music, or writing letters home. Most important, Hostess Houses were places where they could receive family members and—under matronly supervision—female visitors. All four Texas training camps and four of the aviation fields had YWCA Hostess Houses.[23] Reversing its usual role, the Y now sought to safeguard men from women—whose roles were also reversed. The boyish recruits, separated from their families and alone and lonely in strange surroundings, were depicted as the vulnerable potential victims of predatory prostitutes.

Complying with the War Department's policy of segregating troops, the CTCA made an attempt to provide dual recreational facilities. But services and amenities for African American soldiers were everywhere inadequate, and especially so in the South. In Texas there was no Hostess House for black servicemen until the war was nearly over; the CTCA and the YWCA finally began organizing "negro work" in San Antonio in July 1918. Until that point, Texas women had ignored the national YWCA's efforts at interracial cooperation. In 1918, however, the Colored Work Committee of the War Work Council succeeded in setting up a one-room hostess "hut" at Camp Travis in San Antonio through the efforts of the preceptress at Prairie View State College; a second room was later opened where visiting wives and children could rest. The hut received more than two hundred visitors during its first week in operation, and nearly two thousand during its last.[24]

Plans for a facility at Camp Logan outside Houston were dashed, however, by the race riot on August 23, 1917. An African American infantry battalion from Illinois brought in for guard duty resented and flouted the city's segregation ordinances. Strained relations between the black soldiers and white police erupted into open hostility after a soldier intervened in the police beating of an African American woman, and rumor spread that a second black infantryman had been killed over the incident. Sixteen whites and four blacks were killed when angry African American soldiers marched on the city, and white Houston reacted with reflexive outrage. Unable to get further support across the color line, the organizer from the Colored Work Committee and the local black clubwomen instead used money donated in the African American community to open a Colored Recreation Center that served as a combination YWCA and off-base Hostess House. In addition to the regular Y clubs and athletic activities, the center sponsored parties and "Sunday friendly hours" for soldiers. It became the state's first African American or "Blue Triangle" YWCA and was officially accorded branch status in the city association in 1920.[25]

While the YWCA served soldiers and airmen on base, clubwomen undertook to provide similar "safe" spaces in town for those off duty. Following the CTCA's suggestion that servicemen needed places "where they could meet good girls and motherly women," the TFWC's War Work Council attempted to provide a Recreational Canteen for every Texas cantonment. Delegates to the 1917 TFWC convention, heeding Anna Pennybacker's plea to "give until it hurts," raised thirteen thousand dollars in pledges from the floor to launch the undertaking. By offering billiards, dances, and refreshments in a wholesome atmosphere, the clubwomen hoped to divert young men from seeking the same attractions in saloons, pool parlors, and cheap dance halls where they could encounter women who sold or bartered sex. Texas club leaders described the centers as substitutes for the family parlor: "homes where enlisted men may go when off duty and in town, to rest and read or write, to play and sing, or to talk to good women if they wish."[26]

In the four cantonment towns—San Antonio, Fort Worth, Houston, and Waco—clubwomen set up canteens that all reported attendance of several thousand men a week. Three smaller ones served the airfields outside Dallas and Cleburne and the regular army post near Laredo. Each canteen was overseen by a maternal "commandant" who relied on five to seven hundred volunteers from her city federation to prepare and serve food, raise operating expenses, and see to upkeep and repairs.

In Houston, for example, each of the twenty-eight clubs in the city federation provided food and chaperonage one day per month; a supervising hostess paid by the WCCS had overall charge. The most popular attractions were the twice weekly dances; only young women approved by the local War Service Board were admitted and the chaperones served a hot supper instead of liquor. The Laredo Woman's Club spent four hundred dollars converting its own club rooms into a canteen, but the common practice in the cantonment cities was a cooperative arrangement with the War Camp Community Service, which operated its own Soldiers' Clubs. The WCCS donated part of the equipment and operating expenses and the women's club canteen sometimes shared the same building with the Soldiers' Club. Each organization's responsibilities were spelled out in a written contract.[27]

Women's organizations also collaborated with the CTCA's social hygiene component, whose mission was to suppress organized vice around the training camps and to disabuse servicemen of the popular notion that sexual activity was necessary to male health and virility. As a military necessity the army and the government now preached male continence, which women's organizations had been advocating since Frances Willard and the WCTU first called for a "white life for two." CTCA lecturers stressed that military efficiency depended upon each soldier keeping "fit to fight" by shunning disease-carrying prostitutes. In its Social Hygiene Division the CTCA created a Woman's Work Section to do community education explaining the consequences and prevention of venereal disease.[28] Through this collaboration Texas women moved from the periphery of the social hygiene movement to a more active role in combatting prostitution.

The CTCA's imprimatur elevated the prewar campaign against sexual vice to a patriotic crusade. Assisted by an advisory committee that included several women's war organizations, the Public Health Committe of the GFWC, the Association of Collegiate Alumnae, and the National Women's Trade Union League, the Woman's Work Section spoke to women's organizations and junior and senior high schools. The GFWC asked clubs to donate a least two days of the year's program to social hygiene. Most important, the war gave women anti-vice crusaders a powerful new ally in the federal government. Under the authority of the Selective Service Act, Secretary of War Newton Baker prohibited liquor and prostitution within a five-mile radius of military posts and camps. The ruling affected some fifty military points in Texas, and where civil authorities chose to ignore it, women's organizations brought the dereliction to the War Department's attention.[29]

They mobilized after delegates to the Texas Equal Suffrage Association convention in May 1917 discussed reports of vice conditions in the cantonment towns. The convention authorized TESA President Minnie Fisher Cunningham to coordinate an effort to force local authorities into compliance with Secretary Baker's directive. She at once contacted the War Department and, through the presidents of other state women's organizations, issued a call for a mass meeting. On June 5 some three hundred women assembled in San Antonio, one of the few American cities still licensing and inspecting prostitutes and easily recognizable as "Community D" in *Social Hygiene*'s April exposé of Texas towns. Roughly seventy thousand men were on active duty there at a permanent army base, several airfields, and the Camp Travis cantonment.[30]

When San Antonio city officials solemnly assured the women's mass meeting that the reservation district had been closed, Cunningham produced the report of a freshly completed investigation by the TESA's Elizabeth Speer indicating the contrary. (Shortly thereafter a CTCA investigator estimated that five thousand prostitutes were working in San Antonio and confirmed that Fort Sam Houston had the highest rate of venereal infection—228 per 1,000—of any U.S. Army camp.) The presidents of the sixteen organizations represented at the mass meeting then formed the Texas Women's Anti-Vice Committee, with Cunningham as president and the WCTU's Nannie Webb Curtis as secretary, to work for the enforcement of "white zones" around the camps. Taking advantage of the Army's "Fit to Fight" campaign, they spoke of military efficiency, but at the same time reiterated their longstanding concern that "clean-minded, cleanly raised" young men would eventually infect wives and children with venereal diseases contracted in camp. The assembled women then fired off a telegram informing Secretary Baker in Washington that his directive was being only half-heartedly enforced in San Antonio.[31]

The Women's Anti-Vice Committee spent the summer publicizing the problem by holding mass meetings around the state and forming local committees to pressure civic officials to enforce the law. Where the authorities were uncooperative, the anti-vice committees were advised to flood the War Department with letters of protest.[32] Elizabeth Speer, on her first visit to the base hospital at Camp Bowie in Fort Worth, discovered that slightly more than a third of the patients were being treated for venereal disease; when she returned ten days later with Minnie Fisher Cunningham, the proportion had risen to almost half. The president of the Fort Worth Chamber of Commerce told her unapologetically that city officials did not intend to take action against prostitutes and saloons except as they were forced to by the War Department.[33]

Military officers were often no more predisposed than civilians to enforce the War Department prohibitions. Speer found the commanders at Camp MacArthur in Waco "as bad as the local authorities": one officer claimed that Secretary Baker's order was only for publication, not enforcement, and another hospitably offered her party a glass of beer. "Experience has taught us," Speer concluded in a circular letter, "that Secretary Baker's recommendations or the promise of any civil authority to be effective will have to be followed up by the Mothers of Texas."[34]

When the Women's Anti-Vice Committee ran out of operating funds in the fall and was forced to disband, individual members continued the effort through the Texas Social Hygiene Association. Minnie Fisher Cunningham became a vice president and Elizabeth Speer the field secretary, sending regular reports to Raymond Fosdick at CTCA headquarters. By then collaboration between the reformers and the War Department, including Baker's threat to move the revenue-generating cantonments out of areas that refused to comply, had permanently shut down the remaining vice districts.[35] Between 1917 and 1919 Houston, El Paso, Waco, San Antonio, Fort Worth, and Wichita Falls officially put out the red lights.[36]

The war emergency also prompted the state legislature to pass laws that women's organizations had been demanding for decades. Pressure from the anti-vice reformers advanced the WCTU's longstanding battle to raise the age of consent beyond an easily ignored "women's" issue. A special 1918 legislative session called to deal with wartime problems extended the age to eighteen. War also resolved the issue of statewide prohibition, which a coalition of both sexes had been demanding in Texas for two generations. At last the drys had an unassailably patriotic rationale: prohibition as a "war measure" to conserve grain and protect the boys in uniform. The leaders of the progressive-prohibitionist wing of the state Democratic party, seeing a golden political opportunity, increased their pressure on the young "wet" governor, William P. Hobby, to change his stand. They argued persuasively that if he endorsed prohibition to safeguard the soldiers and made it clear that his first priority was winning the war, the about-face could be pulled off without jeopardizing his chances for election in 1918.[37]

While Hobby wavered, women's organizations voiced the same demand in a spate of resolutions. At its 1917 convention the TESA unanimously endorsed prohibition "to stop the criminal waste of food which is needed by our soldiers and allies." The Women's Anti-Vice Committee at its June 1917 mass meeting telegraphed Washington demanding prohibition as a war measure. The TCM board of managers did the same, and the TFWC passed a prohibition resolution in convention.[38]

Lacking the politicians' privileged access to the governor's ear, women made their demand for action publicly. Vigorously contested local option elections in major cities, the last "wet" strongholds, offered vast municipal stages for the public temperance roles that women had long been playing in smaller communities. In Dallas the Women's Prohibition League brought together three thousand women to work for a dry city. Members marched in a huge prohibition parade, accompanied by children with placards that read:

> I can't vote,
> Neither can Ma;
> If Dallas goes wet
> Blame it on Pa.

On election day the Women's Prohibition League converged on the polls. They offered hourly prayers, handed out prohibition cards, and worked in relays to serve coffee, tea, and sandwiches all day long.[39]

Dallas went dry in September 1917, and Austin scheduled a vote the following January. WCTU president Nannie Webb Curtis, addressing a mass prohibition rally to kick off the campaign, urged Austin women to "go to it as the women of Dallas did," leaving beds unmade, meals uncooked, and floors unswept. After reminding her listeners that motherhood was the biggest business on earth and that mothers who had invested years in raising their sons were entitled to get them back from military service as "clean" as they went in, Curtis organized a huge Woman's Committee for Prohibition.[40]

Subcommittees worked in each of the city's seven wards, while others oversaw strategy and publicity. The signal event of the campaign was a "women's parade" just before the election, an elaborate and hugely expanded demonstration of the marches that bands of temperance women had so often made down Main Streets in small towns. Thronging the wide avenues of the capital city, five hundred women, both white and black, accompanied by an equal number of men and several hundred children, advanced on the statehouse. The women, whose names the press printed in long columns under a banner headline, sang temperance songs and carried American flags and white temperance standards, sparing no effort to link prohibition with patriotism. Soldiers rode atop a city water wagon under a banner urging "Vote Pro and Swat the Kaiser." A float of young girls carried one that proclaimed "No Sugar for Us, but the Breweries Get It." University of Texas coeds, each holding a letter of the alphabet, spelled out "Prohibition."[41]

At the election two days later members of the Woman's Committee for Prohibition were out in force in every ward, telephoning, chauffeuring, bringing lunch to poll workers. Acting as "spotters" for strangers voting illegally and wets who might attempt to cast more than one ballot, the "kodaking" subcommittee captured suspicious voters on film. Prohibition carried, reversing a 1916 defeat. Less than a month later Governor Hobby, under pressure from public opinion and the War Department, announced that he would ask a special session of the legislature to outlaw the sale of liquor within ten miles of military bases. It did so, as well as ratifying the Eighteenth Amendment mandating national prohibition and passing a state prohibition law that would take effect sooner than the federal one. War, which convinced many former wets that prohibition was a patriotic necessity, finally brought the dry victory for which women like Curtis had worked for years.[42]

❀

For women themselves, the most obvious and heralded wartime change was their new status as voters. In 1919 Congress at last passed the federal suffrage amendment, bestowing full political citizenship with accolades for women's patriotism and war service. Texas women were partially enfranchised even before the fighting ended; in March 1918, the legislature granted them the right to vote in primary elections. It was one of the few successes for the suffrage movement in the South, and made voters of Texas women in the only election that counted in a one-party state—the Democratic primary.[43] Since Texas had long since instituted the white primary to exclude African Americans, it was also a form of suffrage for which legislators could vote without being accused of betraying the white race.

Legislators and suffragists alike attributed the suffrage victory to the "war emergency." Although this explanation, which both sides propounded for sound political reasons, does not fit the facts, World War I *did* alter the context of the debate to the suffragists' advantage. Most obviously, homefront mobilization completed middle-class women's conquest of public space, fatally weakening the old separate spheres argument against female voting. Austin suffragist Jane Yelvington McCallum's diary entries for 1917–18 are a virtual inventory of the new public roles women assumed through war voluntarism. In addition to running a household and mothering five half-grown children, she sold war bonds and thrift stamps, distributed food pledge cards, learned to can, and promoted it in the countryside. McCallum helped select women to boost conscription, served as secretary of the Woman's Committee for Prohibition, and worked in the local anti-vice league. For the Red Cross, she collected money, recruited volunteers, and blistered her feet marching in a parade—"and I *know* my face was dirty," she confided ruefully.[44]

Unmindful of tender feet and smudged faces, women were simply everywhere after the spring of 1917—in communal canning kitchens, in the streets, on speaker's platforms, and especially in meetings. On one memorably exhausting day McCallum recorded attending five, including one of the Austin Equal Suffrage Association. While new war-inspired committees and organizations proliferated, established voluntary associations added special war work councils that obligated members to assume additional offices and extra public responsibilities. The TFWC's was typical: a state war work council subdivided into district councils, which were further broken down into community councils comprised of all the local club presidents cooperating under a general chairwoman. The goal was to make every clubwoman "an enlisted soldier in the Federation army."[45]

Through both old and new organizations middle-class women became highly visible fund raisers for the federal government. They stationed themselves regularly on the streetcorners to sell thrift stamps, and canvassing in four Liberty Loan drives put women on public platforms in every part of the state. Newspaperwoman Margie Neal observed that before the war "not more than three" of her fellow townswomen in the East Texas community of Carthage had been willing to make a public talk, but "through various types of war work we had a number emerge as confident if not trained public speakers." Neal made her own first speech selling Liberty Bonds from the back of a pickup truck in the town square. Jane McCallum found herself called upon to pitch bonds to a labor union meeting. In sparsely populated West Texas, Lavinia Engle raised an audience in one town by directing the fire engine to drive around the square clanging its bell.[46] It seemed self-evident that the ballot could not take women farther out of the home than the war had already.

War work also helped suffragists polish their public image. Neal, McCallum, and Engle, all activists for the cause, wordlessly promoted votes for women by their very presence before an audience. The NAWSA, for which Engle had been traveling in Texas as full-time organizer, had a War Service Department organized and running even before Congress declared war. Carrie Chapman Catt's insistence that suffragists take up war work without relaxing their efforts for the ballot increased their burdens but also broadened their opportunities. State chapters like the TESA formed Emergency Committes and followed Catt, who served on the Woman's Committee of the CND, and Anna Howard Shaw, its chairwoman, in assuming prominent war-support roles. Vernice Reppert of Dallas, the TESA's press chairwoman, chaired the Woman's Liberty Loan Committee of the Eleventh Federal Reserve District. Minnie Fisher Cunningham ran the TESA while heading the state's Third and Fourth Liberty Loan drives and the Texas Women's Anti-Vice Committee.[47]

Shouldering a full load of war work gave suffragists an unparalleled opportunity to attract positive publicity. The Harris County [Houston] Equal Suffrage Association handed out thousands of free potato slips and cabbage plants for victory gardens, operated a Liberty Loan booth, and volunteered at the Recreational Canteen. In Dallas, where suffragists organized their own Red Cross auxiliary, the ESA's press secretary saw to it that members doing patriotic work were specifically identified as suffragists in news coverage. Jane McCallum, who handled publicity for the Austin ESA, had by July of 1917 persuaded the *Austin American* to let her write a weekly column called "Suffrage Notes." Among other things, McCallum used the column to stress that Texas suffragists, as NAWSA affiliates, were in no way connected with the militants of the National Woman's Party, who were refusing to do war work, and worse, picketing the White House. The NAWSA suffragists, by contrast, were showing themselves to be patriots and ladies.[48]

War work brought the TESA new members and sympathizers. The "white zone" work for military cantonments was a notable example. The TESA's leadership role in the Texas Women's Anti-Vice Committee demonstrated to any who doubted that suffragists shared the high moral values that the culture expected women to embody. More significantly, anti-vice work helped dramatize gender inequality to previously apolitical women. It drew middle-class ladies into confrontations with a male government that refused to acknowledge responsibility for public health and morals, denied women sufficient protection under the laws, and turned a deaf ear to maternal protests. Perceiving that anti-vice activism could be a catalyst for demanding the vote, Minnie Fisher Cunningham assured Carrie Chapman Catt that "we are hitching 'Suffrage' to every bit of it," and making "many converts." One who saw the light at the Women's Anti-Vice Committee's mass meeting in June 1917 told Cunningham: " 'I have never belonged to a Suffrage Club but I am going home to join one!' "[49]

Although the women did not lack male allies, "white zone" work and gender consciousness went hand in hand. San Antonio suffragists forged a citywide coalition of protesting women that combined the moral ardor of nineteenth-century social purity feminism with the progressives' conviction that female officials were better qualified than males to deal with women and youth. Led by Equal Franchise League president Rena Maverick Green, they requested—without success—that the city use some of the money formerly paid to the six doctors who examined licensed prostitutes to aid those evicted by the closing of the red-light district. The city also refused their demand for policewomen to monitor parks and places of public amusement where young runaways and camp followers with "khaki fever" might slip into casual prostitution. Policewomen with the authority to go into court and monitor the cases of women arrested for streetwalking would have enabled Green and her fellow workers to find out if the arrestees were getting fair hearings. The group wanted to know what happened to prostitutes after arraignment in order to devise a plan of follow-up assistance.[50]

Frustrated by the city's intransigence, the anti-vice women sought immediate help for the evicted prostitutes through the Associated Charities, and then took their protest to the San Antonio streets. At a mass meeting on November 30, 1917, they demanded that twelve policewomen be hired and formed themselves into a Woman's City Committee to pursue a solution to the continuing vice problem. Rena Maverick Green of the Equal Franchise Society was elected president. Faced with unrelenting female pressure, city officials compromised and hired six policewomen, whom the Woman's City Committee itself chose, and authorized another twenty volunteers. Less than a month later, all six policewomen were dismissed. The mayor claimed that the patrols were no longer needed because "the city was getting so good," a rationalization that Green derided: "They were finding out too much, I think."[51]

Anger over the situation helped develop suffrage sympathies in women who had not felt a personal need of the ballot. Women of every persuasion "are all working together under the city committee," Green reported to Minnie Fisher Cunningham, "and getting large doses of suffrage unawares." Green and Eleanor Brackenridge used San Antonio Equal Franchise Society money to help finance the Woman's City Committee; they were convinced, as was the EFS membership, that anti-vice work was "the most vital suffrage work we can do at the present time." The object lesson was that women, if they only had the ballot, could elect a city government committed to protecting public morals and health. With so many women up in arms against city hall, Green predicted that San Antonio would shortly be ready for a trained suffrage organizer.[52]

Finally, the Great War added new weapons to the suffragists' arsenal of arguments. They were quick to point out that their disfranchisement contradicted the democratic principles for which America was fighting abroad; democracy should begin at home. And having responded unselfishly to the government's call to save food, raise money, support the Red Cross, and myriad other projects, suffragists said plainly that they were entitled to reciprocal consideration. As they busied themselves distributing Herbert Hoover's food conservation pledge cards, Jane McCallum used her "Suffrage Notes" newspaper column to ask that Hoover, in return, urge Congress to pass the federal suffrage amendment.[53]

Nevertheless, neither women's increased public visibility, nor the broadening of the suffragists' base of support, nor patriotic work on the homefront was responsible for the TESA's success in securing primary suffrage. Texas offers a cautionary example against accepting uncritically the rhetoric of either politicians or suffragists. Political exigency and a split in the state Democratic party put suffrage across in Texas. The timing had nothing to do with the war and everything to do with the fact that former governor James Ferguson, who was impeached in 1917, launched a strong bid to regain the office in 1918. A self-styled populist and an adamant antiprohibitionist, Ferguson had a large and loyal constituency among poor farmers, "wet" ethnic minorities, and urban laborers—and the solid financial backing of the politically powerful brewing interests. A party divided into feuding wet and dry factions and a bitter election contest unexpectedly gave the Texas suffragists the political leverage they needed to play pressure group politics in a one-party state.

As a wet and an outspoken antisuffragist, Ferguson had long been an anathema to voluntarist women, who had rendered quiet assistance in the legislative investigation that culminated in his impeachment. Now Minnie Fisher Cunningham took advantage of Ferguson's comeback to make a behind-the-scenes bargain with the leaders of the progressive-prohibitionist wing of the Democratic party. She pointed out that if women were allowed to vote in the gubernatorial primary their numbers would be sufficient to stop Ferguson, and she promised to mobilize the support of organized women to elect Acting Governor Hobby in his own right. The prohibitionists, with reluctant cooperation from wet conservatives who feared Ferguson's demagogic appeal to tenant farmers and labor, pushed the primary suffrage bill through the 1918 special legislative session.[54]

In return, the suffragists organized a massive drive to register the new women voters. Astutely linking registration and voting to war patriotism, they urged every woman to turn out in defense of her home and not be a "slacker." The WCTU, which had done relatively little active suffrage work, declared that its mission would be to take the registration campaign to the missionary societies and "teach our duties to religious women." Some 386,000 women signed up during the seventeen-day registration period, and untold numbers of "Women's Hobby Clubs" were organized to campaign for the incumbent. Hobby won easily, the press and the progressives crediting women with making the election a landslide.[55]

Texas women were granted the vote because politicians needed their votes, not because their patriotism changed men's minds. The war *did*, however, provide a rationalization that the legislators could use to justify themselves publicly. The progressives who had persuaded Hobby to change his position on the liquor issue had astutely predicted that it could be pulled off with "a show of patriotism" that would smother charges of "flopping to the pros overnight."[56] The same strategy worked for suffrage, as southern-bred Woodrow Wilson had already demonstrated by abandoning his states' rights stance and taking up the NAWSA's claim that women deserved the vote in recompense for their war service.

The superheated passions of wartime provided the suffragists with the same kind of political cover that their opponents had long and successfully exploited with the "negro problem." Cunningham and the TESA avoided mentioning race because it was an issue on which the suffragists knew they could not win, but they took full advantage of one on which they could: anti-German prejudice and the loyalty question. Cooperating with dry politicians and the Anti-Saloon League in the fight for prohibition had taught women the effectiveness of linking the German-dominated brewing industry with disloyalty. The WCTU's Nannie Webb Curtis had declared that brewery profits supported the German army and that every open saloon was "an active agent of the Kaiser." Jane McCallum had been cleverer and less hyperbolic. In a widely distributed poem penned for the Austin local option campaign she lamented the influence of German-American voters and brewery money—"the Hun at the polls with the sold"—on Texas elections.[57]

The same manipulation of patriotism and prejudice surfaced in the campaign for the vote. The TESA leaders worked publicly to construct a patriotic screen for the politically expedient agreement that they were privately negotiating with James Ferguson's enemies in the Democratic party. Using women's clubs, sympathetic newspaper editors, and friends in the legislature to help advance their arguments, they stressed that "enemy aliens" could vote for the next Congress, while loyal American women could not. Nationalism served the suffragists as effectively as racism had formerly served the conservatives who were now their reluctant allies. Just as their opponents had conjured the threat of the negro at the polls to hold them back, the suffragists used the Hun at the polls to push themselves forward.[58]

Some of the women seem to have worried genuinely about disloyalty. Harris County ESA President Hortense Ward, who was prominently involved, told Minnie Fisher Cunningham that she was "desperately in earnest . . . I know the danger is there." But as a practical tactician, Ward was quick to seize the political opportunity embedded in the national eruption of German-bashing. The fact that "first paper" aliens, whose citizenship applications were still pending, were allowed to vote in Texas was added ammunition. Planning strategy with Cunningham, Ward emphasized the need to "stress the German vote" and "spread the dope." Jane McCallum's poem "Women Workers' Woes," deftly parodying Robert Service's "A Song of Winter Weather," was similarly blunt:

> It isn't the "slackers" we fear;
> It isn't the Sammies that fight; . . .
> It's the strafing we get
> From the Kaiser's own set
> At the polls
> polls
> polls[59]

The Hobby campaign, having decided to focus on the loyalty issue and Ferguson's ties to the German-American brewing industry as the most effective way of building a coalition against him, made the most of the suffragists' rationale. Women could compensate for the votes of some one hundred thousand absent soldiers, who were disfranchised by the state constitution as long as they remained in uniform, and for the disloyal ones of numberless German sympathizers. Hobby went on the hustings claiming that women had been admitted to the primaries "to offset the votes of those whose carcasses are in this country but whose souls are in Germany." Former governor Tom Campbell declared that "every slacker and every pro-German" would cast a ballot for Ferguson, "and it is up to the good women of this State to kill those votes."[60] It was an image perfectly calibrated to the xenophobic paranoia gripping the nation.

Exulting in "these piping times of victory" in 1918, Texas suffragists celebrated not a watershed of war but victory in a long engagement they had fought with ingenuity and determination.[61] As significant as the legislative act itself was the fact that prosuffrage women were numerous enough to back up Minnie Fisher Cunningham's promise of political support; Ferguson himself conceded that women apparently voted ten to one for Hobby. Following NAWSA strategy, the TESA had built a broad constituency and applied itself to learning practical politics. "Our object," Annette Finnigan had reported in 1914, "has been to make the Texas Woman Suffrage Association a political organization, working along political lines, and conducted in a businesslike manner." To that effect, local affiliates, with chairwomen and working committees organized down to the city, county, and precinct level, compiled detailed files on the voting records and political backgrounds of their congressmen and state legislators.[62]

Building its own political "machine" through these multiple layers of organization, the TESA steadily gained the strength to play politics seriously. Minnie Fisher Cunningham put the association's legislative files at the disposal of James Ferguson's opponents as they sought allies during the investigation that led to impeachment proceedings in 1917. In 1918, when TESA's sponsor of the primary suffrage bill asked for a breakdown of his legislative collegues by their suffrage views—supportive, opposed, or undecided—to use in lining up votes, Cunningham had the information immediately at hand. And when an antisuffrage legislator from Dallas said that only a petition from five thousand of his townswomen would change his stance, she had the Dallas ESA to do the job. It took them only four days, and they got *ten* thousand signatures for good measure.[63] Party politics supplied the opportunity, and war the rationalization, but the suffragists' success in 1918 was of their own laborious making.

For African American women, the TESA's triumph raised hopes immediately crushed by county Democratic executive committees upholding the white primary. In Austin black women were permitted to register but told they would not be allowed to vote. In Fort Worth, a party of six "well-dressed" women was refused entirely. Hobby campaign leaders in Waxahachie initially sought to bar African American women, fearing that the Fergusonians would accuse them of planning to vote black women as Democrats; the tax collector reversed himself after seeking an opinion from the state attorney general. The Orange tax collector and sheriff refused a group of black women so rudely that they sought relief in court. Their attorney was chairman of the local Hobby club, and the judge, a Ferguson man, threw out the case. El Paso permitted African American women to register, but the president of the Equal Suffrage League was unable to persuade the Democratic Executive Chairman to appoint them as election clerks in their precincts.[64]

In Houston, however, when the tax collector refused to register black women, the newly chartered Houston branch of the National Association for the Advancement of Colored People struck back. An African American attorney on its executive committee informed the tax collector's office that a protest would be prepared; in the branch secretary's words, "we were going to the limit that our women might register." Before they could deliver the protest, the tax collector telephoned that a "mistake" had been made in interpreting the law, and that black women would be permitted to register after all. A separate table was set up at the courthouse, and some 1,200 African American women signed up.[65]

Thirty-one NAACP branches formed in Texas in 1918–19, as African Americans attempted to defend themselves against hostile and exploitative whites who resented African Americans in uniform and black economic gains due to the wartime labor shortage. Black clubwomen, who had always spoken out against segregation and lynching through the National Association of Colored Women, were at the forefront in organizing several Texas branches. NACW President Mary B. Talbert spent the fall of 1918 in Texas and Louisiana, speaking, organizing, and raising money for the NAACP. Talbert and Carrie E. Adams, president of the Texas Association of Colored Women's Clubs and a member of the Beaumont NAACP, led a drive that doubled membership there. Together Talbert and the TACWC vice president, Mrs. H. E. Williams, chartered the Corsicana branch. In some Texas branches women constituted 40 percent or more of the membership.[66]

Most black women had to wait until after the ratification of the Nineteenth Amendment in 1920 to cast their first ballots; the state's white primary law effectively subverted their Fourteenth Amendment voting rights. But in Houston they and their male allies in the NAACP peacefully forced a white city official to uphold the letter of the law. "We won a signal victory, as small as it may seem," the branch secretary wrote jubilantly to NAACP headquarters, "for many of our women had been turned away from the office. But they are registering NOW!"[67] In a city where racial tensions had culminated in violence and bloodshed less than a year earlier, it was a quiet triumph.

Conclusion:
Gender and Public Cultures

A QUARTER of a century after Bride Neill Taylor reported on the Texas Congress of Women, her optimistic prediction had been fulfilled: the southern woman was at last "up with the procession." In the empty political space created by the southern tradition of weak government, the progressive women of Texas carved out a significant public role. White women constructed a network of federated voluntary associations through which they worked locally for civic improvement and lobbied in Austin for state-mandated social change. African American women built a parallel but largely separate culture of clubs and societies, translated their long tradition of mutual association at the community level into a state federation of women's clubs, and helped organize the state's first NAACP branches. Public woman, who had been barely visible in Texas when the Women's Congress convened in 1893, was everywhere by World War I.

The growth of this female public culture made possible a sustained and successful suffrage movement in the 1910s. Clubs nurtured the municipal housekeeping and social motherhood ethos that became the most popular and persuasive suffrage arguments and helped nudge some nonsuffragists toward the beginnings of feminist consciousness. White clubwomen discovered the real face of sex discrimination through their attempts to found a women's industrial college, pass a married women's property law, serve on school boards, and secure a gender-equal distribution of Smith-Lever money from the Agricultural Extension Service. The ferment of social reform in the Progressive Era facilitated a reconciliation between the ideology of domesticity and the demands of feminism that helped make suffrage a mass movement.

Through membership in a network of national voluntary associations southern ladies discovered social activism and developed perspectives that challenged regional conservatism. Their thumbnail biographies proudly noted Virginia ancestors and the Confederate military service of their husbands and fathers, but they stood with the General Federation of Women's Clubs rather than with the New South industrialists on labor issues. Living in a segregated society and sharing the racial attitudes of the era, they sought the ballot in the name of maternalism rather than white supremacy. Brought up to revere states' rights, they worked assiduously for the federal suffrage amendment.

Through their voluntarist politics, elite white women implicitly criticized the New South Creed of industrial progress promulgated by men of their own class. Female voices were among the loudest for child labor laws, minimum wage and maximum hour laws for working women, higher school taxes, longer school terms, and compulsory attendance. All were innovations that contradicted the southern tradition of low taxes, limited government, and local control. All would cost money, increase the power of the state at the expense of individual communities and local male elites, and restrain the freedom of business and industry to exploit labor.

Advocating expanded power and responsibility for the state put progressive women squarely at odds with the southern political tradition, which insisted that a weak state best guaranteed human liberty. Women's experience in voluntary associations helped shape their much more positive, proactive view of government.[1] Disfranchised though they were, federated women had more direct experience with participatory democracy than many men. Local clubs and societies were accustomed to cooperating productively with state federations in a relationship that in many ways paralleled the one between local and state government. Women expected state authority to enhance rather than inhibit their own power in community work. Just as federation gave local clubs access to additional resources and new offices, a proactive state would require new positions, such as factory inspectors, pure food inspectors, and truant officers, that women themselves might fill.

Because voluntary associations rather than electoral politics structured female public culture, Texas women were likewise more progressive—perhaps it would be more accurate to say less reactionary—on racial matters. African American historians have justly exposed the discrimination that black women suffered in white-led organizations, and southern women have been held especially culpable. Anna Pennybacker undeniably expressed the views of most white women when she wrote to a Minnesota friend: "Social equality is simply unthinkable to me. Mixture of blood is a most obnoxious thought."[2] But it does not greatly advance our understanding of southern women to contrast them simply with their northern counterparts, who had wider social and political latitude within which to act. A more realistic standard of measurement would compare southern women not against Frances Willard and Jane Addams but with white southern men.

Consider the interplay between gender and race when female and male public cultures faced off at a local option election in East Texas. The writer complaining about the WCTU is a local antiprohibitionist leader communicating with an official of the Texas Brewers' Association, which spent money freely to "fix" minority voters: "The women and children, both black and white, marched and sang and prayed, and absolutely grabbed the voters, to keep them from voting. . . . We cannot get women who will make counter-demonstrations. It most certainly has a wonderful influence on the voters, especially in the smaller towns. Can't we stop it? Our committee was bluffed, and we lost several votes, that I saw, not to mention those who heard of it and stayed away."[3] Shared gender and class interests motivated a political protest that breached racial boundaries, and very effectively, as the rest of the antisuffragist's complaint reveals: "When a negro would come, they would ask him if he was 21, or if he had a tax receipt, and if he had to swear his vote they would tell him . . . that if he swore falsely it meant two years in the pen. The negro usually quit right there, and our committee laid right down and stood for it."

Joining forces did not signify that the white women were less committed to white supremacy or the black ones less resolved to resist subordination, only that each group needed the other's cooperation to succeed. The black women would have been more likely to know which African American men had been paid off or were underage, just as the white women knew which of their own friends and neighbors were likely to vote against prohibition. The temperance women of both races were disgusted with their menfolk, white men who bought votes and black men who sold them—the only interracial cooperation that southern male political culture recognized. The women worked together in the name of righteous morality, intimidating not just the vulnerable black men but the powerful white ones who "laid right down and stood for it" as well.

The WCTU's interracialism may have been limited and patronizing, but on the men's side of the prohibitionist movement there was no cooperation at all across the racial divide. The two male organizations, the Texas Local Option Association, and the clergy-led Anti-Saloon League (which absorbed the former in 1908) were entirely white and outspokenly racist. While the women of the WCTU and the men of the Anti-Saloon League alike denounced the manipulated voting of blacks and Hispanics by political bosses, they assigned culpability differently. The WCTU criticized the white bosses; the Anti-Saloon League blamed the "criminal class of negroes" and the "ragamuffin greasers" of the border counties. After a statewide prohibition amendment narrowly lost in 1911, the Anti-Saloon League voiced its approval of a proposal to eliminate the Hispanic vote by disfranchising illiterates. It raged against "that horde of tamale vendors and peon princes" who were "nothing more or less than Indians who can scarcely be classed as even semi-civilized."[4]

The WCTU, by contrast, began an earnest if not spectacularly successful attempt to organize unions in the wet, Hispanic-dominated southern counties. Following the tradition of outreach to African Americans, it organized a Department of Foreign-Speaking People, whose superintendent was responsible for "mobilizing the Mexican."[5] Exclusion from male political culture freed women from the competition for votes, giving them the latitude to explore collaboration, however tentative, across racial-ethnic lines. Voluntarist women could expect their causes to succeed only by increasing the number of their allies. White men had the additional alternative of eliminating their rivals, the option they had exercised in disfranchising blacks.

A similar dichotomy is evident in the campaigns for and against suffrage: there was no equivalent among female suffragists in Texas of the flagrant race-baiting that their male political opponents displayed at every opportunity. Antisuffragist politicians kept up a ceaseless counterfactual chant that woman suffrage in any form—partial, state-granted, or by federal amendment—would overturn the race settlement and bring on a new invasion of federal troops. As Elna Green has pointed out, antisuffragists demanded not just white supremacy but white monopoly.[6] Forced on the defensive, suffragists reiterated endlessly that it was impossible under the state's election laws for hordes of African American women to overrun the polls; a small number of black women would be added to the small number of black men who could meet the voting qualifications.

If the suffragists failed to condemn black disfranchisement and Jim Crow, their statements were at least truthful. In the persuasive, educational mode of voluntary association politics, they enumerated the benefits of the proposed change; their male opponents demagogued the race issue in the tradition of one-party southern politics. A typical editorial diatribe claimed that woman suffrage would put the ballot "in the hands of 300,000 negro women and prostitutes," forcing pure white women to "elbow their way through gangs of negro women." By 1919, with ratification of the Nineteenth Amendment pending, race obliterated other arguments among male antisuffragists. The Alabama-based Men's Organization Opposed to Woman Suffrage flooded Texas with ugly propaganda accusing the national suffrage leaders of advocating racial intermarriage and warned of the sexual danger to white women if black-majority counties fell under "negro domination."[7]

Female antisuffragists, however, largely rejected this approach. There was comparatively little rhetorical racism among the small group of organized antisuffragist women, the Texas Association Opposed to Woman Suffrage, founded in 1916. The women of the TAOWS might easily have cloaked themselves in the devastatingly effective language of bigotry and pleaded for male protection. But in common with the women of the TESA, those of the opposition chose the familiar strategy of voluntarist politics, "educating public opinion." Like any other voluntary association, the TAOWS adopted a constitution, by-laws, and plan of work at its first meeting. In the tradition that clubwomen had followed for decades, it announced "a campaign of education through the publication and circulation of such information . . . as will lead to a full knowledge and understanding of the subject."[8]

Like the TESA, the TAOWS was a state branch of a national organization headquartered in the North; it articulated the ideas and distributed the literature of the National Association Opposed to Woman Suffrage. Thus while their male allies ruthlessly exploited the "negro bogey," TAOWS members published long statistical pieces purporting to show that enfranchised women in other states had failed to eliminate red-light districts, raise working women's wages, and usher in prohibition. The NAOWS demons, "feminism, sex antagonism, socialism, and Mormonism," resonated much more strongly in the North, but the TAOWS echoed and emphasized them. Its leaders did not inject the white supremacy claim until very late in the Texas suffrage campaign, and then only as one argument of many.[9]

Winning the right to participate with men in electoral politics did not lessen women's commitment to their own voluntarist public culture. Men resisted admitting them to the inner circles of power, and many women found the realities of electoral politics distasteful. In the 1920s women of both races continued to pursue through proliferating voluntary associations the social reform agenda formulated during the progressive decades. The National American Woman Suffrage Association metamorphosed into the League of Women Voters, with a mandate not only to educate the new female voters but to press for reforms such as compulsory education laws in every state and protective labor legislation for women and children.[10]

In Texas a Woman's Joint Legislative Council (the WCTU, TFWC, and TCM united with the Business and Professional Women's Clubs and the new League of Women Voters) carried on the lobbying work for public school improvement, prohibition enforcement, and health care. As in the Progressive Era, the women of the JLC were inspired by a national association, the Women's Joint Congressional Committee, that coordinated the Washington lobbying of ten major women's groups. The WJCC's first achievement was persuading Congress to pass the 1921 Sheppard-Towner Act authorizing federal funds for state maternal and infant health care programs, an idea first proposed by Julia Lathrop and the Children's Bureau. The first triumph of the Texas JLC was persuading the reluctant legislature to appropriate the matching funds necessary to implement Sheppard-Towner.[11]

At the same time, black women's race work took on added significance as the Texas NAACP succumbed to intimidation from state government and the rise of the Ku Klux Klan. By 1921 only seven of the more than thirty Texas branches founded in 1918–19 survived, but the TACWC continued to grow in numbers and effectiveness and to work quietly for what the NAACP, as a northern-led organization, no longer dared pursue openly. Under the administration of Carrie Adams (1916–20) the TACWC had committed itself to securing a training school for delinquent African American girls, as an alternative to incarceration at the state women's prison. By 1926 the TACWC had paid off the purchase price of a house and barn on a ten-acre property in San Antonio and had begun the even more difficult task of persuading the state to assume the operating costs. And for the first time, the organization had cooperation and assistance from its white counterparts. The TFWC, which had ignored black clubwomen before the war, and the new JLC both endorsed the training school; the TFWC made it part of a "program of cooperation" with the TACWC.[12]

Through their voluntary associations, women took the lead in the tentative movement for interracial cooperation that emerged slowly in the 1920s. Membership in national organizations, as historian Glenda Gilmore has pointed out, gave white southern women the opportunity "to see past the parochial racism that surrounded them." Firmly resisting the idea of "social equality," women like Anna Pennybacker were nevertheless troubled by the belief that "we have not done our full duty by the negro." World War I sharpened tensions between white and black men, but it fostered positive interaction between women, nudging them across racial boundaries as they cooperated in canning demonstration programs, childsaving work, and fundraising drives. Suffragist Margie Neal recalled that selling Liberty Bonds prompted the first speech of her life to a "colored" audience: she addressed the "very responsive" women of an African Methodist Episcopal Church.[13]

After the war white women extended their efforts, through religious and secular voluntary associations, to build a narrow bridge across the chasm of race. Although questioning white supremacy was still unimaginable, they worked quietly with African American women to address social problems. In 1921 the TFWC created a standing committee, Condition of Our Colored People, within its Department of Social and Industrial Conditions. Former suffragist Jessie Daniel Ames chaired the new committee (later renamed Interracial Relations), at the same time serving as head of the Texas women's division of the Atlanta-based Commission on Interracial Cooperation.

In the 1920s the TFWC for the first time began to invite TACWC presidents to address its conventions. In 1926 the program on home economics included Mary Evelyn V. Hunter of Prairie View Normal College, who described the home demonstration work being done by her staff of eighteen agents and asked the white clubwomen's help in training more. By the end of the decade, the chair of the TFWC's Interracial Relations Committee was articulating a vision that years of voluntary association labor had gradually enabled white women to see: social progress for the state was impossible without addressing the needs of both races. To that end, the white clubwomen were working to build libraries in black schools, helping to support "Negro Health Week," and lobbying the legislature for a tuberculosis hospital for African Americans.[14]

Most significantly, white women took up black women's challenge to speak out against lynching, so long justified in the name of protecting white womanhood and the most enduring symbol of the reactionary South. In 1930 Jessie Daniel Ames, by then relocated to Atlanta, would chart a bold new direction for white women's public culture by founding the Association of Southern Women for the Prevention of Lynching. Deploring mob violence as she discussed the race problem with her northern friend, Anna Pennybacker had written in 1918, "above all things, I want my state and my section of the country to have a clean conscience." Ames and the ASWPL would work to fulfill Pennybacker's hope.

Notes

Abbreviations

AAAPSS	*Annals of the American Academy of Political and Social Science*
AHC-APL	Austin History Center, Austin Public Library
CAH-UT	Center for American History, University of Texas at Austin
CET	Conference for Education in Texas
DMN/GDN	*Dallas Morning News/Galveston Daily News*
HMRC	Houston Metropolitan Research Collection, Houston Public Library
NACWC	National Association of Colored Women's Clubs
NAWSA	National American Woman Suffrage Association
TAOWS	Texas Association Opposed to Woman Suffrage
TCM	Texas Congress of Mothers
TFWC	Texas Federation of Women's Clubs
TWU	Texas Woman's University, Denton
WCTU	Woman's Christian Temperance Union

Introduction

1. *Dallas Morning News,* October 27, 1893.

2. Suzanne Lebsock, "Women and American Politics, 1880–1920," in *Women, Politics, and Change,* edited by Louise A. Tilly and Patricia Gurin (New York, 1990), 35; William H. Chafe, *The Paradox of Change: American Women in the Twentieth Century* (New York, 1991), 16. See also Nancy Schrom Dye's introduction to *Gender, Class, Race, and Reform in the Progressive Era,* edited by Noralee Frankel and Nancy Schrom Dye (Lexington, Ky., 1991).

3. Evan Anders, "Populism and Progressivism," in *A Guide to the History of Texas,* edited by Light Townsend Cummins and Alvin R. Bailey Jr. (New York, 1988); Anne Firor Scott, "An Historian's Odyssey," in her *Making the Invisible Woman Visible* (Urbana, Ill., 1984), xviii.

4. Kathryn Kish Sklar, *Florence Kelley and the Nation's Work: The Rise of Women's Political Culture, 1830–1900* (New Haven, Conn., 1995).

5. See Jean E. Friedman, *The Enclosed Garden: Women and Community in the Evangel-ical South, 1830–1900* (Chapel Hill, N.C., 1985), and Suzanne Lebsock, *The Free Women of Petersburg: Status and Culture in a Southern Town, 1784–1860* (New York, 1984), 239–44, on the late appearance of female social reform in the South. See also Elizabeth Fox-Genovese in *Within the Plantation Household: Black and White Women of the Old South* (Chapel Hill, N.C., 1988), especially chap. 1, which argues that women in slaveholding so-ciety were divided by race and class rather than united by gender. Elizabeth R. Varon, "Tippecanoe and the Ladies, Too: White Women and Party Politics in Antebellum Vir-ginia," *Journal of American History* 82 (Sept. 1995): 494–521, finds Whig women actively interested in politics but concludes that they channeled partisanship into support for the Confederacy rather than into women's rights.

6. See for example, Darlene Rebecca Roth, *Matronage: Patterns in Women's Organiza-tions, Atlanta, Georgia, 1890–1940* (New York, 1994); Elizabeth Hayes Turner, *Women, Culture and Community: Religion and Reform in Galveston, 1880–1920* (New York, 1997); and Marsha Wedell, *Elite Women and the Reform Impulse in Memphis, 1875–1915* (Knoxville, Tenn., 1991).

7. Paula Baker, "The Domestication of Politics: Women and American Political Soci-ety, 1780–1920," *American Historical Review* 89 (June 1984): 620–47.

8. Nancy F. Cott, "What's in a Name? The Limits of 'Social Feminism'; or, Expanding the Vocabulary of Women's History," *Journal of American History* 76 (Dec. 1989): 809–29.

9. Glenna Matthews, *The Rise of Public Woman: Woman's Power and Woman's Place in the United States, 1630–1970* (New York, 1992), esp. 3–11.

10. Elsa Barkley Brown, "Womanist Consciousness: Maggie Lena Walker and the In-dependent Order of Saint Luke," *Signs* 14 (Spring 1989): 610–33.

11. Terry G. Jordan, "A Century and a Half of Ethnic Change in Texas," *Southwestern Historical Quarterly* 89 (Apr. 1996): 392–404; Cynthia E. Orozco, "Beyond Machismo, La Familia, and Ladies Auxiliaries: A Historiography of Mexican-Origin Women's Par-ticipation in Voluntary Associations and Politics in the United States," *Perspectives in Mexican-American Studies* (1994): 1–34. Orozco points out that it has been more com-mon for Mexican American women to organize with men along class lines and that these mixed-gender associations "are primarily a post–World War II phenomenon" (p. 4).

12. Catherine Clinton, ed., *Half-Sisters of History: Southern Women and the American Past* (Durham, N.C., 1994). See for example, Anastatia Sims, *The Power of Femininity in the New South: Women and Politics in North Carolina, 1883–1930* (Columbia, S.C., 1997), which finds a more conservative female public culture in North Carolina than I have de-scribed in Texas.

Chapter 1: "The Coming Woman in Politics"

1. "An Appeal to the Christian Women of San Antonio," *San Antonio Daily Express,* Aug. 28, 1886; May Baines, *A Story of Texas White Ribboners* (n.p., [1935?]), 26.

2. *Denison Democrat,* Feb. 12, 1882, scrapbook 15, reel 32, WCTU series, *Temperance and Prohibition Papers* (Ohio Historical Society, Michigan Historical Collections, and

Woman's Christian Temperance Union, 1977, microfilm). On women's "sphere" in the South, see Anne Firor Scott, *The Southern Lady: From Pedestal to Politics, 1830–1930* (Chicago, 1970), Jean E. Friedman, *The Enclosed Garden: Women and Community in the Evangelical South, 1830–1900* (Chapel Hill, N.C., 1985), and George C. Rable, *Civil Wars: Women and the Crisis of Southern Nationalism* (Urbana, Ill., 1991), 285–88.

3. E. L. Dohoney, who secured the opera house for Willard's lecture, recalled in his autobiography, *An Average American* (Paris, Tex., 1907), that "at the time, the preachers of the South regarded the Woman's Christian Temperance Union as a Northern fanaticism, and were afraid of it." On the status of women in evangelical churches, see Virginia Shadron, "Out of Our Homes: The Woman's Rights Movement in the Methodist Episcopal Church, South, 1890–1918" (Master's thesis, Emory University, 1976); John Patrick McDowell, *The Social Gospel in the South: The Woman's Home Mission Movement in the Methodist Episcopal Church, South, 1886–1939* (Baton Rouge, 1982), 6–35, 116–43; Norman H. Letsinger, "The Status of Women in the Southern Baptist Convention in Historical Perspective," *Baptist History and Heritage* 12 (Jan. 1977): 37–44; and Patricia Summerlin Martin, "Hidden Work: Baptist Women in Texas, 1880–1920" (Ph.D. diss., Rice University, 1982), 276.

4. Ruth Bordin, *Woman and Temperance: The Quest for Power and Liberty, 1873–1900* (Philadelphia, 1981), 76–81; scrapbooks 14 and 15, reel 32, WCTU series, *Temperance and Prohibition Papers.* Yearly membership figures are printed in the corresponding secretary's report in Annual Meeting Minutes, reel 2 (1885–88), and reel 3 (1889–92). On the WCTU in the South, see Scott, *The Southern Lady*, 144–60, and Friedman, *Enclosed Garden,* 118–121.

5. *Morrison and Fourmy's General Directory of the City of Houston, 1887–88* (Galveston, 1887), 50–52; *Directory of the City of Houston, 1913* (Houston, 1913), 69, 73.

6. Annual Meeting Minutes, 1892, reel 3, WCTU series, *Temperance and Prohibition Papers,* quotation at p. 249.

7. On the origins of the club movement, see Karen Blair, *The Clubwoman as Feminist: True Womanhood Redefined, 1868–1914* (New York, 1980); Theodora Penny Martin, *The Sound of Our Own Voices: Women's Study Clubs, 1860–1910* (Boston, 1987); and Anne Firor Scott, *Natural Allies: Women's Associations in American History* (Urbana, Ill., 1992), chap. 5.

8. Betty T. Chapman, "From the Parlor to the Public: New Roles for Women in Houston, 1885–1918," *Houston Review* 15:1 (1993): 31–44.

9. Minutes, May 30, 1893, Ladies' Reading Club Records and "Address of Mrs. M. Looscan to the Ladies' Reading Club of Houston, Texas, on its Tenth Anniversary, Apr. 1895," Adele Briscoe Looscan Papers, both in Houston Metropolitan Research Collection, Houston Public Library (hereafter cited as HMRC).

10. "Editor's Study," *Harper's New Monthly Magazine* 87 (Oct. 1893): 801. On Anthony's protest, see Eleanor Flexner, *Century of Struggle: The Woman's Rights Movement in the United States* (1959; rept. New York, 1974), 170–72.

11. Frances K. Pohl, "Historical Reality or Utopian Ideal? The Woman's Building at the World's Columbian Exposition, Chicago, 1893," *International Journal of Women's Studies*

5 (Sept./Oct. 1982): 289–311; Estelle Freedman, "Separatism as Strategy: Female Institution Building and American Feminism, 1870–1930," *Feminist Studies* 5 (Fall 1979): 520–21; Scott, *Natural Allies,* 128–29.

12. May Wright Sewell, ed., *The World's Congress of Representative Women* (Chicago, 1894), 2–3.

13. Gayle Gullett, "'Our Great Opportunity': Organized Women Advance Women's Work at the World's Columbian Exposition of 1893," *Illinois Historical Journal* 87 (Winter 1994): 259–76; Jeanne Madeline Wiemann, *The Fair Women* (Chicago, 1981), 523–49. The papers are gathered in Sewell, ed., *World's Congress of Representative Women.*

14. Rebecca Henry Hayes to Laura Clay, Feb. 13, 1893, Clay Papers, King Library, University of Kentucky, Lexington; Hayes, "Texas," in *Proceedings of the Twenty-seventh Annual Convention of the National American Woman Suffrage Association,* edited by Harriet Taylor Upton (Warren, Ohio, [1895]) 91. I am indebted to Marjorie Spruill Wheeler for drawing my attention to the Hayes letter.

15. Darlene Rebecca Roth, in *Matronage: Patterns in Women's Organizations, Atlanta, Georgia, 1890–1940* (New York, 1994), and Anne Firor Scott in *The Southern Lady* and *Natural Allies,* have stressed this point, emphasizing the effect of national fairs in stimulating the growth of women's organizations.

16. *Dallas Morning News,* October 23, 27 (quotation), 1893.

17. Ibid.; Jacqueline Van Voris, *Carrie Chapman Catt: A Public Life* (New York, 1987), 29.

18. *Dallas Morning News,* Oct. 29, 1893. On Elizabeth Fry, see Elizabeth Brooks, *Prominent Women of Texas* (Akron, Ohio, 1896), 149.

19. Ann Massa, "Black Women in the 'White City,' " *Journal of American Studies* 8 (Dec. 1974): 319–37; Weimann, *The Fair Women,* 111–12 (quotation).

20. "The Texas Girl at Oread," *Dallas Morning News,* July 3, 1899. On Colored People's Day, see ibid., Oct. 24, 1893.

21. "Woman's Congress . . . Its Name Changed to State Council of Women of Texas," and "The State Council," unidentified newspaper clippings [1894], Texas Equal Suffrage [*sic*] Association Scrapbook, pp. 36, 38, [Jane Y.] McCallum Family Papers, Austin History Center, Austin Public Library (hereafter cited as AHC-APL); *Dallas Morning News,* Nov. 2, 1895. Current Topics Club quotation appears in Mary S. Cunningham, *The Woman's Club of El Paso: Its First Thirty Years* (El Paso, 1978), p. 2.

22. Mrs. J. C. Terrell, "Succinct History of the Woman's Club Movement," *Dallas Morning News,* Nov. 22, 1903. Mrs. J[ane] C[unningham] Croly, *The History of the Woman's Club Movement in America* (New York, 1898), lists no Texas clubs founded earlier than 1886.

23. Cunningham, *Woman's Club of El Paso.*

24. Stella L. Christian. ed., *History of the Texas Federation of Women's Clubs* [vol. 1] (Houston, 1919), 5–8, traces the origin of the Texas Federation of Women's Clubs to the State Council of Women. TFWC yearbooks do not supply founding dates for clubs, but see *The Club Monthly,* edited by the Tyler Twentieth Century Club, copy at the Center for American History, University of Texas at Austin (hereafter cited as CAH-UT) for

suggestive evidence. Extant issues of vol. 1, Dec. 1897–Mar. 1898, at CAH-UT contain reports from twenty clubs that specify founding dates; only one of these was organized before 1891. See the issue for Mar. 1898, p. 34, for the Congress of Clubs.

25. The convention was postponed in 1897 because of a public health scare, and no more meetings were announced. I am indebted to Jackie McElhaney for pointing out the notice in the *Dallas Morning News*, Oct. 18, 1897.

26. Robert H. Wiebe, *The Search for Order, 1877–1920* (New York, 1967); Charlotte Perkins Gilman, *Women and Economics* (Boston, 1898), 166.

27. NAWSA's Southern Committee, headed by Laura Clay of Kentucky, is described in Marjorie Spruill Wheeler, *New Women of the New South: The Leaders of the Woman Suffrage Movement in the Southern States* (New York, 1993), 115–20.

28. The earliest membership figures for the Texas Federation were published in *Yearbook of the Texas Federation of Women's Clubs, 1901–1902*, 40. The state WCTU reported 1,654 active members in 1901 and 2,119 in 1912; see "Annual Meeting Minutes," reel 6, WCTU series, *Temperance and Prohibition Papers*, and "Proceedings of the Thirteenth Annual Convention of the Woman's Christian Temperance Union of Texas," in Texas Woman's Press Association Scrapbook, CAH-UT. Comparative national figures appear in Bordin, *Woman and Temperance*, 3, 140. The GFWC counted 20,000 members at its first biennial convention in 1892, against 150,000 in the national WCTU; by 1910 the GFWC had roughly three-quarters of a million members, the WCTU less than a quarter million. These figures, however, derive from self-reported and variable data. Bordin calculates half a million clubwomen in 1910, while Mary I. Wood's *History of the General Federation of Women's Clubs* (New York, 1912), 353, claims one million. Three-quarters of a million is probably more accurate, since reports of the 1912 Biennial used 800,000 as the figure.

29. See Chapman, "From the Parlor to the Public," 33, n.7, on Houston, and Elizabeth Hayes Turner, *Women, Culture and Community: Religion and Reform in Galveston, 1880–1920* (New York, 1997), which found that in Galveston WCTU women tended to come from the evangelical churches and the lower range of the middle class, while clubwomen were more likely to be in the higher socio-economic strata.

30. Bordin, *Woman and Temperance*, provides the best description of the WCTU, supplemented by her *Frances Willard: A Biography*. Baines, *A Story of Texas White Ribboners*, is the only history of the Texas WCTU and contains numerous errors. Archival sources for this organization are very thin. See especially the minute books in Records of the W.C.T.U. of Canadian, Texas, 1904–54, Southwest Collection, Texas Tech University, Lubbock; and *Yearbook of the Woman's Christian Temperance Union of Texas, November 1904–October 1905* in the George Purl Childers Papers, CAH-UT. This is the only Texas WCTU yearbook I have located.

31. Even the unions that remained loyal to the Texas WCTU after the suffrage split in 1888 did no work for the ballot. The situation was similar in other southern states. The North Carolina WCTU nominally endorsed the ballot in the 1890s but did not work for it. In Georgia, declining membership and clerical pressure to withdraw from the national body forced the WCTU to declare in 1893 that suffrage was not in the best interest of the

temperance cause. In Alabama, the national organizer had to reassure the nervous orga-nizing convention of 1884 that each state could define its own work without subscribing to the "advanced" views of the national organization. The state union refused to go on record for suffrage until 1914. Anastatia Sims, "Feminism and Femininity in the New South: White Women's Organizations in North Carolina, 1883–1930" (Ph.D. diss., University of North Carolina at Chapel Hill, 1985); Mrs. J. J. Ansley, *History of the Georgia Woman's Christian Temperance Union from its Organization, 1883–1907* (Columbus, Ga., 1914), 141–50, 174–79; and Mary Martha Thomas, *The New Woman in Alabama: Social Reforms and Suffrage, 1890–1920* (Tuscaloosa, Ala., 1992), 14–15, 17–18.

32. On the benefits of federation, see Blair, *Clubwoman as Feminist,* 97–98, and Theda Skocpol, *Protecting Soldiers and Mothers: The Political Origins of Social Policy in the United States* (Cambridge, Mass., 1992), 448.

33. "Texas," [*The Signal,* 1882], scrapbook 15, reel 32, and Annual Meeting Minutes, reel 2, p. 113 [1886], reel 5, p. 204 [1897], p. 195 [1898], p. 200 [1899], p. 199 [1900], WCTU series, *Temperance and Prohibition Papers; Union Signal,* June 21, 1883, p. 11, and Oct. 29, 1885, p. 8. Black ministers seem to have been as divided as their white counterparts on the WCTU. Mrs. Eliza Peterson, the president of Texas No. 2, found them equally likely to help or hinder.

34. Although there are no organizational records for the WCTU in Texas, and its leaders left no papers, brief annual reports submitted to the National by the white union are available in the *Temperance and Prohibition Papers.* The black union did not send reports; the only information on it appears in the "WCTU Notes" column of the *Dallas Morning News,* which unfortunately never mentioned total membership figures. See Jan. 25, 1909, for the state convention. After 1909, when Eliza Peterson became National Superintendent of Colored Work and began traveling throughout the South, these items ceased to appear. Nothing is known about Peterson except that she was a music teacher; see Ruthe Winegarten, *Black Texas Women: A Sourcebook* (Austin, 1996), 262, and Winegarten, *Black Texas Women: 150 Years of Trial and Triumph* (Austin, 1995), 78, 79, 190.

35. E. E. Peterson to Mrs. Booker T. Washington, Apr. 28, 1899, published in *National Association Notes* 3 (June 1899), reel 23, *Records of the National Association of Colored Women's Clubs,* part 1 (Bethesda, Md., 1993, microfilm); *National Association Notes* 3 (Feb. 1900), ibid.

36. No records have been found for the Texas Association of Colored Women's Clubs. Brief information on the organization appears in Elizabeth Lindsay Davis, *Lifting as They Climb* (Washington, D.C., 1933), 397–98; Charles Wesley Harris, *The History of the National Association of Colored Women's Clubs, A Legacy of Service* (Washington, D.C., 1984), 519–23; Andrew Webster Jackson, *A Sure Foundation and a Sketch of Negro Life in Texas* (Houston, [1944?]), and Winegarten, *Black Texas Women,* 190–93, and *Black Texas Women: A Sourcebook,* 133–35.

37. Stephanie J. Shaw, "Black Club Women and the Creation of the National Association of Colored Women," *Journal of Women's History* 3 (Fall 1991): 10–25; Anne Firor Scott, "Most Invisible of All: Black Women's Voluntary Associations," *Journal of Southern History* 56 (Feb. 1990): 3–22; Dorothy Salem, *To Better Our World: Black Women and*

Organized Reform, 1890–1920, vol. 14 of *Black Women in United States History,* edited by Darlene Clark Hine (Brooklyn, 1990); Loretta Barnett Floris Cash, "Womanhood and Protest: The Club Movement among Black Women, 1892–1922" (Ph.D. diss., SUNY-Stony Brook, 1986); Tullia K. Brown Hamilton, "The National Association of Colored Women, 1896–1920," (Ph.D. diss., Emory University, 1978).

38. Pauline Periwinkle [Isadore Callaway], "Civic Improvement," *DMN/GDN,* Jan. 21, 1907. On the TFWC's growth see Megan Seaholm, "Earnest Women: The White Woman's Club Movement in Texas, 1880–1920" (Ph.D. diss., Rice University, 1988), and Christian, *History of the Texas Federation of Women's Clubs.*

39. Wood, *History of the General Federation,* 109–11.

40. Ibid., 139, 145–48, 172–74; Mrs. A. O. Granger, "The Work of the General Federation of Women's Clubs against Child Labor," *Annals of the American Academy of Political and Social Science* 25 (May 1905): 516–21. (Hereafter cited as *AAAPSS.*)

41. Minutes, Fifth Annual Meeting, Nov. 17, 1902, Texas Federation of Women's Clubs Records (uncataloged), Texas Woman's University Library, Denton, Texas; Pauline Periwinkle [Isadore Callaway], "Work of the Biennial," *DMN/GDN,* May 26, 1902; Christian, *History of the Texas Federation of Women's Clubs,* 88 (quotation). The Dallas Federation's "espionage" is recounted in Mrs. J. C. Roberts to Anna Pennybacker, June 24, 1902, TFWC Records; I am indebted to Jackie McElhaney for sharing a copy from her files.

42. Olga Kohlberg to Pennybacker, Feb. 16, 1906, Mrs. Percy V. [Anna J. H.] Pennybacker Papers (recataloging in process), CAH-UT; *Houston Post,* Nov. 30, 1910; *Dallas Morning News,* Jan. 16, 26, Mar. 20, 1911.

43. Clubwomen's efforts on behalf of child labor legislation are typically accorded only brief mention in the secondary literature. See for example, Walter I. Trattner, *Crusade for the Children: A History of the National Child Labor Committee and Child Labor Reform in America* (Chicago, 1970), 34, and Dewey W. Grantham, *Southern Progressivism: The Reconciliation of Progress and Tradition* (Knoxville, Tenn., 1983), 178–99; the latter notes without elaboration the presence of women in the reform coalitions in nearly every state. For details on two southern states, see Thomas, *New Woman in Alabama,* chap. 5, and Judith N. McArthur, "Saving the Children: The Women's Crusade against Child Labor, 1902–1918," in *Women and Texas History: Selected Essays,* edited by Fane Downs and Nancy Baker Jones (Austin, 1993).

44. Mrs. J. C. Roberts to Anna Pennybacker, June 24, 1902, TFWC Records; John F. Worley and Co., *Dallas Directory for 1902* (Dallas, 1902), 53.

45. Josephine K. Henry, "The New Woman of the New South," *Arena* 11 (1894–95): 355.

46. Christian, *History of the Texas Federation of Women's Clubs,* 8–9. For biographical information see Terrell's obituaries in *Fort Worth Star-Telegram,* Oct. 17, 1920, and *Marshall Messenger,* Oct. 18, 1920.

47. Peter Molyneaux, "A Miracle of Faithfulness," *Texas Club Woman,* June 8, 1914, pp. 2–4, is a good brief account of Pennybacker's early life. See also Helen Knox, *Mrs. Percy V. Pennybacker: An Appreciation* (New York, 1916), Rebecca Langworthy Richmond, *A Woman of Texas: Mrs. Percy V. Pennybacker* (San Antonio, 1941), and the collection of obituaries in the Pennybacker Papers.

48. On Brackenridge's life see Johnowene B. Crutcher Menger, "M. Eleanor Brackenridge, 1837–1924, a Third Generation Advocate of Education," (Master's thesis, Trinity University, 1964); Marin B. Fenwick, *Who's Who among the Women of San Antonio and Southwest Texas* (San Antonio, 1917), 19, 42; and the biographical file at the Daughters of the Republic of Texas Library at the Alamo, San Antonio.

49. M. Eleanor Brackenridge to Anna Pennybacker, July 24, 1901, TFWC Records.

50. *Dallas Morning News,* May 2–4, 1901.

51. Mrs. Percy V. Pennybacker, "The Eighth Biennial Convention of the General Federation of Women's Clubs," *AAAPSS* 28 (Sept. 1906): 79.

52. Quoted in Pauline Periwinkle [Isadore Callaway], "The General Biennial" and "Clubdom," *DMN/GDN,* May 19, 1902.

53. Wood, *History of the General Federation,* 161, 195, 216, 218; Molyneaux, "Miracle of Faithfulness," 4; Anna J. H. Pennybacker, "The Endowment Fund," *General Federation Bulletin* 9:5 (Feb. 1912): 298–99.

54. "Texas Bulletin," *General Federation Bulletin* 10:1 (Apr. 1912), 47–48.

55. Unidentified newspaper clipping, Scrapbook, 1912–16, Pennybacker Papers (hereafter cited as GFWC Scrapbook); "Polly" [Isadore Callaway] to "My Dear," Mar. 7, 1912 (quotation), both in Pennybacker Papers.

56. Special Committee to the Clubs of the Texas Federation of Women's Clubs, Mar. 20, 1912, Pennybacker Papers. The Terrell-Pennybacker correspondence does not mention the size of the campaign chest, but see Past Presidents' Association, Dallas Federation of Women's Clubs, *History of the Dallas Federation of Women's Clubs,* 2 vols. (Dallas, n.d.), 1:67–68, which asserts that the Special Committee raised $2,000 by assessing each club a $10–$20 contribution.

57. "Our New York State Candidate," *General Federation Bulletin* 10:2 (May 1912), 86–87. Unfortunately, there are no papers for Fanny Carpenter and no mention of the contest in the New York State Federation Papers at Elmira College.

58. "Polly" to "My Dear," Mar. 7, 1912.

59. M. Y. Terrell to Pennybacker, Mar. 23 [1912]; Terrell to Mrs. Dancy, May 7 [1912]; Terrell to "Lady P," undated, (quotation); "Pauline" [Isadore Callaway] to "My Dear" and "Dear Friend" [Pennybacker], undated, all in Pennybacker Papers.

60. Terrell to Dancy, May 7; Pauline to "Dear Friend," Pennybacker Papers.

61. Rheta Childe Dorr, *What Eight Million Women Want,* (Boston, 1910), 289; Blair, *Clubwoman as Feminist,* 111.

62. "Digest of Resolutions from the Inception of the New York State Federation of Women's Clubs," compiled by Eleanor F. Hahn; Della A. Stewart and Cornelia F. Bidell, *A Record of Golden Years,* unpublished ts., chap. 5 (unpaged), both in New York State Federation of Women's Club Records, Elmira College Library, Elmira, New York. Hay's successor was another staunch suffragist, Nettie Rogers Schuler, a future NAWSA secretary.

63. Sarah Platt Decker to Mary Terrell, Mar. 15, [1912]; Grace Julian Clark to Anna Pennybacker, Mar. 12, 1912; Pennybacker to Clark, Mar. 16, 1912; Terrell to Pennybacker, Mar. 19, 23, 1912; I. C. S. [Ida C. Saunders] to Terrell, undated [1912]; "Pauline" [Isadore Cal-

laway] to "My Dear" [Pennybacker], undated; "Clever Generalship of Two Fort Worth Club Women Wins for Texas Leader," *Fort Worth Star-Telegram,* July 5, 1912, GFWC Scrapbook; all in Pennybacker Papers.

64. Ida Saunders to Pennybacker, June 13, 1912; M.Y.T. to "Lady P." [June 1912], Pennybacker Papers. On "General" Terrell, see Pennybacker to Saunders, July 20, 1912, ibid.

65. Terrell to Pennybacker, July 23, 1912 (quotation), and "Ready for the Biennial," unidentified San Francisco newspaper clipping, June 24, 1912, GFWC Scrapbook, Pennybacker Papers; "Official Report of the Biennial," *General Federation Bulletin* 10:4 (July 1912), 282, 291.

66. "Ready for the Biennial"; "Conservation of Childhood Theme," undated *San Francisco Chronicle* clipping, GFWC Scrapbook, Pennybacker Papers.

67. "Bomb is Cast into Convention by Committee on Nominations" (quotation); "Mrs. Pennybacker and Mrs. Carpenter Placed in Nomination by the Committee"; unidentified newspaper clippings, GFWC Scrapbook, Pennybacker Papers.

68. Saunders to Pennybacker, May 4, 1912; Terrell to Pennybacker, July 23, 1912, Pennybacker Papers.

69. "Flood of Tears and Gold Starts," unidentified San Francisco newspaper clipping, GFWC Scrapbook, Pennybacker Papers. See Molyneaux, "Miracle of Faithfulness," for a touchy defense of Pennybacker's motives: "Some of the newspapers described this as a 'shrewd piece of politics.' It was nothing of the kind. It was simply an expression of the woman herself. It was a purely unstudied and spontaneous act that was characteristic of her. If it influenced anyone to vote for her, it did so legitimately, for it was a revelation of character and not an effect."

70. "Official Report of the Biennial," 298; Terrell to Pennybacker, July 23, 1912.

71. Wood, *History of the General Federation,* 250 (Moore quotation); Dorr, *What Eight Million Women Want,* 327; Grover Cleveland, "Woman's Mission and Woman's Clubs," *Ladies' Home Journal,* May 1905, pp. 3–4; *Dallas Morning News,* Jan. 15, 1906; *History of the Dallas Federation of Women's Clubs* 1:31.

72. See Elisabeth S. Clemens, "Organizational Repertoires and Institutional Change: Women's Groups and the Transformation of U.S. Politics, 1890–1920," *American Journal of Sociology* 98 (Jan. 1993): 783–86, on language and lobbying; and Paula Baker, "The Domestication of Politics: Women and American Political Society, 1780–1920," *American Historical Review* 89 (June 1984): 620–47, for a discussion of women's influence in reshaping political culture. Elizabeth York Enstam makes the point for Texas in "They Called it 'Motherhood': Dallas Women and Public Life, 1895–1918," in *Hidden Histories of Women in the New South,* edited by Virginia Bernhard et al. (Columbia, Mo., 1994).

73. Mrs. Cone Johnson to Anna Pennybacker, Jan. 4, 1906 (quotation), and Mar. 25, 1906; Johnson to Mary Terrell, Jan. 20, 1906, Pennybacker Papers. For biographical details, see Alice Jean Cooksey, "'Her Life Shines Out Upon the Way': Birdie Robertson Johnson," (Master's thesis, University of Texas at Arlington, 1985).

74. Margaret Nell Price, "The Development of Leadership by Southern Women through Clubs and Organizations" (Master's thesis, University of North Carolina, 1945),

136; Scott, *The Southern Lady,* 161. Pennybacker and Terrell embody Scott's observation that "For those with real ambition clubs and women's groups were one of the few available roads to anything approaching real power" (162).

75. Terrell, "Succinct History of the Woman's Club Movement"; Jane Addams, Frances Kellor, and Isabella W. Blaney, "Why Every Woman Should be a Progressive," *General Federation Bulletin,* Sept. 1912, 412–13. See also, "What Republican Women are Doing," October 1912, 32–35; "Mrs. Borden Harriman, Leader in Philanthropy and Friend of Labor," ibid., 36–38; and "The Socialist Party," December 1912, 165–69.

Chapter 2: Domestic Revolutionaries

1. Mary Kavanaugh Eagle, ed., *The Congress of Women Held in the Woman's Building, World's Columbian Exposition, Chicago, U.S.A., 1893* (Philadelphia, 1894), 28; Laura S. Wilkinson, "Household Economics," ibid., 234.

2. Caroline L. Hunt, *The Life of Ellen H. Richards* (Boston, 1912), 221–26; Robert Clarke, *Ellen Swallow: The Woman Who Founded Ecology* (Chicago, 1973), 128–30; Delores Hayden, *The Grand Domestic Revolution: A History of Feminist Designs for American Homes, Neighborhoods, and Cities* (Cambridge, Mass., 1981), 159.

3. Susan Strasser, *Never Done: A History of American Housework* (New York, 1982), 72–73; Ruth Schwartz Cowan, *More Work for Mother: The Ironies of Household Technology from the Open Hearth to the Microwave* (New York, 1985), 90–91, and "Ellen Swallow Richards: Technology and Women," in *Technology in America: A History of Individuals and Ideas,* edited by Carroll W. Pursell Jr. (Cambridge, Mass., 1981), 142–50; Ellen Richards, "Ten Years of the Lake Placid Conference on Home Economics; Its History and Aims," in Lake Placid Conference on Home Economics, *Proceedings of the Tenth Annual Conference* (Lake Placid, N.Y., 1908), 21 (quotation).

4. Feminist historians wrote dismissively of home economics in the 1970s, judging by its results in the twentieth century rather than its goals in the nineteenth. Revisionist scholarship stresses its careerist origins and importance to municipal housekeeping. See Glenna Matthews, *'Just a Housewife': The Rise and Fall of Domesticity in America* (New York, 1987), 148–52, 159, 62; Sarah Stage and Virginia B. Vincenti, *Rethinking Home Economics: Women and the History of a Profession* (Ithaca, N.Y., 1997); Janice C. Steinschneider, *An Improved Woman: The Wisconsin Federation of Women's Clubs, 1895–1920* (New York, 1994), 23–24; and Sallie A. Marston, "Transforming the Boundaries: Power and Resistance among Turn-of-the-Century American Women," paper presented at the Ninth Berkshire Conference on the History of Women, Vassar College, June 1993.

5. See "Dr. Leslie Waggener's Address," *Dallas Morning News,* June 7, 1896, for female enrollment at the University of Texas. The State Council of Women discussion is reported in *Dallas Morning News,* Oct. 20, 1896.

6. Joyce Antler, *The Educated Woman and Professionalism: The Struggle for a New Feminine Identity* (New York, 1987), 95–97; Barbara Miller Solomon, *In the Company of Educated Women: A History of Women and Higher Education in America* (New Haven, 1985), 86; John L. Rury, "Vocationalism for Home and Work: Women's Education in the United

States, 1880–1930," in *The Social History of American Education*, edited by B. Edward Mc-Clellan and William J. Reese (Urbana, Ill., 1988), 233–41.

7. Ellen H. Richards, *Euthenics: The Science of Controllable Environment* (Boston, 1910), 150.

8. Mary I. Wood, *History of the General Federation of Women's Clubs* (New York, 1912), 86; Linda Hull Larned, "The National Household Economic [*sic*] Association," *Journal of Home Economics* 1 (Apr. 1909), 185–86.

9. Maria Daniel, "Attitude of Women's Clubs in Texas toward the Study of Home Economics," in Lake Placid Conference on Home Economics, *Proceedings of the Sixth Annual Conference* (Lake Placid, N.Y., 1906), 33–36; Emma Seifrit Weigley, "It Might Have Been Euthenics: The Lake Placid Conferences and the Home Economics Movement," *American Quarterly* 26 (Mar. 1974): 79–96; Ellen H. Richards, "Domestic Science: What It Is and How to Study It at Home," *The Outlook*, Apr. 24, 1897, pp. 1078–80.

10. Elizabeth York Enstam, "They Called it 'Motherhood': Dallas Women and Politics, 1895–1920," in *Hidden Histories of Women in the New South*, edited by Virginia Bernhard et al. (Columbia, Mo., 1994), 71–72. On women and urban reform, see also Suellen Hoy, "'Municipal Housekeeping': The Role of Women in Improving Urban Sanitation Practices, 1880–1917," in *Pollution and Reform in American Cities, 1870–1930*, edited by Martin V. Melosi (Austin, 1980), and Hoy, *Chasing Dirt: The American Pursuit of Cleanliness* (New York, 1995), 72–78; Marlene Stein Wortman, "Domesticating the Nineteenth-Century American City," *Prospects: An Annual of American Cultural Studies* 3 (1977): 531–72; and Anne Firor Scott, *Natural Allies: Women's Associations in American History* (Urbana, Ill., 1992), chap. 6.

11. Elizabeth Hayes Turner, "Women's Culture and Community: Religion and Reform in Galveston, 1880–1920" (Ph.D. diss., Rice University, 1990), 359–87.

12. Flora Huntly, "Business Methods Applied to the Home," *Texas Motherhood Magazine*, Nov. 1911, 110–11.

13. Marion Talbot and Sophonisba P. Breckinridge, *The Modern Household* (Boston, 1912), 40–42.

14. Pauline Periwinkle [Isadore Miner], "The Higher Education of Women an Imperative Need of the Time" (quotations); "Reasons Why Girls Should be Trained in Domestic Science"; and "Dean Talbot's Evidence on the Importance of Domestic Training," *DMN/GDN*, June 7, July 12, 19, 1896.

15. Quoted in Fanny L. Armstrong, *To the Noon Rest: The Life, Work, and Addresses of Mrs. Helen M. Stoddard* (Butler, Ind., 1909), 187.

16. Addams is quoted in Ellen H. Richards, "The Social Significance of the Home Economics Movement," *Journal of Home Economics* 3 (Apr. 1911): 120. Richards's pamphlet, "Food and Its Relation to Intemperance," appears in "Annual Meeting Minutes, 1893," reel 5, pp. 267–70, WCTU series, *Temperance and Prohibition Papers*.

17. Samuel H. Preston and Michael R. Haines, *Fatal Years: Child Mortality in Late Nineteenth-Century America* (Princeton, 1991), 52.

18. Ibid., 189; Pauline Periwinkle [Isadore Callaway], "Reasons Why Girls Should be Trained in Domestic Science"; "Conclusion Drawn Few Mothers Wise," *DMN/GDN*,

Jan. 4, 1915 (quotation). On middle-class women's embrace of "scientific motherhood," see Rima D. Apple, *Mothers and Medicine: A Social History of Infant Feeding, 1890–1950* (Madison, Wis., 1987), chap. 6.

19. Jacquelyn McElhaney, "Pauline Periwinkle: Prodding Dallas into the Progressive Era," in *Women and Texas History: Selected Essays,* edited by Fane Downs and Nancy Baker Jones (Austin, 1993), 43–44.

20. Armstrong, *To the Noon Rest,* 184, 187 (quotation), 188, 195. On professionalism, see Wiebe, *Search for Order,* chap. 5, and Burton J. Bledstein, *The Culture of Professionalism: The Middle Class and the Development of Higher Education in America* (New York, 1976).

21. Armstrong, *To the Noon Rest,* 184–85, 188; Stella L. Christian, *History of the Texas Federation of Women's Clubs* [vol. 1] (Houston, 1919), 39–40; Joyce Thompson, *Marking a Trail: A History of Texas Woman's University* (Denton, 1982), 2, 9 n.2; Mrs. J. C. Terrell, "Succinct History of the Woman's Club Movement," *Dallas Morning News,* Nov. 22, 1903. "Pauline Periwinkle" columns appear in *DMN/GDN,* Feb. 20, Apr. 17, 1899.

22. Helen Stoddard, "Location of the College of Industrial Arts," ts., Stoddard Papers, Texas Woman's University; Thompson, *Marking a Trail,* 3; E. V. White, *Historical Record of the Texas State College for Women: The First Forty-Five Years, 1903–1948* (Denton, 1948), 5–7.

23. Armstrong, *To the Noon Rest,* 189; Christian, *History of the Texas Federation of Women's Clubs,* 86, 142, 168; Thompson, *Marking a Trail,* 15–16, 27; *Second Biennial Report of the Board of Regents of the College of Industrial Arts from September 1, 1904 to August 31, 1906* (Austin, 1906), 37–41; *Third Biennial Report of the Board of Regents of the College of Industrial Arts from September 1, 1906 to August 31, 1908* (Austin, 1908), 11. First-hand accounts of women's activity can be found on the woman's page of *DMN/GDN,* Mar. 13, 27, 1905, and Feb. 18, 1907. See also M. E. B. [Mary Eleanor Brackenridge], "Industrial Arts for Women," *Fort Worth Record,* Mar. 10, 1907.

24. *DMN/GDN,* Mar. 27, 1905, and Feb. 18, 1907; *Bulletin of the College of Industrial Arts* 12 (Dec. 1905), 49. The full text of the Education Committee's report appears in *Second Biennial Report of the Board of Regents,* 42–44.

25. Glenda Elizabeth Gilmore, *Gender and Jim Crow: Women and the Politics of White Supremacy in North Carolina, 1896–1920* (Chapel Hill, N.C., 1996), 36–43.

26. Ruthe Winegarten, *Black Texas Women: 150 Years of Trial and Triumph* (Austin, 1995), 111–12, and *Black Texas Women: A Sourcebook* (Austin, 1996), 85–91 (quotation at 85); Leedel W. Neyland, *Historically Black Land-Grant Institutions and the Development of Agriculture and Home Economics, 1890–1990* (Tallahassee, 1990), 195, 201.

27. Mrs. B. T. Washington, "The Negro Home," address made at the Interracial Conference Held in Memphis, Tennessee, Oct. 1920, reel 6 *NACWC Records,* part 1; Gilmore, *Gender and Jim Crow,* 47. On African Americans and home economics, see Paula Giddings, *When and Where I Enter: The Impact of Black Women on Race and Sex in America* (New York, 1984), 99–100, and Dorothy Salem, *To Better Our World: Black Women in Organized Reform, 1890–1920* (Brooklyn, 1990), 64–66; and Cynthia Neverdon-Morton, *Afro-American Women of the South and the Advancement of the Race, 1895–1925* (Knoxville, Tenn., 1989), 23–28, 34–36.

28. Christian, *History of the Texas Federation of Women's Clubs*, 109, 111, 119; Texas Federation of Women's Clubs, *Yearbook, 1904–1905*, 23; Marilyn McAdams Sibley, *George Washington Brackenridge: Maverick Philanthropist* (Austin, 1973), 180; *Fifteenth Biennial Report of the Board of Regents of the University of Texas, 1910–1911, 1911–1912* (Bulletin of the University of Texas, no. 258, Dec. 8, 1912), 27. On Gearing, see Lucy Rathbone, "Mary E. Gearing—Pioneer," *Journal of Home Economics* 39 (Jan. 1947): 5–6; *The University of Texas Record* 11 (Jan. 1912): 204, and the biographical files at CAH-UT and Texas Woman's University.

29. *The Texas Clubwoman*, Feb. 21 and 28, 1914, describes a typical Home Economics Week in detail and includes the texts of numerous lectures. See also Christian, *History of the Texas Federation of Women's Clubs*, 298, 346.

30. See Mary S. Hoffschwelle, "The Science of Domesticity: Home Economics at George Peabody College for Teachers, 1914–1939," *Journal of Southern History* 57 (Nov. 1991): 659–80, for a case study on this theme.

31. Mrs. Cree T. Work, "The Home Economics Movement," *Dallas Morning News*, Mar. 29, 1909. I am indebted to Kim Grover-Haskin and Glenna Mae Lehrmann at Blagg-Huey Library, Texas Woman's University, for tracking down Mrs. Work's given name.

32. Wood, *History of the General Federation*, 195; Oscar E. Anderson Jr., *The Health of a Nation: Harvey W. Wiley and the Fight for Pure Food* (Chicago, 1958); James Harvey Young, *Pure Food: Securing the Federal Food and Drugs Act of 1906* (Princeton, N.J., 1989), 185–86.

33. Wood, *History of the General Federation*, 210. For firsthand accounts of the GFWC's role, see Sarah Platt Decker, "The Meaning of the Woman's Club Movement"; Mrs. Percy V. Pennybacker, "The Eighth Biennial of the General Federation of Women's Clubs"; and the testimonial by Wiley, all in *AAAPSS* 28 (Sept. 1906): 4, 6, 82, 92–93.

34. Pauline Periwinkle [Isadore Callwway], "Hats and Tobacco . . . Tax Bachelors; Women Vote," *DMN/GDN*, Feb. 11, 1907.

35. Pauline Periwinkle [Isadore Callaway], "Work of Pure Food Committee Endorsed," *DMN/GDN*, May 11, 1908, and "Way to a Man's Heart," July 31, 1905 (quotation).

36. Martha Lavinia Hunter, *A Quarter of a Century History of the Dallas Woman's Forum, 1906–1931* (Dallas, 1932), 4; Walter B. Whitman, "The Adulteration of Food in Texas," *Holland's Magazine*, Oct. 1906, 5–7. The series ran from September 1906 through March 1907.

37. Mrs. Cree T. Work, "Pure Food Legislation," *Bulletin of the College of Industrial Arts* 16 (Dec. 1906): 46–48; *Dallas Morning News*, Mar. 29, 1909 (first quotation), and Jan. 21, 1907 (second quotation).

38. *Dallas Morning News*, Jan. 21, Mar. 11, 1907; Outlook Committee "To the Clubwomen of the T.F.W.C.," undated [1907], TFWC Papers.

39. *Dallas Morning News*, Jan. 7, 21, 1907; Mar. 29, 1909.

40. Mrs. Cree T. Work, "A Pure Food Law and Its Administration," *Holland's Magazine*, Jan. 1907, 6, 31; Helen M. Stoddard, "A Protest from Housekeepers," *Holland's Magazine*, Mar. 1907, 7; *Dallas Morning News*, Jan. 21, Feb. 18 (Periwinkle column), 25, and Mar. 11,

1907; Walter B. Whitman to Mrs. S. J. Wright, Jan. 12, 1907, TFWC Papers. The endorsements were published in the February issue of *Holland's*.

41. *Dallas Morning News*, Mar. 29, 1909; Texas Legislature, House, *Journal*, 30th Leg., reg. sess., 1907, pp. 593–95, 947–49.

42. "Abbott Was Chemistry Teacher," *Texas Magazine*, May 1911, 59–60; Work, "A Pure Food Law and Its Administration." See William A. Link, *The Paradox of Southern Progressivism, 1880–1930* (Chapel Hill, N.C., 1992), especially chap. 1, on the lack of strong state bureaucracies to oversee public health in the South.

43. Mrs. Cree T. Work, "Co-operation of Women's Clubs with our State Dairy and Food Commissioner," *Bulletin of the College of Industrial Arts* 20 (Nov. 1907): 28–29, and "The Work of the Pure Food Commissioner," ibid., 27. Megan Seaholm, "Earnest Women: The White Woman's Club Movement in Texas, 1880–1920" (Ph.D. diss., Rice University, 1988), 306–9, provides additional detail on club cooperation.

44. Pauline Periwinkle [Isadore Callaway], "Work of Pure Food Committee Endorsed," *DMN/GDN*, May 11, 1908.

45. Abbott is quoted in Work, "Co-operation of Women's Clubs with our State Dairy and Food Commissioner," 28–29; the Fort Worth commissioners in Seaholm, "Earnest Women," 309.

46. Turner, "Women's Culture and Community," 377–83 (quotation at 380).

47. Mrs. Julian Heath, "Work of the Housewives' League," *AAAPSS* 48 (July 1913): 121–26; *Houston Daily Post*, Apr. 1, 2, 1915; Mrs. W. M. [May Harper] Baines, *Houston's Part in the World War* (Houston, 1919), 105–8.

48. Ruth A. Allen, *The Labor of Women in the Production of Cotton*, University of Texas Bulletin no. 3134 (Austin, 1931), 40–74 (quotations at p. 40). On farm wives see M. Rebecca Sharpless, "Fertile Land, Narrow Choices: Women on Cotton Farms of the Texas Blackland Prairie, 1900–1940" (Ph.D. diss., Emory University, 1993).

49. William L. Bowers, *The Country Life Movement in America, 1900–1920* (Port Washington, N.Y., 1974), 63; United States Department of Agriculture, Office of the Secretary, *Social and Labor Needs of Farm Women*, Report no. 103 (Washington, D.C., 1915), 16. See also Marilyn Irvin Holt, *Linoleum, Better Babies, and the Modern Farm Woman, 1890–1930* (Albuquerque, 1995), chap. 1.

50. Pauline Periwinkle [Isadore Callaway], "Civic Improvement," *DMN/GDN*, Jan. 21, 1907.

51. Christian, *History of the Texas Federation of Women's Clubs*, 298, 311. On the TFWC's outreach to rural women, see M. Rebecca Sharpless, "Town Women, Country Women: The Club Women's Movement and Home Demonstration in Texas, 1914–1930," paper presented at the Texas State Historical Association annual meeting, Austin, Texas, 1992 (copy in author's possession).

52. Texas Farm Women, *Constitution and By-Laws* (Houston, 1914), 9, 3 (quotation). No founding date is given for the organization.

53. Earl William Crosby, "Building the Country Home: The Black County Agent System, 1906–1940" (Ph.D. diss., Miami University, 1977), 56–57; Kathleen C. Hilton,

"'Both in the Field, Each with a Plow': Race and Gender in USDA Policy, 1907–1929," in Bernhard et al., eds., *Hidden Histories of Women in the New South*. Southern congressmen, led by the bill's cosponsor, Senator Hoke Smith of Georgia, successfully defeated attempts to require that black colleges share administrative authority and to stipulate that the work be carried out without racial discrimination.

54. Kate Adele Hill, *Home Demonstration Work in Texas* (San Antonio, 1958), 132–35 (quotation). For biographical information on Mary Evelyn V. Hunter, see Winegarten, *Black Texas Women: A Sourcebook*, 253–54.

55. William Hard, "The Woman with the Pails," *The Delineator*, Mar. 1915, pp. 7–8; *Dallas Morning News*, Mar. 22, 1915.

56. Helen Louise Jackson to "Dear Sir," Mar. 3, 1915, box 3, folder 22, Agricultural Extension Service Records, Texas A&M University Library, College Station, Texas; David F. Houston to Maggie Barry, Feb. 13, 1915, box 3, folder 12, ibid.

57. *Dallas Morning News*, Jan. 25, Mar. 22, 1915; Anna Pennybacker to Ousley, Nov. 21, 1914 (quotation), box 3, folder 22, Agricultural Extension Service Records.

58. Clarence Ousley, Speech to District Federation of Women's Clubs, Bryan, Texas [Apr. 1915], ts., box 3, folder 22, Agricultural Extension Service Records.

59. David F. Houston to Ousley, Apr. 17, 1916, box 3, folder 12, ibid.

60. *Dallas Morning News*, Oct. 29, 1915; Maggie Barry to Clarence Ousley, Nov. 22, 1914, box 3, folder 22, Agricultural Extension Service Records.

61. *Dallas Morning News*, Mar. 22, 1915.

62. Pauline Periwinkle [Isadore Callaway], "Hats and Tobacco"; Work, "Pure Food Law and its Administration."

63. Maggie Barry to Clarence Ousley, Nov. 22, 1914, box 3, folder 22, Agricultural Extension Service Records. A copy of the TFWC resolution can be found in the same folder; it was also published in *Dallas Morning News*, Jan. 25, 1915. Kalb and the Texas Farm Women seem not to have stated any position on this issue.

64. Houston to Barry, Feb. 13, 1915; Houston to Ousley, Apr. 17, 1916.

65. Maggie W. Barry to Pat Neff, June 2, 1921, box 3, folder 12, Agricultural Extension Service Records; Ousley, Speech to District Federation of Women's Clubs, p. 3 (first quotation), 6, (second quotation). A similar pattern seems to have obtained in most states: women's programs received less money, fewer home demonstration agents were hired, and they were paid less than the agricultural agents. See Joan M. Jensen, "Canning Comes to New Mexico," in *New Mexico Women: Intercultural Perspectives*, edited by Joan M. Jensen and Darlis A. Miller (Albuquerque, 1986), 207–8.

66. *Galveston Daily News*, July 13, 1917; Helen Knox to Anna Pennybacker, July 24, Aug. 5, 1917, Pennybacker Papers; Minnie Fisher Cunningham to "Dear Suffragist," July 21, 1917, box 34, McCallum Papers (part 2); Eula Whitehouse, Louise Megee, and Gertrude Goldsmith to "My Dear—," July 24, 1917 (quotation), ibid.

67. See Cowan, *More Work for Mother*, for the fullest exploration of this theme. Matthews, *'Just a Housewife,'* 159–71, analyzes the evolution and disappointments of home economics.

68. Mrs. Philip North Moore, "Women's Clubs Training Women for the Larger Citizenship," in *The Woman Citizen and the Home,* vol. 12 of *The Woman Citizen's Library,* edited by Shailer Mathews (Chicago, 1914), 3118.

69. Christian, *History of the Texas Federation of Women's Clubs,* 310.

70. Work, "Pure Food Law and Its Administration," 6.

Chapter 3: Every Mother's Child

1. Sheila M. Rothman, *Woman's Proper Place: A History of Changing Ideals and Practices, 1870 to the Present* (New York, 1978), 98–99; Dorothy G. Ross, *G. Stanley Hall: The Pyschologist as Prophet* (Chicago, 1972), 279–89; Molly Ladd-Taylor, *Mother-Work: Women, Child Welfare, and the State, 1890–1930* (Urbana, Ill., 1995), 46–47.

2. Susan Strasser, *Never Done: A History of American Housework* (New York, 1982), 232; Elizabeth Dale Ross, *The Kindergarten Crusade: The Establishment of Preschool Education in the United States* (Athens, Ohio, 1976), 1–13; Rothman, *Woman's Proper Place,* 100, 103; Elizabeth Harrison, *A Study of Child Nature from the Kindergarten Standpoint,* 8th ed. (Chicago, 1895), 12 (quotation).

3. Olga Kohlberg, Speech to Woman Pioneers' Luncheon, Feb. 14, 1924, ts., Kohlberg biographical file, El Paso Public Library.

4. Mary. S. Cunningham, *The Woman's Club of El Paso: Its First Thirty Years* (El Paso, 1978), 8–10; "Kindergarten Report," *Texas Motherhood Magazine,* Nov. 1910, 34–35; Mary King Drew, *History of the Kindergarten Movement in Texas* (Dallas, 1942), 12–13.

5. "Fort Worth Kindergarten Association," *Texas Motherhood Magazine,* June 1910, 15–16; Karen Wolk Feinstein, "Kindergartens, Feminism, and the Professionalization of Motherhood," *International Journal of Women's Studies* 3 (Jan./Feb. 1980): 28–38.

6. Elizabeth York Enstam, "They Called It 'Motherhood': Dallas Women and Public Life, 1895–1918," in *Hidden Histories of Women in the New South,* edited by Virginia Bernhard et al. (Columbia, Mo., 1994), 71–72.

7. *Yearbook of the Texas Federation of Women's Clubs, 1902–1903* (n.p. [1902]), 18; Megan Seaholm, "Earnest Women: The White Woman's Club Movement in Texas, 1880–1920" (Ph.D. diss., Rice University, 1988), 282–94.

8. James L. Leloudis, *Schooling in the New South: Pedagogy, Self, and Society in North Carolina, 1880–1920* (Chapel Hill, N.C., 1996), 78.

9. Newer studies are beginning to rectify this omission; see William A. Link, *The Paradox of Southern Progressivism, 1880–1939* (Chapel Hill, N.C., 1992), 138–41; James L. Leloudis, "School Reform in the New South: The Women's Association for the Betterment of Public School Houses in North Carolina, 1902–1919," *Journal of American History* 69 (Mar. 1983): 886–909; and Joseph F. Kett, "Women and the Progressive Impulse in Education," in *The Web of Southern Social Relations,* edited by Walter J. Fraser Jr., R. Frank Saunders Jr., and Jon L. Wakelyn (Athens, Ga., 1985).

10. Russell Sage Foundation, Division of Education, *A Comparative Study of Public School Systems in the Forty-Eight States* (New York, 1912), 32, 11; C. E. Evans, "The

Conference for Education in Texas" [1911], box 4J294, Conference for Education in Texas Records, CAH-UT. Hereafter cited as CET Records.

11. On the southern school crusade and the Conference for Education in the South, see Charles William Dabney, *Universal Education in the South* (Chapel Hill, N.C., 1936), 2 vols; C. Van Woodward, *Origins of the New South, 1877–1913* (Baton Rouge, 1951), 396–406; Hugh C. Bailey, *Liberalism and the New South: Southern Social Reformers and the Progressive Movement* (Coral Gables, Fla., 1969), 131–52; Dewey W. Grantham, *Southern Progressivism: The Reconciliation of Progress and Tradition* (Knoxville, Tenn., 1983), 247–60; and Link, *Paradox of Southern Progressivism*, 125–33;

12. Frederick Eby, *The Development of Education in Texas* (New York, 1925), 220; F. M. Bralley, "Report of the First Year's Work of the Conference for Education in Texas," *Texas School Journal* 25 (June 1908): 4–8.

13. Pauline Periwinkle [Isadore Callaway], "Women for Dallas City School Board," *DMN/GDN*, Mar. 23, 1908.

14. Wood, *History of the General Federation*, 87, 124–28.

15. Theda Skocpol, *Protecting Soldiers and Mothers: The Political Origins of Social Policy in the United States* (Cambridge, Mass., 1992), 333–34; David J. Rothman and Sheila M. Rothman, eds., *National Congress of Mothers: The First Conventions* (New York, 1987), 6–10; National Congress of Parents and Teachers, *Golden Jubilee History, 1897–1947* (Chicago, 1947), 20–31.

16. Ladd-Taylor, *Mother-Work*, 44–55.

17. National Congress of Parents and Teachers, *Golden Jubilee History*, 52, 58; Ladd-Taylor, *Mother-Work*, 55–63; Convention Minutes, 1915, Box 32A, Texas Congress of Mothers and Parent-Teacher Associations Archives, Texas PTA Headquarters, Austin, Texas (hereafter cited as Texas PTA Archives). Nothing more is known about this exchange; the newspapers covered the white congress in detail but ignored the black one. No archives or publications have been found for the black congress in Texas.

18. Skocpol, *Protecting Soldiers and Mothers*, 334; National Congress of Parents and Teachers, *Golden Jubilee History*, 44. For biographical information on Ella Porter, see *The Texas Clubwoman*, Nov. 1909, p. 8 (copy in CAH-UT); Sinclair Moreland, *The Texas Woman's Hall of Fame* (Austin, 1917), 102–5; *Woman's Who's Who of America*, 654; and the Ella Porter biographical file, Daughters of the Republic of Texas Library at the Alamo, San Antonio.

19. For private expressions of the tension between leaders of the two organizations, see Mary Barnum to Anna Pennybacker, June 23, July 18, and Oct. 30, 1913, Pennybacker Papers; Ella Porter to Mrs. S. J. Wright, Nov. 22, 1909, TFWC Records; and Porter to Pennybacker, Mar. 28, 1912, Pennybacker Papers.

20. Stella L. Christian, *History of the Texas Federation of Women's Clubs* [vol. 1] (Houston, 1919), 244, 250; Texas Federation of Women's Clubs, *Yearbook, 1911–1912* (San Antonio, [1911]), 59–60. On the organization's motivation, see Mrs. [Ella Dancy] Dibrell to Miss M. Greenwood Hardy, Nov. 9, 1910, and Mrs. Eli Hertzberg to Mrs. S. J. Wright, Dec. 2, 1909, TFWC Records.

21. Mrs. J. N. Porter, "Texas Congress of Mothers and Parent-Teacher Associations," *Texas Motherhood Magazine,* June 1910, 8–9. A published account of the convention can be found in *The Texas Clubwoman,* Nov. 1909. The Texas Congress has not published an organizational history; general information appears in Lucille Moore, "History and Development of the Texas Congress of Parents and Teachers" (Master's thesis, University of Texas at Austin, 1946).

22. Christian, *History of the Texas Federation of Women's Clubs,* 147–49; Seaholm, "Earnest Women," 290; Constitution and By-laws, Texas Congress of Mothers, Box 32A, Texas PTA Archives.

23. Porter, "Texas Congress of Mothers and Parent-Teacher Associations," 9.

24. C. E. Evans, "The Conference for Education in Texas," [1911], and F. M. Bralley to Prof. F. Z. T. Jackson, Aug. 30, 1907, boxes 4J294, 4J279, CET Records. On the TFWC's role in the school levy campaign, see Christian, *History of the Texas Federation of Women's Clubs,* 194; Mrs. Joseph B. Dibrell to "Dear Madam President" [1908], TFWC Records; and C. E. Evans to Mrs. F. W. McAllister, Nov. 9, 1909, box 4J281, CET Records. (The same GFWC guidelines were shaping campaigns in other states. See for example, Nancy K. Forderhase, "'The Clear Call of Thoroughbred Women,'" *Register of the Kentucky Historical Society* 83 [Winter 1985]: 19–35.) For Periwinkle columns, see *DMN/GDN,* Dec. 16, 1907, Oct. 12, 1908.

25. "Report of Austin Mothers' Clubs," *Texas Motherhood Magazine,* June 1910, 15. Reports from Texarkana and Floresville are in ibid., 16, 17.

26. Every issue of *Texas Motherhood Magazine,* published by the Congress of Mothers, contains reports from the local clubs on their activities; see June 1910, 12–13, for the Houston clubs. I am indebted to the Texas Congress of Mothers and Parent-Teacher Associations for permitting me to examine the magazines at its Austin headquarters.

27. Mrs. William Alphin, "Twinkles from Lone Star," *National Association Notes,* June 1913, 18, *NACWC Records,* part 1, reel 23.

28. *Texas Motherhood Magazine,* June 1910, 17 (Goliad), 16; *The Survey,* Dec. 11, 1909, 364 (Waco).

29. *Dallas Morning News,* Jan. 16, Feb. 6, 1911. See Seaholm, "Earnest Women," 289, on the Woman's Shakespeare Club, and club reports in *Texas Motherhood Magazine.*

30. Pauline Periwinkle [Isadore Callaway], "For Kindergartens" and "Clubs Pledge Help," *DMN/GDN,* Feb. 27, 1905, Dec. 17, 1906; Christian, *History of the Texas Federation of Women's Clubs,* 167, 187–88, 195, 349, 362; "Fort Worth Kindergarten Association," *Texas Motherhood Magazine,* June 1910, 15; Mrs. George Steere, "Kindergarten Report," ibid., Nov. 1914, 147; Texas Federation of Women's Clubs, *Yearbook, 1908–9,* 52–54.

31. See Leloudis, "School Reform in the New South," and *Schooling in the New South,* 154–76, for a full description of the WABPS. Athough he claims that the organization had a Texas branch, I have found no evidence of one; it may have existed only on paper.

32. See for example the following correspondence in the CET Records: C. E. Evans to Mrs. W. A. Callaway, July 9, 1909, box 4J281; Evans to Mrs. S. J. Wright, Jan. 11, Mar. 24, Apr. 28, 1910, box 4J282; Evans to "Dear Madam," Mar. 29, 1910, ibid.; Evans to Wright,

July 8, 1910, Mrs. Fred Fleming to Evans, Sept. 16, 1910, Evans to Wright, Sept. 21, 1910, box 4J283; Lee Clark to Maggie W. Barry, Nov. 6, 1911, box 4J284; Clark to Mrs. J. N. Porter, Jan. 17, 1912, box 4J285.

33. Mrs. J. N. Porter to Lee Clark, Feb. 21, 1912, and Clark to Porter, Feb. 26, 1912, box 4J285, CET Records; Executive Board Minute Book, box 4J291, ibid.

34. *A Call to the Citizens of Texas*, CET Bulletin no. 30 (quotation at p. 3), box 4J294, CET Records; [A. Caswell Ellis], "The Relation of Education to Industrial Development," ts., box 2P92, Alexander Caswell Ellis Papers, CAH-UT; Ellis, *The Relation of Education to Industrial Development of the State*, CET Bulletin no. 25, and "The Financial Value of a Common School Education," both in box 4J294, CET Records.

35. "To the Friends of Education in Texas," Aug. 26, 1912, ts., box 4J294, CET Records. See also the following CET bulletins in the same location: Dr. T. R. Sampson, *The Conference for Education in Texas: Its Purpose, Program, and Policy*, no. 31; *Country High Schools*, no. 32 (Aug. 24, 1910); *Rural High Schools*, no. 9 (Feb. 15, 1909), quotation at p. 3.

36. Pauline Periwinkle [Isadore Callaway], "For Kindergartens," *DMN/GDN*, Feb. 27, 1905 (quotation), and Feb. 4, 1907.

37. See for example Rothman, *Woman's Proper Place*, 101–2, on the usefulness of kindergartens in "Americanizing" immigrants, and Ross, *Kindergarten Crusade*, chaps. 2 and 3.

38. *Dallas Free Kindergarten and Industrial Association, Annual Report, 1903–1904*, Texas and Dallas History Collection, Dallas Public Library; Pauline Periwinkle [Isadore Callaway], "Kindergarten Talk," *DMN/GDN*, Jan. 5, 1903.

39. Mrs. Julius Runge, "History of the Kindergarten Movement in Galveston," *DMN/GDN*, May 29, 1899.

40. For details of the Runge Free Kindergarten, see Elizabeth Hayes Turner, "Women's Culture and Community: Religion and Reform in Galveston, 1880–1920" (Ph.D. diss., Rice University, 1990), 250–57.

41. [Mrs. Morris Liebman], "A Plain Talk about the Kindergarten and a Report of the Work in Dallas of the Dallas Free Kindergarten Training School and Industrial Association," undated ts. [ca. 1914?], Mrs. Morris Liebman Papers, Dallas Historical Society.

42. Jackie McElhaney, "'The Only Clean, Bright Spot They Know,'" *Heritage News: A Journal Devoted to the History of North Central Texas* 11 (Fall 1986): 20–22 (quotation at p. 22). By 1910 the burden of meeting operating expenses led the women to consider the possibility of finding male partners to raise half the monthly budget of $600. Eventually the Federated Charities Finance Association took over most of the responsibility. See Dallas Free Kindergarten, Training School, and Industrial Association, Minute Book, 1910–11, p. 42, Dallas Historical Society, and "Dallas Free Kindergarten Caring for 120 Children with Thirty Babies in the Day Nursery," *Dallas Morning News*, Sept. 30, 1917, clipping in Liebman Papers.

43. "Kindergarten Report," *Texas Motherhood Magazine*, Nov. 1910, 35 (quotation). On kindergartens and Progressivism, see Michael Steven Shapiro, *Child's Garden: The Kindergarten Movement from Froebel to Dewey* (University Park, Pa., 1983), chap. 10.

44. The Progressive school reformers' enthusiasm for vocational curricula has been sharply criticized by revisionist historians as a middle-class attempt to produce tractable workers for an industrial society. For an overview of the debate see Jeffrey E. Mirel, "Progressive School Reform in Comparative Perspective," in *Southern Cities, Southern Schools: Public Education in the Urban South,* edited by David N. Plank and Rick Ginsberg (Westport, Conn., 1990), 152–74.

45. Annual Meeting Minutes, box 32A, Texas PTA Archives; Texas Federation of Women's Clubs, *Yearbook, 1909–1910,* 34, and *Yearbook, 1911–1912,* 16; Mrs. J. B. Dibrell, "The Clubwoman is a Vital Factor in the Development of the Child of Today, the Man of Tomorrow," in *Proceedings of the Second Annual Session of the Conference for Education in Texas, May 8–9, 1909,* 16–17; Pauline Periwinkle [Isadore Callaway], "Social Workers' Greatest Problem . . . Insufficient Schooling," *DMN/GDN,* Sept. 9, 1912.

46. Jacquelyn Masur McElhaney, "Childhood in Dallas, 1870–1900" (Master's thesis, Southern Methodist University, 1982), 30–31 (quotation); Jesse O. Thomas, *A Study of the Social Welfare Status of the Negroes in Houston, Texas* (Houston, 1929), 62–67.

47. Mario T. Garcia, *Desert Immigrants: The Mexicans of El Paso, 1880–1920* (New Haven, Conn., 1981), 110–26.

48. *Houston Daily Post,* July 21, 1902; *DMN/GDN,* Sept. 29, Nov. 18, 1902, and Oct. 20, 1902 (Periwinkle column).

49. *Houston Daily Post,* July 21, 1902 (Pennybacker quotation); Minutes, Fifth Annual Meeting, 1902, Texas Federation of Women's Clubs, TFWC Records; Christian, *History of the Texas Federation of Women's Clubs,* 88, 194, 246, 311; Annual Meeting Minutes, 1911, 1912, 1914, 1915, box 32A, Texas PTA Archives.

50. On the CET position, see C. E. Evans to H. H. Banister, Jan. 4, 1910; Evans to Owen Lovejoy, Feb. 11, 1910; and Evans to W. A. Beasley, Mar. 18, 1910, all in box 4J282, CET Records. For women's opinions, see Minutes, Fifth Annual Meeting, 1902, TFWC Records, and Grace Zimmer, "Equipping the Child for Life," *Texas Motherhood Magazine,* July 1912, 63–65.

51. Harry F. Estill, *Plea for Compulsory Education,* Conference for Education in Texas Bulletin no. 32 (Austin, [1913]); Mrs. Henry B. Fall, "Texas," in General Federation of Women's Clubs, *Official Report, Twelfth Biennial Convention* (n.p., 1914), 325.

52. *Dallas Morning News,* Jan. 23, 25, Feb. 15, 1915; "Social Gains by the Texas Legislature," *Survey,* May 29, 1915, p. 191; TFWC Education Committee, "Compulsory Education" mailing cards, box 2P359, Ellis Papers, and "Significant Facts about Compulsory Education," Pennybacker Papers; Eby, *Development of Education in Texas,* 230–31.

53. Christian, *History of the Texas Federation of Women's Clubs,* 346.

54. Mrs. Edwardts [*sic*] Calahan Dodd to Anna Pennybacker, 190?, Pennybacker Papers; Pauline Periwinkle [Isadore Callaway], "School Sanitation," *DMN/GDN,* Apr. 8, 1907.

55. Pauline Periwinkle [Isadore Callaway], "School Problems," *DMN/GDN,* Feb. 25, 1907, Apr. 6, 1908 (quotation); "Women Eligible for Most Offices in Texas," *Dallas Morning News,* May 3, 1918.

56. *Dallas Morning News,* May 14, 1888. If any women became candidates in the nineteenth century their names have not come to light.

57. Michael V. Hazel, "A Mother's Touch: The First Two Women Elected to the Dallas School Board," *Heritage News: A Journal Devoted to the History of North Central Texas* 12 (Spring 1987): 9–12.

58. Pauline Periwinkle [Isadore Callaway], "School Problems"; "Rights vs. Courtesy," *DMN/GDN,* Jan. 28, 1907; "Women Make Good on School Boards," ibid., Apr. 6, 1908.

59. Mrs. Cree T. Work, "What May Be Accomplished by Closer Cooperation between Women's Clubs and School Authorities," *Bulletin of the College of Industrial Arts,* 27 (Sept. 1909): 31; Pauline Periwinkle [Isadore Callaway], "Women for Dallas City School Board," *DMN/GDN,* Mar. 23, 1908.

60. Enstam, "They Called it 'Motherhood,' " 87–89; *Dallas Morning News,* Apr. 7, 1908.

61. *San Antonio Daily Express,* Mar. 14, 16, 19, 1909.

62. Hazel, "A Mother's Touch," 11–12.

63. Work, "What May Be Accomplished," 31.

64. *San Antonio Light,* Mar 27, 1913, and Apr. 5, 9, 1913.

65. Charles S. Meek, "Women as School Board Members," *Proceedings of the Thirty-ninth Annual Meeting of the Texas State Teachers' Association* (n.p., 1918), 28.

66. *San Antonio Light,* Mar. 28, 30, 1913.

67. Mrs. Eli Hertzberg, Mrs. J. N. Porter, "The Co-operation of Women's Organizations with the Conference for Education in Texas," *Proceedings of the Fifth General Session of the Conference for Education in Texas,* 1912, p. 82, 85 (Porter quotation).

Chapter 4: Cities of Women

1. Glenna Matthews, *The Rise of Public Woman: Woman's Power and Woman's Place in the United States, 1630–1970* (New York, 1992), 4–8.

2. Gail Lee Dubrow, "Women and Community," in *Reclaiming the Past: Landmarks of Women's History,* edited by Page Putnam Miller (Bloomington, Ind., 1992), 89–93; Martha Lavinia Hunter, *A Quarter of a Century History of the Dallas Woman's Forum, 1906–1931* (Dallas, 1932), 33; Darlene Rebecca Roth, *Matronage: Patterns in Women's Organizations, Atlanta, Georgia, 1890–1940* (New York, 1994), 120–23.

3. Megan Seaholm, "Earnest Women: The White Woman's Club Movement in Texas, 1880–1920" (Ph.D. diss., Rice University, 1988), 272–78; Karen Blair, *The Clubwoman as Feminist: True Womanhood Redefined, 1868–1914* (New York, 1980), 100–101; Olga Kohlberg, "Speech to Women Pioneers' Luncheon," p. 5, Kohlberg Biographical File, El Paso Public Library.

4. Betty T. Chapman, "From the Parlor to the Public: New Roles for Women in Houston, 1885–1918," *Houston Review* 15:1 (1993): 36–38.

5. *History of the Dallas Federation of Women's Clubs* 1:1, 4.

6. Alice J. Rhoades, "Early Women Librarians in Texas," *Texas Libraries* 47 (Summer 1986): 46: "Julia Ideson," in Texas Federation of Women's Clubs, *Who's Who of the*

Womanhood of Texas (Fort Worth, 1923–24), 194; Harriet Smither, "Julia Bedford Ideson," *Proceedings of the Philosophical Society of Texas, 1945* (Dallas, 1946), 56–58.

7. See Elizabeth Hayes Turner, "Women's Culture and Community: Religion and Reform in Galveston, 1880–1920" (Ph.D. diss., Rice University, 1990), chap. 4, for an analysis of women's benevolent institutions in Galveston.

8. *Dallas Morning News,* Mar. 23, 1903 (first quotation); "Canadian," scrapbook clipping [1904] from *Texas White Ribbon,* Records of the WCTU of Canadian, Texas, 1904–54, Southwestern Collection, Texas Tech University, Lubbock (second quotation).

9. The South's contribution to the settlement movement has been little explored. Older scholarship judged it a weak echo of the northern phenomenon, largely an extension of the free kindergarten enthusiasm and of Methodist mission evangelism; see Allan Davis, *Spearheads for Reform: The Social Settlements and the Progressive Movement, 1890–1914* (New York, 1967), 23, and Milton D. Speizman, "The Movement of the Settlement House Idea into the South," *Southwestern Social Science Quarterly* 44 (Dec. 1963): 237–46. Adopting the position of the National Federation of Settlements at the time, older studies denied that church-affiliated houses, which predominated below the Mason-Dixon line, were genuine settlements. For a contrasting view that accepts missions as "true" settlements, see Anne Firor Scott, *The Southern Lady: From Pedestal to Politics, 1830–1930* (Chicago, 1970), 142–43, and Elisabeth Lasch-Quinn, *Black Neighbors: Race and the Limits of Reform in the American Settlement House Movement, 1890–1945* (Chapel Hill, N.C., 1993), 48–54.

10. Work on social settlements as female-dominated communities, the institutional bases from which educated, unmarried women built careers as social reformers, has focused on the experience of well-known northern women. See Helen Lefkowitz Horowitz, "Hull House as Women's Space," *Chicago History* 12:4 (1984): 40–55; Kathryn Kish Sklar, "Hull House in the 1890s: A Community of Women Reformers," *Signs* 10 (Summer 1985): 658–77; Delores Hayden, *The Grand Domestic Revolution: A History of Feminist Designs of American Homes, Neighborhoods, and Cities* (Cambridge, Mass., 1981), 162–78; Dubrow, "Women and Community," 103–10; Estelle Freedman, "Separatism as Strategy: Female Institution Building and American Feminism, 1870–1930," *Feminist Studies* 5 (Fall 1979): 512–29; and Mina Carson, *Settlement Folk: Social Thought and the American Settlement Movement* (Chicago, 1990). By contrast Ruth Hutchinson Crocker's *Social Work and Social Order: The Settlement Movement in Two Industrial Cities, 1889–1930* (Urbana, Ill., 1992), examining three Indiana houses, argues that "second tier" settlements in medium-sized cities are more typical of the movement than Hull House and Henry Street, and that men held most of the leadership posts.

11. Frances Ingram, "The Settlement Movement in the South," *World Outlook* 37 (May 1937): 14 (quotation). Theda Skocpol, *Protecting Soldiers and Mothers: The Political Origins of Social Policy in the United States* (Cambridge, Mass., 1992), 346, cites the 60 percent figure. Robert A. Woods and Albert J. Kennedy, eds., *Handbook of Settlements* (1911; rept. New York, 1970), lists settlement houses in Alabama, Georgia, Louisiana, Mississippi, North Carolina, South Carolina, Tennessee, Texas, and Virginia; my calculation is

derived from counts of the male and female residents and volunteers listed for each house.

12. *Dallas Morning News,* Jan. 25, 1903.

13. Dallas Free Kindergarten and Industrial Association, *Annual Reports,* 1903–4, 1909–10, Texas and Dallas History Collection, Dallas Public Library. *Handbook of Settlements,* 294–95; *The Texas Club Woman,* Apr. 27, 1914, 4.

14. *Handbook of Settlements,* 60, 205; Kathryn Kish Sklar, "Who Funded Hull House?" in *Lady Bountiful Revisited: Women, Philanthropy, and Power,* edited by Kathleen D. McCarthy (New Brunswick, N.J., 1990), 94–115; *Dallas Morning News,* Jan. 25, 1903, and Sept. 30, 1917 (a clipping of the latter is in the Mrs. Morris Liebman Papers, Dallas Historical Society).

15. Dallas Free Kindergarten and Industrial Association, *Annual Reports;* Pauline Periwinkle [Isadore Callaway], "Hull House, Chicago," *DMN/GDN,* Oct. 5, 1903, and "A Welfare Center," ibid., Mar. 25, 1907.

16. Corinne S. Tsanoff, *Neighborhood Doorways* (Houston, 1957), 1–7; B. H. Carroll Jr., *Standard History of Houston, Texas* (Knoxville, Tenn., 1912), 287.

17. Constitution and By-Laws, box 1, Evangelia Settlement Records, Texas Collection, Baylor University.

18. *Handbook of Settlements,* 5; John Patrick McDowell, *The Social Gospel in the South: The Woman's Home Mission Movement in the Methodist Episcopal Church, South, 1886–1939* (Baton Rouge, 1982), 13–14; Mabel Katharine Howell, *Women and the Kingdom* (Nashville, 1928), 185–89, 191 (quotation).

19. Noreen Dunn Tatum, *A Crown of Service: A Story of Woman's Work in the Methodist Episcopal Church, South, from 1878–1940* (Nashville, 1960), 271–76; Virginia A. Shadron, "Out of Our Homes: The Woman's Rights Movement in the Methodist Episcopal Church, South, 1890–1918" (Master's thesis, Emory University, 1976), 25–27, 42, 57–58.

20. Jubilee Committee, Woman's Missionary Society, Texas Conference, *History of Woman's Work, Texas Conference, Methodist Episcopal Church, South* (n.p., 1928), 87.

21. Vicki Ruiz, "Dead Ends or Gold Mines?: Using Missionary Records in Mexican-American Women's History," *Frontiers* 12:1 (1991): 38, 49–51 (quotation at p. 50).

22. History Committee, Woman's Missionary Society, North Texas Conference, *History of Woman's Work, North Texas Conference, Methodist Episcopal Church, South* (n.p., 1929), 88; Tatum, *Crown of Service,* 275; *Texas Christian Advocate,* Mar. 25, 1915, 7; *History of Woman's Work, Texas Conference, Methodist Episcopal Church, South,* 89; Mrs. T. A. Brown, *Our Golden Jubilee: Historical Sketch of the Women's Missionary Society, West Texas Conference* (n.p., 1928), 40: Howell, *Women and the Kindgom,* 191.

23. Richard F. Selcer, *Hell's Half Acre: The Life and Legend of a Red-Light District* (Fort Worth, 1991), 255–62; Patricia Ward Wallace, *Waco: Texas Crossroads* (Woodland Hills, Calif., 1983), 33; David C. Humphrey, "Prostitution and Public Policy in Austin, Texas, 1870–1915," *Southwestern Historical Quarterly* 86 (Apr. 1983): 473–516; *History of Woman's Work, North Texas Conference, Methodist Episcopal Church, South,* 86; Tatum, *Crown of Service,* 273.

24. Mary E. Odem, *Delinquent Daughters: Protecting and Policing Adolescent Female Sexuality in the United States, 1885–1920* (Chapel Hill, N.C., 1995), 8–37; Helen Gardener, "A Battle for Sound Morality: Final Paper," *Arena* 14 (Nov. 1895): 408.

25. Fanny Armstrong, *To the Noon Rest: The Life, Work, and Addresses of Helen M. Stoddard* (Butler, Ind., 1909), 62, 78–84.

26. Odem, *Delinquent Daughters,* 110–11; Elizabeth York Enstam, "They Called it 'Motherhood': Dallas Women and Public Life, 1895–1918," in *Hidden Histories of Women in the New South,* edited by Virginia Bernhard et al. (Columbia, Mo., 1994), 86.

27. Mabel Dodge Luhan's biographer notes, for example, that Luhan contracted gonorrhea from one of her lovers and that two of her husbands had syphilis. Lois Rudnick, "The Male-Identified Woman and Other Anxieties: The Life of Mabel Dodge Luhan," in *The Challenge of Feminist Biography: Writing the Lives of Modern American Women,* edited by Sara Alpern et al. (Urbana, Ill., 1992), 134–36.

28. John C. Burnham, "The Progressive Revolution in American Attitudes toward Sex," *Journal of American History* 59 (Mar. 1973): 893–97; Mark Thomas Connelly, *The Response to Prostitution in the Progressive Era* (Chapel Hill, N.C., 1980), 67–90; Allan M. Brandt, *No Magic Bullet: A Social History of Venereal Disease in America* (New York, 1985), 14–19; John D'Emilio and Estelle B. Freedman, *Intimate Matters: A History of Sexuality in America* (New York, 1988), 203–6.

29. Rachelle Yarros, "The Secret Plague," *The Texas Club Woman,* Feb. 28, 1914; *Dallas Morning News,* Feb. 6, 1911.

30. Jeffrey P. Moran, "'Modernism Gone Mad': Sex Education Comes to Chicago," *Journal of American History* 83 (Sept. 1996): 481–513.

31. Elisabeth Israels Perry, *Belle Moskowitz: Feminine Politics and the Exercise of Power in the Age of Alfred E. Smith* (New York, 1987), 67; Annual Meeting Minutes, Oct. 10–12, 1910, Texas PTA Archives.

32. Mary I. Wood, *History of the General Federation of Women's Clubs* (New York, 1912), 266, 274, 275, 282–84; Ruth Rosen, *The Lost Sisterhood: Prostitution in America, 1900–1918* (Baltimore, 1982), 52–53; GFWC, *Official Report, Twelfth Biennial Convention* (n.p., 1912), 141–44; Maggie Barry, "Personal Hygiene in the Normal Schools," *Dallas Morning News,* Mar. 27, 1911.

33. Mary Ritter Beard, *Women's Work in Municipalities* (New York, 1915), 98.

34. Beard, *Women's Work in Municipalities,* 221; TCM Annual Meeting Minutes, Oct. 10–12, 1910, Texas PTA Archives; Hortense Ward, "Some Laws Needed for the Home and Child," [Texas] *Motherhood Magazine,* Dec. 1914, 14–19 (quotation at p. 18).

35. *The Stylus,* Jan. 27, 1912, 6; Thomas Clyde Mackey, *Red Lights Out: A Legal History of Prostitution, Disorderly Houses, and Vice Districts, 1870–1917* (New York, 1987), 197–205; Humphrey, "Prostitution and Public Policy in Austin," 506–14.

36. *Dallas Morning News,* Nov. 4, 1913. See Mary P. Ryan, *Women in Public: Between Banners and Ballots, 1825–1880* (Baltimore, 1990), chap. 3, for a discussion of the politics of prostitution and public space.

37. Thomas C. Mackey, "Thelma Denton and Associates: Houston's Red Light Reservation and a Question of Jim Crow," *Houston Review* 14:2 (1992): 139–52.

38. Edward L. Ayers, *The Promise of the New South: Life after Reconstruction* (New York, 1992), 136–46.

39. The debate began with C. Vann Woodward's *The Strange Career of Jim Crow* (New York, 1955), which argued that southern race relations were relatively flexible after the Civil War and that widespread segregation did not appear until the 1890s. For an over-view of the literature see Howard N. Rabinowitz, "More Than the Woodward Thesis: Assessing the Strange Career of Jim Crow," *Journal of American History* 75 (Dec. 1988): 842–56, and Woodward, "*Strange Career* Critics: Long May They Persevere," ibid., 857–68. Glenda Elizabeth Gilmore, *Gender and Jim Crow: Women and the Politics of White Su-premacy in North Carolina, 1896–1920* (Chapel Hill, N.C., 1996), chap. 4, exposes white supremacists' deliberate manipulation of gender images.

40. Woodward, *The Strange Career of Jim Crow*, 3d rev. ed., 97; Howard N. Rabinowitz, *The First New South, 1865–1920* (Arlington Heights, Ill., 1992), 138; August Meier and El-liot Rudwick, "The Boycott Movement against Jim Crow Streetcars in the South, 1900–1906," *Journal of American History* 55 (Mar. 1969): 756–75.

41. *Austin Statesman*, Mar. 16, 1906; Alwyn Barr, *Black Texans: A History of Negroes in Texas, 1528–1971* (Austin, 1973), 82.

42. Jesse O. Thomas, *A Study of the Social Welfare Status of the Negroes in Houston, Texas* (Houston, 1929), 96–97, 78 (first quotation), 79 (third quotation); Elizabeth York Enstam, "The Forgotten Frontier: Dallas Women and Social Caring, 1895–1920," *Legacies: A History Journal for Dallas and North Central Texas* 1 (Spring 1989): 23–24 (second quotation).

43. Tsanoff, *Neighborhood Doorways*, 9; Thomas, *Study of the Social Welfare Status*, 85. On the response of the settlement movement to blacks, see Lasch-Quinn, *Black Neigh-bors*, especially chap. 1. Throughout the South, "Bethlehem House" designated the black counterparts (with interracial boards) of the Wesley House mission settlements founded by the Women's Missionary Society of the Methodist Episcopal Church, South. The Texas Methodists, however, did not claim the Houston settlement, which was secular and appears to have copied the name and board structure.

44. Minutes of the Fifth Biennial Meeting of the National Association of Colored Women, 1908, pp. 41–42, reel 23, *Records of the National Association of Colored Women's Clubs*, part 1; Mrs. William Alphin, "Twinkles from the Lone Star," *National Association Notes*, June 1913, p. 18, ibid.; Winegarten, *Black Texas Women: A Sourcebook*, 289.

45. Mrs. Morris White, "The Texas Federation of Colored Women's Clubs," Jan.–Feb. 1915, pp. 9–11 (quotation); Mrs. William Alphin, "From the Lone Star State," *National As-sociation Notes*, May 1913, pp. 7–8; "Texas," *National Association Notes*, December 1911, pp. 4–5, all on reel 23, *Records of the National Association of Colored Women's Clubs*, part 1. The NACW reported membership dues paid by state federations but not member-ship figures. See Minutes of the Eleventh Biennial Convention, 1918, reel 1, ibid., which shows that, among southern federations, only Florida and Mississippi paid less than Texas.

46. White, "Texas Federation of Colored Women's Clubs," p. 10. A small collection of the Married Ladies Social, Art, and Charity Club records has been preserved at the

Houston Metropolitan Research Center, Houston Public Library, but nearly all of it pertains to the years after 1950.

47. White, "Texas Federation of Colored Women's Clubs, " p. 9; Stephanie J. Shaw, "Black Club Women and the Creation of the National Association of Colored Women," *Journal of Women's History* 3 (Fall 1995): 10–25 (quotation p. 18); Winegarten, *Black Texas Women: 150 Years,* 189, 195; Alphin, "Twinkles from Lone Star." The first black clubhouse in Texas appears in the record in 1926. Purchased by the Wichita Falls City Federation of Colored Women's Clubs, it served as a meeting place for other black organizations as well. See Winegarten, *Black Texas Women: 150 Years,* 197.

48. Transcript of interview with Christia Adair, Black Women Oral History Project, Schlesinger Library, Radcliffe College, copy in box 4, folder 2, Adair Papers, HMRC.

49. Carroll, *Standard History of Houston, Texas,* 306; Nancy Hadley, "The 'Hello' Girls of Houston," *Houston Review* 9:2 (1987): 85–86. Alice Kessler-Harris estimates that 3.3 percent of working women nationally were unionized in 1900. After 1902 this figure began to drop, reaching a low of 1.5 percent in 1910. See Kessler-Harris, *Out to Work: A History of Wage-Earning Women in the United States* (New York, 1982), 152.

50. Hadley, "'Hello' Girls"; Stephen H. Norwood, *Labor's Flaming Youth: Telephone Operators and Worker Militancy, 1878–1923* (Urbana, Ill., 1990), 132–33.

51. Susan Porter Benson, *Counter Cultures: Saleswomen, Managers, and Customers in American Department Stores, 1890–1940* (Urbana, Ill., 1986), 180; Joanne J. Meyerowitz, *Woman Adrift: Independent Wage Earners in Chicago, 1880–1930* (Chicago, 1988), xvii; Lynn Y. Weiner, *From Working Girl to Working Mother: The Female Labor Force in the United States, 1820–1980* (Chapel Hill, N.C., 1985), 20; Chapman, "From the Parlor to the Public," 35 n. 12; Dept. of Commerce, Bureau of the Census, *Twelfth Census of the United States Taken in the Year 1900, Population,* vol. 2 (Washington, D.C., 1902), clv. See Scott, *The Southern Lady,* chap. 5, on the movement of southern women into the workforce.

52. Weiner, *From Working Girl to Working Mother,* 5, 22, 25; Jane Addams, "Some Reflections on the Failure of the Modern City to Provide Recreation for Young Girls," *Charities and the Commons,* Dec. 5, 1908, 365.

53. Alice Kessler Harris, *Women Have Always Worked* (Old Westbury, N.Y., 1981), 63–64; Hadley, "'Hello' Girls of Houston": 84–85; Carroll, *Standard History of Houston, Texas,* 309–12; John H. Regan, "How 3500 Houston Women and Girls Earn Daily Bread," *Houston Chronicle,* Jan. 26, 1913.

54. Leslie Woodcock Tentler, *Wage-Earning Women: Industrial Work and Family Life in the United States, 1900–1930* (New York, 1979), 115–25; Meyerowitz, *Woman Adrift,* xvii–xix; Weiner, *From Working Girl to Working Mother,* 36, 52–53.

55. U.S. Dept. of Labor, *Boarding Homes and Clubs for Working Women,* by Mary S. Ferguson, Bulletin no. 15 (Washington, 1898), cited in Weiner, *From Working Girl to Working Mother,* 52; *History of Woman's Work, Texas Conference, Methodist Episcopal Church, South,* 86–89. (The nine businessmen, including department store owner Abe M. Levy, who comprised the Women's Co-operative Home board of trustees undoubtedly had financial as well as philanthropic motives for supporting it.)

56. *Texas Supplement of the Association Monthly,* Mar. 1910, pp. 1–12, Apr. 1910, pp. 1–2, and May 1909, pp. 8–9; Young Women's Christian Association, Houston, *Fifty Golden Years of the Young Women's Christian Association of Houston* (n.p., n.d.), 3; Elizabeth Wilson, *Fifty Years of Association Work among Women, 1866–1916* (New York, 1916), 360. For the history of the association, see Mary S. Sims, *The National History of an Institution— the Young Women's Christian Association* (New York, 1936), and Anne Firor Scott, *Natural Allies: Women's Associations in American History* (Urbana, Ill., 1992), 104–10.

57. Kathy Peiss, *Cheap Amusements: Working Women and Leisure in Turn-of-the-Century New York* (Philadelphia, 1986), is the best assessment of "working girl" culture. See also Peiss, "'Charity Girls and City Pleasures: Historical Notes on Working-Class Sexualtiy, 1880–1920," in *Powers of Desire: The Politics of Sexuality,* edited by Ann Snitow, Christine Stansell, and Sharon Thompson (New York, 1983), 74–87; and James R. McGovern, "The American Woman's Pre-World War I Freedom in Manners and Morals," *Journal of American History* 55 (Sept. 1968): 315–33.

58. For representative criticism of the YWCA's attempt to impose middle-class morals and mores on working women see Meyerowitz, *Woman Adrift,* 46–88; Weiner, *From Working Girl to Working Mother,* 53–59; Tentler, *Wage-Earning Women,* 126–29; and Peiss, *Cheap Amusements,* 166–78.

59. *Texas Supplement of the Association Monthly,* May 1909, p. 9, Mar. 1911, p. 15, Jan.–Mar. 1912 (Special Yearbook Number), pp. 19–24; *Houston Chronicle,* Feb. 2, 1913, p. 25; Elizabeth Hayes Turner, "Issues of Protection and Class: Galveston Women in the Progressive Era," paper presented at the Women and Texas History Conference, Austin, October 1990, p. 12 (copy in author's possession). On saloons and working-class culture, see Madelon Powers, "The 'Poor Man's Friend': Saloonkeepers, Workers, and the Code of Reciprocity in U.S. Barrooms, 1870–1920," *International Labor and Working-Class History* 45 (Spring 1994): 3–12; Raymond Calkins, *Substitutes for the Saloon* (Boston, 1901), chap. 1.

60. "Reports of the Texas Associations," *Texas Supplement of the Association Monthly,* Jan.–Mar. 1912, pp. 20 (first quotation), 24 (second quotation); March 1911, p. 15.

61. *Texas Supplement of the Association Monthly,* Dec. 1910, pp. 8–9. See Meyerowitz, *Woman Adrift,* 48–49, on the YWCA's image of the working woman as "endangered orphan."

62. *Texas Supplement of the Association Monthly,* Jan-Mar. 1912, pp. 19, 22; Mar. 1911, p. 15; *A Greater San Antonio Demands a Greater Young Woman's Christian Association,* [San Antonio, 1914], n.p.; Turner, "Issues of Protection and Class," 10; "Miss Helen Knox," in *Who's Who of the Womanhood of Texas,* vol. 1, 1923–24 (n.p., 1924), 98.

63. Elsie Dorothy Harper, *The Past Is Prelude* (New York, 1963), 5, 13; *Texas Supplement of the Association Monthly,* Jan.–Mar. 1912, pp. 23, 19; Eva Goldsmith, "Objections Raised to Minimum Wage Bill," *Houston Labor Journal,* Feb. 20, 1915.

64. "Miss Eva Goldsmith Argues," *Galveston Daily News,* Jan. 26, 1913. I have been unable to discover any source of biographical information on Eva Goldsmith other than newspaper reports.

178   *Notes to Pages 95–99*

65. *Houston Labor Journal,* Feb. 1, 8, Mar. 15, Apr. 12, 1913; and Feb. 6, 13, 20, 27, Mar. 6, 1915; *Proceedings of the Sixteenth Annual Convention of the Texas State Federation of Labor* (Austin, 1913), 62–63, 77–78, 80; *Sixth Biennial Report, Joint Labor Legislative Board of Texas for the Thirty-Third Legislature* (Austin, 1913), 15; *Proceedings of the Eighteenth Annual Conference of the Texas State Federation of Labor* (Austin, 1915), 57, 63–64.

66. See for example, Nancy F. Cott, "What's in a Name? The Limits of Social Feminism; or, Expanding the Vocabulary of Women's History," *Journal of American History* 76 (Dec. 1989): 809–29.

67. *Galveston Daily News,* July 7, 1916; Eva Goldsmith to Minnie Fisher Cunningham, July 2, 1916, box 14, folder 7, McCallum Papers (part 2).

68. Matthews, *Rise of Public Woman,* 11.

Chapter 5: "I Wish My Mother Had a Vote"

1. "Eighty Years Young Today: Women of San Antonio to Honor One Who Has Made Their Interests Her Own," photocopy of unidentified newspaper clipping, M. Eleanor Brackenridge biographical file, Daughters of the Republic of Texas Library at the Alamo, San Antonio.

2. A. Elizabeth Taylor, "The Woman Suffrage Movement in Texas," *Journal of Southern History* 27 (May 1951): 194–215, reprinted in Ruthe Winegarten and Judith N. McArthur, eds., *Citizens at Last: The Woman Suffrage Movement in Texas* (Austin, 1987), 13–48; *San Antonio Express,* Apr. 2, 1913; Elizabeth Hayes Turner, " 'White-Gloved Ladies' and 'New Women' in the Texas Woman Suffrage Movement," in *Southern Women: Histories and Identities,* edited by Virginia Bernhard et al. (Columbia, Mo., 1992), 134, 140; *Dallas Morning News,* Mar. 16, Apr. 8, May 30, 1913; M. Eleanor Brackenridge to Minnie Fisher Cunningham, June 15, 1916, box 14, folder 2, Jane Y. McCallum Family Papers, AHC-APL.

3. Taylor, "Woman Suffrage Movement in Texas," 30; Louise Boyer Murphy to Henry B. Stevens, Sept. 15, 1913, and Murphy to Agnes Ryan, Nov. 18, 1913, National American Woman Suffrage Association Papers, reel 19, container 29 (Library of Congress, microfilm); *Dallas Morning News,* Oct. 1, 28, 29, 1914, and Oct. 7, 23, 24, 1915. Michael McGerr has pointed out that in embracing a ritual of popular politics such as parades, suffragists were appropriating for their own purpose a public ritual that men had abandoned. See Michael McGerr, "Political Style and Women's Power, 1830–1930," *Journal of American History* 77 (Dec. 1990): 864–85.

4. "Minutes of the First Session of the Texas Equal Rights Association," (lists forty-eight charter members), reprinted in Winegarten and McArthur, eds., *Citizens at Last,* 87–93; Helen M. Stoddard, "Texas," in *The History of Woman Suffrage,* edited by Susan B. Anthony and Ida Husted Harper, 4 vols. (Rochester, N.Y., 1902), 4:931 (reports fifty-two members); Taylor, "Woman Suffrage Movement in Texas," 18–19; *Dallas Morning News,* June 9, 1894, and June 7, 8, 1895.

5. *San Antonio Daily Express,* July 30, 1889; "Struggling for Freedom," *Dallas Morning News,* [date handwritten as May 10, 1893; should be May 11], TESA [*sic*] Scrapbook, McCallum Papers.

6. "Women Suffragists Meet," undated clipping, *Fort Worth Gazette*, TESA [*sic*] Scrapbook, p. 21–22 (quotation); "Struggling for Freedom," *Dallas Morning News*, June 7, 1895.

7. "Minutes of the First Session of the Texas Equal Rights Association"; *Dallas Morning News*, June 8, 1894.

8. Five of the signers of the call were identified by their WCTU affiliations: Elizabeth Fry, Sarah Acheson, Elizabeth Tracy, Mrs. W. S. Herndon, and Mary Pendergast. Three others are known to have been members: Rebecca Henry Hayes, Grace Danforth, and Ellen Lawson Dabbs. Bettie Gay of the Texas Farmers' Alliance was a temperance advocate, but it is not known if she was actually a WCTU member. The nine TERA officers actually represented only eight women because Sarah Trumbull held two positions: first vice president and state organizer. The only officer for whom no information is available is Margaret Watson of Beaumont, the recording secretary. The names of the signers of the call and the officers appear in "Minutes of the First Session of the Texas Equal Rights Association." The Fry quotation appears in *San Antonio Daily Express*, July 30, 1889.

9. "Mrs. Wells' Address," *Houston Post*, Apr. 1, 1915.

10. Turner, "'White-Gloved Ladies,'" 145.

11. Johnowene B. Crutcher Menger, "M. Eleanor Brackenridge, 1837–1924, a Third Generation Advocate of Education," (Master's thesis, Trinity University [San Antonio], 1964), 44–45, 71, 78–79; John William Leonard, ed., *Woman's Who's Who of America, 1914–15* (New York, 1914), 121.

12. *Morrison & Fourmy's General Directory of the City of Houston, 1887–88* (Galveston, 1887), 44, 50, 51–52, 54; *Directory of the City of Houston, 1913* (Houston, 1913), 54–56, 67–71, 73.

13. See "To the Women of Granger," unidentified newspaper clipping, TESA Scrapbook, p. 5; "Woman Suffragists," ibid., p. 9.

14. Kathleen Elizabeth Lazarou, *Concealed Under Petticoats: Married Women's Property and the Law of Texas, 1840–1913* (New York, 1986), 15–80; *Dallas Morning News*, June 8, 1894.

15. [Lawrence Neff], "Legal Rights and Wrongs of Woman," *The New South*, Jan. 1912, p. 2; Pauline Periwinkle [Isadore Callaway], "Clubs Pledge Help," *DMN/GDN*, Dec. 17, 1906. Callaway also wrote a number of blistering columns on the subject. See "Are You a Foreigner?" Mar. 30, 1903; "Shiftless Husbands," Mar. 20, 1905; "Rights vs. Courtesy," Jan. 28, 1907; "Ignorance of Laws," May 6, 1907; and "When Is a Citizen Not a Citizen?" Jan. 11, 1909.

16. Christian, *History of the Texas Federation of Women's Clubs*, 194; Hortense Ward, "The Legal Status of Married Women in Texas," *Houston Chronicle*, Apr. 1, 1911 (pamphlet copy in Pennybacker Papers, CAH-UT). Biographical information on Ward appears in I. Sterling, "Being a Woman Lawyer," *The Stylus*, Sept. 21, 1912, p. 3, and Sept. 28, 1912, pp. 5, 15; Sinclair Moreland, *Texas Women's Hall of Fame* (Austin, 1917), 117–19; *Woman Citizen*, Feb. 18, 1918, p. 233; and the collection of obituaries in Houston Scrapbooks: Biography, in the HMRC.

17. Joan Hoff, *Law, Gender, and Injustice: A Legal History of U.S. Women* (New York, 1991), 121–35; Ellen Carol DuBois, ed., *Elizabeth Cady Stanton, Susan B. Anthony:*

Correspondence, Writings, Speeches (New York, 1981), 163. See also Carole Shammas, "Reassessing the Married Women's Property Acts," *Journal of Women's History* 6 (Spring 1994): 9–30.

18. Mary I. Wood, *History of the General Federation of Women's Clubs* (New York, 1912), 271; Theda Skocpol, *Protecting Soldiers and Mothers: The Political Origins of Social Policy in the United States* (Cambridge, Mass., 1992), 350, 433–35; Erman J. Ridgeway, "Conversazione," *Delineator*, Sept. 1911, p. 57; William Hard, "Help from Clubwomen," *Delineator*, Oct. 1912, p. 223 (quotation).

19. Hard, "Discovering the Laws about Women: A Nationwide Movement Which Will Make History," *Delineator*, May 1912, p. 389, and "Watch the Results," p. 172; Hard, "Real Work Begins to Secure Better Law for Home," ibid., Apr. 1912, pp. 288 (first quotation), 287 (second quotation).

20. Hard, "Will Texas Do Better by its Married Women?" *Delineator*, Nov. 1912, pp. 317–18. The campaign and its legislative results are described in Hard, "650,000 Wives Get their Own Money," ibid., August 1913, 18–19. On the TFWC's and TCM's adoption of married women's property rights as a legislative goal, see Maggie Barry to Anna Pennybacker, Oct. 24, 1912, Pennybacker Papers, CAH-UT; and Annual Meeting Minutes, 1912, and Executive Board Minutes, Nov. 16, 1912, box 32A, Texas PTA Archives.

21. Instead of working cooperatively the TFWC and TCM backed rival bills, apparently because TFWC president Ella Dibrell resented the publicity that *The Delineator* accorded Hortense Ward and the Congress of Mothers. The competition replayed the two organizations' previous rivalry over school mothers' clubs and resulted in a legislative compromise that gave the women somewhat less than they had originally hoped for. The husband's joinder was still required in order for a wife to sell or transfer her real estate, stocks, and bonds. Anna Pennybacker to William Hard, Nov. 26, 1912; Hard to Pennybacker, Dec. 3, 1912; Pennybacker to Hard, Dec. 6, 1912; all in Pennybacker Papers. For an analysis of the 1913 law, see Lazarou, *Concealed Under Petticoats*.

22. Hortense Ward, "Shall Women Have Adequate Laws?" *Texas Magazine*, Jan. 1913, p. 239 (first quotation); Jane Addams, "Why Women Should Vote," *Ladies' Home Journal*, Jan. 1910, pp. 21–22 (second quotation), reprinted in *The Social Thought of Jane Addams*, edited by Christopher Lasch (New York, 1965); "Woman's Vote Will Cover Texas," *Galveston News*, June 14, 1914 (third quotation), clipping in Oscar B. Colquitt Papers, CAH-UT.

23. Sara Hunter Graham, "The Suffrage Renaissance: A New Image for a New Century," in *One Woman, One Vote: Rediscovering the Woman Suffrage Movement*, edited by Marjorie Spruill Wheeler (Troutdale, Oreg., 1995), and Sara Hunter Graham, *Woman Suffrage and the New Democracy* (New Haven, 1996), chap. 3. The ten legislative standards on the Wheel of Progress were: an industrial welfare commission; a fourteen-year age minimum for child labor; compulsory statewide education; an eight- or nine-hour day for women workers; minimum wage; mothers' pensions for widows; equal guardianship rights for mothers; raising the age of consent to eighteen; red-light abatement; and prohibition. See also Suzanne M. Marilley, *Woman Suffrage and the Origins of Liberal Feminism in the United States* (Cambridge, Mass., 1996), 187–210.

24. Aileen S. Kraditor, *The Ideas of the Woman Suffrage Movement, 1890–1920* (New York, 1965), chap. 3. Kraditor devoted a sentence and a footnote to the growth of the woman's club movement as a factor in the shift to expedient arguments. Her analysis lays more stress on declining faith in democracy and the rise of the Progressive movement. See Genevieve G. McBride, *On Wisconsin Women: Working for Their Rights from Settlement to Suffrage* (Madison, Wis., 1993), chap. 8, for a perceptive discussion of clubwomen's impact on the suffrage movement.

25. Alisa Kraus, *Every Child a Lion: The Origins of Maternal and Infant Health Policy in the United States and France, 1890–1920* (Ithaca, N.Y., 1993), chap. 4; Richard E. Meckel, *Save the Babies: American Public Health Reform and the Prevention of Infant Mortality* (Baltimore, 1990), 146–48, 151; "Better Babies," [Texas] *Motherhood Magazine*, Apr. 1914, 74; May 1914, 135; October 1914, 36–37. A sample "Better Babies Score Card" prepared by the *Woman's Home Companion* can be found in box 2P359, Alexander Caswell Ellis Papers, CAH-UT. The judges were usually doctors who rated the youngsters' physical development and health on a point system and compared weight and length against standardized charts. The prize for the "best baby" was awarded to the one with the most points.

26. "Women in the Home," and "Twelve Reasons Why Mothers Should Have the Vote," NAWSA broadsides, box 9, folder 11, McCallum Papers (part 1); "Better Babies," NAWSA broadside, 1918, box 21, folder 311, Minnie Fisher Cunningham Papers, HMRC; *Dallas Times Herald*, Mar. 9, 1916, clipping in box 3L91, Better Babies Scrapbook, CAH-UT.

27. "Points on Organization Work," box 3, folder 3, McCallum Papers (part 1); Harriett N. Leary to Annette Finnigan, Apr. 18, 1918, McCallum Papers (part 2); Elizabeth York Enstam, "They Called it 'Motherhood': Dallas Women and Public Life, 1895–1918," in *Hidden Histories of Women in the New South*, edited by Virginia Bernhard et al. (Columbia, Mo., 1994), 91. See Nancy F. Cott, *The Grounding of Modern Feminism* (New Haven, Conn., 1987), 16–34, on the shifting ideological emphasis of the women's movement.

28. *San Antonio Daily Express*, July 30, 1889 (Fry quotation); Pauline Periwinkle [Isadore Callaway], "Ties Strings to Woman Suffrage," *DMN/GDN*, Feb. 12, 1912.

29. Suzanne M. Marilley, "Frances Willard and the Feminism of Fear," *Feminist Studies* 19 (Spring 1993): 123–46; "Better Babies" (quotation). O'Neill's Kewpies appeared widely in suffrage fliers illustrating the "give Mother the vote" theme. See Alice Sheppard, *Cartooning for Suffrage* (Albuquerque, 1994), 136.

30. "Woman's Vote Will Cover Texas."

31. Quoted in Karen Blair, *The Clubwoman as Feminist: True Womanhood Redefined, 1868–1914* (New York, 1980), 111; Anna Pennybacker to Olga Kohlberg, Aug. 27, 1912, Pennybacker Papers.

32. "Federation of Women's Clubs Opens Biennial," *Chicago Record-Herald*, June 11, 1914; untitled clipping, *Chicago Evening Post*, June 12, 1914; and "Equal Suffrage to be Discussed at Biennial," unidentified clipping, all in Scrapbook, 1914, Pennybacker Papers. *Chicago Tribune*, June 12–15, 1914.

33. Turner, "'White-Gloved Ladies,'" 152; Annette Finnigan to Mary Garrett Hay, Feb. 22, 1915, and Hay to Finnigan, Mar. 10, 1915, box 11, folder 6, McCallum Papers (part 2).

34. Marin Fenwick to Annette Finnigan, Nov. 21, 1914, box 11, folder 1, McCallum Papers (part 2). Finnigan to Mrs. William Dunne, Mar. 28, Apr. 4, 1915; Dunne to Finnigan, Mar. 29 (quotation), Apr. 14, 1915, all in box 10, folder 1, ibid.

35. Amy Cresswell Dunne to Mrs. Fain, May 6, 1915; and Gussie Ayers Young to Dear Friend [Annette Finnigan], Apr. 6 (first quotation), 25, 1915, all in box 10, folder 1, McCallum Papers (part 2); Molly Ladd-Taylor, *Mother-Work: Women, Child Welfare, and the State, 1890–1930* (Urbana, Ill., 1995), 45, 49; Mrs. Claude DeVan Watts, "Why I Am a Suffragist," *Dallas Times Herald,* Sept. 2, 1917 (second quotation); Mrs. E. A. Watters to Minnie Fisher Cunningham, box 17, folder 266, Cunningham Papers. I am indebted to Elizabeth York Enstam for the Watts quotation.

36. *Dallas Morning News,* Aug. 21, 1916; *Chicago Tribune,* June 13, 1914.

37. Mrs. W. M. [May Harper] Baines, *Houston's Part in the World War* (Houston, 1919), 69.

38. M. Eleanor Brackenridge to Minnie Fisher Cunningham, June 15, 1916, box 14, folder 2, McCallum Papers.

39. Kraditor, *Ideas of the Woman Suffrage Movement,* chap. 7; Marjorie Spruill Wheeler, *New Women of the New South: The Leaders of the Woman Suffrage Movement in the Southern States* (New York, 1993), chap. 4.

40. On suffragists as racial moderates, see Suzanne Lebsock, "Woman Suffrage and White Supremacy: A Virginia Case Study," in *Visible Women: New Essays on American Activism,* edited by Nancy A. Hewitt and Suzanne Lebsock (Urbana, Ill., 1993); Glenda Elizabeth Gilmore, *Gender and Jim Crow: Women and the Politics of White Supremacy in North Carolina, 1896–1920* (Chapel Hill, N.C., 1996), chap. 8; and Elna Green, "'Ideals of Government, of Home, and of Women': The Ideology of Southern White Antisuffragism," in *Hidden Histories of Women in the New South,* edited by Virginia Bernhard et al. (Columbia, Mo., 1994).

41. "Struggling for Freedom" (quotation); Marilley, *Woman Suffrage,* 159–80.

42. Wheeler, *New Women of the New South,* 113–20. On Texas, see *Proceedings of the Twenty-sixth Annual Convention of the National American Woman Suffrage Association, February 15–20, 1894,* edited by Harriet Taylor Upton (Warren, Ohio, [1894]), 47–49.

43. "Minutes of the First Session of the Texas Equal Rights Association," May 10, 1893, and "If I Were Mayor of San Antonio" (first Fry quotation), reprinted in Winegarten and McArthur, eds., *Citizens at Last,* 91, 86; *Dallas Morning News,* Oct. 29, 1893 (second Fry quotation), June 8, 1894. There is a copy of Henry Blackwell's pamphlet, *A Solution to the Southern Question,* in the Erminia Thompson Folsom Papers, Archives Division, Texas State Library. It probably belonged to Erminia Folsom's mother, Marianna, a correspondent of Blackwell and NAWSA organizer from Iowa who spent time in Texas in the 1880s and 1890s. If TERA suffragists were aware of it, they never said so in print.

44. Paul Fuller, *Laura Clay and the Woman's Rights Movement in Kentucky* (Lexington, Ky., 1975), 58–60; "Woman Suffragists . . . Waving the Bloody Shirt," *Dallas Morning News,* June 9, 1894, reprinted in Winegarten and McArthur, eds., *Citizens at Last,* 101–3.

45. For details of the conflict, see TESA [*sic*] Scrapbook, pp. 19, 23, 43–45. Quotation appears in Danforth to Laura Clay, Aug. 3, 1894, Clay Papers, University of Kentucky; thanks to Marjorie Spruill Wheeler for alerting me to this correspondence.

46. *National Woman's Party Papers*, part 2, ser. 1, reel 87, frames, 268, 271, 278 (Bethesda, Md., 1981, microfilm); "Why I am a Suffragist," *Dallas Times Herald*, June 10, 1917.

47. On the split between the states' rights minority and the majority of southern suffragists see Wheeler, *New Women of the New South*, chap. 5.

48. [Elizabeth Herndon Potter] to Mrs. C[unningham], Jan. 22, 1918, box 14, folder 205, Cunningham Papers (first quotation); *Ennis Daily News*, July 29, 1916 (second quotation), reprinted in Winegarten and McArthur, eds., *Citizens at Last*, 181.

49. Mrs. E. Sampson to Mrs. [Maud Wood] Park, June 1918; Belle C. Critchett to Edith Hinkle League, July 1, 1918 (quotation); League to Ruth White, July 8, 1918, and White to League, July 12, 1918, all in box 3, folder 4, McCallum Papers (part 1). The El Paso city directory indicates that Mrs. Sampson was married to a janitor at City Hall; no other information is known about her.

50. Lebsock, "Woman Suffrage and White Supremacy," 65.

51. Kraditor, *Ideas of the Woman Suffrage Movement*, 200–202; Carrie Chapman Catt to Edith Hinkle League, July 17, 1918, box 3, folder 4, McCallum Papers; Paula Giddings, *When and Where I Enter: The Impact of Black Women on Race and Sex in America* (New York, 1984), 161–62.

52. "The South's 'Battalion of Death'—Making the World Safe for Democracy," box 6, folder 2, McCallum Papers (part 1); Lebsock, "Woman Suffrage and White Supremacy," 76.

53. Cunningham to Sampson, Aug. 31, 1918, 3/4, McCallum Papers; Cunningham to Carrie Chapman Catt, Mar. 25, 1918, box 1, folder 9, Cunningham Papers.

54. Cunningham to Kate Gordon, Feb. 16, 1917, box 14, folder 209, Cunningham Papers. Cunningham avoided mentioning race at all; I have found no public or private statements under her signature. She may have been the author of an editorial, "Regarding the Suffrage Amendment," published Dec. 30, 1917, in the progressive *Houston Chronicle*. A reprint is in box 4, folder 7, McCallum Papers, and it is attributed to Cunningham in Willie D. Worley Bowles, "History of the Woman Suffrage Movement in Texas," (Master's thesis, University of Texas at Austin, 1939). The editorial includes several paragraphs reminding readers that black women would be subject to the same restraints operating against black male voters. If Cunningham wrote this piece, she clearly did not want it to appear under her name or TESA auspices, which would only have encouraged a noisy attack by the antisuffragist race-baiters and magnified the issue.

55. Lee N. Allen, "The Woman Suffrage Movement in Alabama," *Alabama Review* 11 (Apr. 1958): 98; Elna C. Green, "Those Opposed: The Antisuffragists in North Carolina," *North Carolina Historical Review* 67 (July 1990): 321.

56. Calculated from the votes reported in *Senate Journal*, 36th Leg., 2d Called Sess., 44–45. This is the vote to move the bill to its third reading; the ratification vote was *viva voce* with the same reported result: 19 yeas and 10 nays. Population figures are taken from

Bureau of the Census, *Statistical Atlas of the United States* (Washington, D.C., 1914), plate no. 199, "Per Cent of Negroes in Total Population of Texas, by Counties, 1910."

57. Votes appear in *Senate Journal*, 35th Leg., 4th Called Sess., 61, and 36th Leg., 2d Called Sess., 44–45; they are tabulated in Judith N. McArthur, "Cracking the Solid South: Texas as a Case Study," paper presented at "Women in Public Life: A Symposium Commemorating 125 Years of Suffrage in Wyoming," Third Annual American Heritage Center Symposium, University of Wyoming, September 1994. J. C. McNealus, one of the two prohibitionists who voted against the Nineteenth Amendment was actually a longtime suffrage supporter who changed his position after the voters turned down a state constitutional amendment earlier in the year.

58. Annette Finnigan to Laura Clay, Feb. 20, 1915, 11/6, McCallum Papers (part 2); Minnie Fisher Cunningham to Alice S. Ellington, July 12, 1917, 3/29, Cunningham Papers; [Jessie Daniel Ames] to Claude D. Teer, Aug. 7, box 18, file unnumbered, McCallum Papers (part 2); Janet G. Humphrey, ed., *A Texas Suffragist: Diaries and Writings of Jane Y. McCallum* (Austin, 1988), 72 (quotation).

59. Anti-Saloon League, *The Brewers and Texas Politics*, 2 vols. (San Antonio, 1916), 1:109–12; "Brewing Propaganda," *New Republic*, Aug. 21, 1915. Carrie Chapman Catt and Nettie Rogers Schuler in *Woman Suffrage and Politics: The Inner Story of the Suffrage Movement* (1926; rept. Seattle, 1969), list Texas as one of the eight states where the "organized German-liquor vote was hurled into woman suffrage referenda campaigns with the unerring accuracy claimed for it." On special interests and national suffrage politics, see David Morgan, *Suffragists and Democrats: The Politics of Woman Suffrage in America* (East Lansing, Mich., 1972). In Tennessee during the fight over ratifying the Nineteenth Amendment, the racist propaganda that had already appeared in Texas circulated in abundance. Tennessee suffragists, however, calculated that the most difficult obstacle would be the deep pockets of the special interests. The women compiled a list of all the prosuffrage legislators they considered susceptible to bribery, and before the final vote was taken all of them had deserted to the antisuffragists. See Anastatia Sims, "'Powers that Pray' and 'Powers that Prey': Tennessee and the Fight for Woman Suffrage," *Tennessee Historical Quarterly* 50 (Winter 1991): 212–16.

60. *Texas White Ribbon*, May 1914, p. 6. See also Turner, "'White-Gloved Ladies,'" 146–48, which compares memberships of the Galveston ESA and WCTU to the same conclusion.

61. *San Antonio Express*, May 7, 9, 1913. On the battleship *Texas*, see *Home and State*, Dec. 9, 1911, and June 1, 1912. The WCTU column in the *Dallas Morning News*, Feb. 22, 1915, describes one of the "heavenly birthday" celebrations.

62. For biographical information on Curtis, see Leonard, ed., *Woman's Who's Who of America*; Moreland, *Texas Woman's Hall of Fame*; May Baines, *A Story of Texas White Ribboners* (n.p., [1935?]), 52–53; *Home and State*, Apr. 5, 1920.

63. Annette Finnigan to Texas Woman [*sic*], Dec. 16, 1918, McCallum Papers, reprinted in Winegarten and McArthur, eds., *Citizens at Last*, 116; "Spanning the Old to the New South: Minnie Fisher Cunningham and Her Heroine Mother," *Texas Observer*, Nov. 21, 1958; and Turner, "'White-Gloved Ladies,'" 152–55.

64. On the "Liquor Trust" image, see K. Austin Kerr, *Organized for Prohibition: A New History of the Anti-Saloon League* (New Haven, Conn., 1985), 24–34. Danforth quotations appear in "Struggling for Freedom," and "Emancipation of Women," *Dallas Morning News,* dateline May 18, [1893], TESA [*sic*] Scrapbook, p. 2.

65. *Dallas Morning News,* May 8 (quotation), 9, 1913; *San Antonio Express,* May 7, 1913; *Home and State,* May 24, 31, 1913.

66. *Dallas Morning News,* Jan. 16, 1911; "Woman's Appeal to the Manhood of Men, the Justice of Manhood. The Helpless Ask a Priceless Boon of Those Who Alone Are Able to Grant It," [1903], E. L. Shettles Papers, CAH-UT. I am indebted to Norman D. Brown for sharing a photocopy of this document.

67. Estelle Hebert Folk to Hally B. Bryan, Mar. 4, 1915, box 2F286, Hally Ballinger Bryan Papers, CAH-UT.

Chapter 6: "These Piping Times of Victory"

1. "War College for Women" program, box 21, folder 311, Cunningham Papers; *Austin American,* June 25–29, 1918.

2. Ida Clyde Clarke, *American Women and the World War* (New York, 1918), 17–35; Mrs. Nevada Davis Hitchcock, "The Mobilization of Women," *AAAPSS* 78 (1918): 24–31.

3. Mrs. O. L. McKnight to Minnie Fisher Cunningham, Oct. 31, 1918, 20/289, Cunningham Papers; Mrs. S. A. Collom to Mrs. Reese Wilson, Aug. 30, 1918, box 2J364, Texas War Records, CAH-UT.

4. Clarke, *American Women and the World War,* 61–65; *Texas White Ribbon,* May 1917, copy in box 2H459, James M. Rockwell Papers, CAH-UT; *Dallas Morning News,* Apr. 25, 1917; Kate Adele Hill, *Home Demonstration Work in Texas* (San Antonio, 1958), 31–32.

5. Anna Pennybacker, *What Our Country Asks of Its Young Women,* Patriotism Through Education Series, no. 3 (New York, 1917), 1–2, copy in 21/311, Cunningham Papers; *Austin American,* June 25, 1917; Mary E. Gearing Biographical Files, CAH-UT, and Blagg-Huey Library, TWU.

6. M. Rebecca Sharpless, "Town Women, Country Women: The Club Women's Movement and Home Demonstration in Texas, 1915–1930," paper presented at Texas State Historical Association Annual Meeting, Austin, 1992, copy in author's possession; *Austin American,* June 25, 1918.

7. J. A. Hallowell to E. A Peden, July 16, 1918 (quotation), box 2J220, Texas War Records; Monthly Report of the Executive Secretary to the Executive Board, Colored Section, Federal Food Administration, Nov. 4, 1918, ibid.

8. *Austin American,* June 25, 1918.

9. Molly Ladd-Taylor, "Hull House Goes to Washington: Women and the Children's Bureau," in *Gender, Class, Race, and Reform in the Progressive Era,* edited by Noralee Frankel and Nancy S. Dye (Lexington, Ky., 1991), 110–26; "Council of Mothers Will Help Win War," unidentified clipping, Lala Fay Watts Papers, in possession of Lillian Watts Green, New Braunfels, Texas; Richard E. Meckel, *Save the Babies: American Public Health Reform and the Prevention of Infant Mortality* (Baltimore, 1990), 201; "Report of the Child

Welfare Department, Woman's Committee of National Defense, State of Texas," box 2J364, Texas War Records.

10. James Johnson, "The Role of Women in the Founding of the United States Children's Bureau," in *'Remember the Ladies': New Perspectives on Women in American History,* edited by Carol V. R. George (Syracuse, 1975), 179–96; Theda Skocpol, *Protecting Soldiers and Mothers: The Political Origins of Social Policy in the United States* (Cambridge, Mass., 1992), 482–94; Alisa Kraus, *Every Child a Lion: The Origins of Maternal and Infant Health Policy in the United States and France, 1890–1920* (Ithaca, N.Y., 1993), 158–71.

11. Jessica P. Pexiotto, "The Children's Year and the Woman's Committee," *AAAPSS* 79 (Sept. 1918): 257–62; U.S. Department of Labor, Children's Bureau, *Children's Year Working Program* (Washington, D.C., 1918), copy in 19/284, Cunningham Papers (quotation at p. 3); Meckel, *Save the Babies,* 200–201. On the Children's Bureau and World War I, see Kriste Lindenmeyer, *"A Right to Childhood": The U.S. Children's Bureau and Child Welfare, 1912–46* (Urbana, Ill., 1997), 71–74.

12. Kraus, *Every Child a Lion,* 257. Fleming was annoyed, however, that Watters and her staff exercised their new functions under their TCM titles and took small notice of the formal jurisdiction of the Woman's Committee. They continued to issue directives on TCM letterhead until the war was nearly over. See Dora Hartzell Fleming to Mrs. Reese Wilson, Sept. 21, 1918; Ella Caruthers Porter to Wilson, Sept. 3, 26, 1918; and Mrs. B. A. Sadler to Wilson, Sept. 20, 1918, all in box 2J364, Texas War Records.

13. "Report of the Child Welfare Department, Woman's Committee of National Defense, State of Texas," p. 4, box 2J364, Texas War Records; Mrs. E. A. Watters and Mrs. Ella Caruthers Porter to "Dear President," undated [1918], ibid. (there are several different form letters, all undated); *Dallas Morning News,* June 1, 1918; *Houston Post,* July 3, 1918; *San Antonio Express,* July 12, 1918.

14. Pexiotto, "Children's Year and the Woman's Committee"; Kraus, *Every Child a Lion,* 258–59; Watters and Porter to "Dear President"; "Report of the Child Welfare Department," pp. 5–6.

15. "Report of the Child Welfare Department," pp. 9, 13, 15. Only two city reports—for San Antonio and Fort Worth—are attached to this document, and San Antonio's is not broken down by race or ethnicity.

16. *Dallas Morning News,* July 1, 19, 1918.

17. "Report of the Child Welfare Department," pp. 8–9; "Council of Mothers to Make Home Survey," unidentified newspaper clipping [1918], Watts Papers.

18. "Children's Year Committee Will Go to Austin for Survey on Legislation," unidentified newspaper clipping, Aug. 1918, Watts Papers; "Report of the Child Welfare Department," p. 8; Watters and Porter to "Dear President."

19. *Austin American,* July 24, 1918 (first quotation); Texas Bureau of Labor Statistics, *Fifth Biennial Report, 1917–18* (Austin, 1918), 18 (second quotation); Texas Congress of Mothers, Dallas Council of Mothers to William P. Hobby, June 5, 1918, Watts Papers; T. C. Jennings to Watts, Sept. 26, 1918, Watts Papers; Mrs. Claude DeVan Watts, "Where Once the Home Was Woman's World, Now the World Is Woman's Home," unidentified clipping, ibid. (third quotation).

20. Robert S. Maxwell, "Texas in the Progressive Era, 1900–1930," in *Texas: A Sesquicentennial Celebration* (Austin, 1984), 191; Lt. George J. Anderson, "Making the Camps Safe for the Army," *AAAPSS* 79 (Sept. 1918): 146.

21. Allan M. Brandt, *No Magic Bullet: A Social History of Venereal Disease in the United States since 1880* (New York, 1985), 53–56; Mark Thomas Connelly, *The Response to Prostitution in the Progressive Era* (Chapel Hill, N.C., 1980), 137–38; Ronald Schaffer, *America in the Great War: The Rise of the Welfare State* (New York, 1991), 98–100: M. J. Exner, "Prostitution and its Relation to the Army on the Mexican Border," *Social Hygiene* 3 (Apr. 1917): 205–20; Janet G. Humphrey, ed., *A Texas Suffragist: Diaries and Writings of Jane Y. McCallum* (Austin, 1988), 75.

22. Raymond B. Fosdick, "The Program of the Commission on Training Camp Activities with Relation to the Problem of Venereal Disease," *Social Hygiene* 4 (Jan. 1918): 71–76; Fosdick, "The War and Navy Departments on Training Camp Activities," *AAAPSS* 79 (Sept. 1918): 130–42; Joseph Lee, "War Camp Community Service," ibid., 189–94. See Nancy K. Bristow, *Making Men Moral: Social Engineering during the Great War* (New York, 1996), for a detailed and analytical study of the CTCA.

23. [CTCA] "Section on Hostess Houses and Rules and Regulations Regarding Women Visitors to Camps," Sept. 1, 1918, box 2G186, Mrs. Walter B. [Estelle Boughton] Sharp Papers, CAH-UT; Young Women's Christian Association, War Work Council, *Report of the Hostess House Committee* (New York, [1919]), 5, 37–41.

24. Bristow, *Making Men Moral*, 146–73; Jane Olcott, comp., *The Work of Colored Women* (New York, 1920), 21.

25. Garna L. Christian, *Black Soldiers in Jim Crow Texas, 1899–1917* (College Station, Tex., 1995), 145–72; Robert V. Haynes, *A Night of Violence: The Houston Riot of 1917* (Baton Rouge, 1976); Olcott, *The Work of Colored Women*, 14, 116–17; "Report of the War Services Commission, Houston Chamber of Commerce, Apr. 21, 1918," box 2G186, Sharp Papers; *50 Golden Years of the Young Women's Christian Association of Houston*, 6.

26. "Report of War Work Adopted at the State Convention in Waco," box 2G186, Sharp Papers (first quotation); Mrs. W. B. Sharp to "Dear Club President," Nov. 19, 1917, ibid.; Christian, *History of the Texas Federation of Women's Clubs*, 365; Mrs. W. B. Sharp, Mrs. Florence Floore, and Mrs. M. Hetty Curry to "Dear Clubwoman," Feb. 8, 1918, Pennybacker Papers (second quotation).

27. "Report of the Seven Canteens Run by the Federation Women of Texas," box 2G181, Sharp Papers; Fannie C. Potter, ed., *History of the Texas Federation of Women's Clubs, 1918–1938* [vol.2] (Dallas, 1941), 59–63; "Statement of Relationships & Agreements between War Camp Community Service Board and the City Federation of Women's Clubs of San Antonio, Texas, in Connection with the Cafe at the Community House," box 2J364, Texas War Records; Mrs. W. M. [May Harper] Baines, *Houston's Part in the World War* (Houston, 1919), 94–95.

28. See Brandt, *No Magic Bullet*, chap. 2, on the "Fit to Fight" Campaign.

29. Katherine Bement Davis, "Women's Education in Social Hygiene," *AAAPSS* 79 (Sept. 1918): 167–77; Anderson, "Making the Camps Safe for the Army," 146; Fosdick,

"Program of the Commission on Training Camp Activities," 73–75; David J. Pivar, "Cleansing the Nation: The War on Prostitution, 1917–21," *Prologue* 12:1 (1980): 29–40.

30. *San Antonio Express,* June 6, 1917; Minnie Fisher Cunningham to "Dear Suffragist," [Conservation Bulletin no. 1], undated [1917], and Cunningham to "Dear Madam President," box 2G181, Sharp Papers.

31. Cunningham to Carrie Chapman Catt, June 20, 1917, 1/8, Cunningham Papers; *San Antonio Express,* June 6, 1917; "Vice Conditions are Horrible in San Antonio," *Home and State,* June 15, 1917; copy of telegram sent to War Department by Order of the Joint Conference at San Antonio, June 5, 1917, box 2G181, Sharp Papers. The sixteen cooperating organizations appear on the Anti-Vice Committee's letterhead in the Sharp and Cunningham Papers: Texas Equal Suffrage Association, Woman's Christian Temperance Union, Texas Women Bankers' Association, Texas Federation of Women's Clubs, Texas Farm Women, Daughters of 1812, United Daughters of the Confederacy, Daughters of the American Revolution, Women's Benefit Association of the Maccabees, Texas Congress of Mothers, Young Women's Christian Association, Daughters of Isabella, Daughters of the Republic of Texas, The King's Daughters, Texas Women's Press Association, and National League for Women's Service.

32. *Houston Post,* June 22, 1917; *Woman Citizen,* July 7, 1917, p. 106; Cunningham to Nannie Webb Curtis, June 19, July 6, 1917, 17/254, Cunningham Papers; [Edith Hinkle League] to Mrs. George F. L. Bishop, June 26, 1917, ibid., and to Lavinia Engle, Aug. 7, 1917, box 34, McCallum Papers (part 2).

33. "Report on Fort Worth," enclosed in Cunningham to Mrs. [Estelle B.] Sharp, [Nov. 1917], box 2G181, Sharp Papers; Cunningham to Sharp, Oct. 31, 1917, ibid.

34. Elizabeth M. Speer to Raymond B. Fosdick, Feb. 12, 1918, 17/264, Cunningham Papers (first quotation); Speer, "Conservation of the Manhood of America and its Effect upon Future Generations," box 2G181, Sharp Papers (second quotation).

35. Bristow, *Making Men Moral,* 98–107.

36. Cunningham to Mrs. E. A. Watters, Oct. 27, 1918, 17/266 Cunningham Papers; Dora Fleming to Anna Pennybacker, Sept. 22, 1917, Pennybacker Papers. Cunningham to Nannie Webb Curtis, Oct. 25, 1917; Cunningham to A. I. Folsom, Oct. 29, 1917; and Elmer Scott to Cunningham, all in 17/264, Cunningham Papers. On the closing of the vice districts, see Thomas Clyde Mackey, *Red Lights Out: A Legal History of Prostitution, Disorderly Houses, and Vice Districts, 1870–1917* (New York, 1987), 239–40; Fosdick, "Program of the Commission on Training Camp Activities," 75; Richard F. Selcer, *Hell's Half Acre: The Life and Legend of a Red-Light District* (Fort Worth, 1991), 269, 271–72; and *Austin American,* July 21, 1917. The CTCA took credit for Houston, even though construction on Camp Logan did not begin until more than a month after the red-light district was abolished.

37. *Woman Citizen,* Apr. 20, 1918, p. 417; M. M. Crane to William P. Hobby, Feb. 2, 1918, box 3N98, folder 4, Martin McNulty Crane Papers, CAH-UT; Thomas B. Love to Hobby, Jan. 26, 1918, Thomas B. Love Papers, Dallas Historical Society. Lewis L. Gould, *Progressives and Prohibitionists: Texas Democrats during the Wilson Era* (Austin, 1974), chap. 8, provides the best assessment of the political situation.

38. Minnie Fisher Cunningham to Charles A. Culberson, May 23, 1917, 14/205, Cunningham Papers; Cunningham to M. H. Wolfe, Aug. 25, 1917, 14/214, ibid.; Texas Women's Anti-Vice Committee to Hon. James Young, Sen. T. P. Gore, June 5, 1917, box 2G181, Sharp Papers; Board of Managers, Minutes, Apr. 21, 1917, box 32A, Texas PTA Archives; Megan Seaholm, "Earnest Women: The White Woman's Club Movement in Texas, 1880–1920" (Ph.D. diss., Rice University, 1988), 467.

39. *Dallas Morning News*, Sept. 6, 10, 11, 1917.

40. *Austin American*, Jan. 7 (quotation), 9, 1918.

41. Ibid., Jan. 20, 1918.

42. Ibid., Jan. 22, 1918; Gould, *Progressives and Prohibitionists*, 231–33, 247; *Woman Citizen*, May 18, 1918, p. 496.

43. For the history of the Texas suffrage movement, see A. Elizabeth Taylor, "The Woman Suffrage Movement in Texas," *Journal of Southern History* 27 (May 1951): 194–215, reprinted in Ruthe Winegarten and Judith N. McArthur, eds., *Citizens at Last: The Woman Suffrage Movement in Texas* (Austin, 1987); John Carroll Eudy, "The Vote and Lone Star Women: Minnie Fisher Cunningham and the Texas Equal Suffrage Association," *East Texas Historical Journal* 14 (Fall 1976): 52–59; Willie Dee Worley Bowles, "History of the Woman Suffrage Movement in Texas" (Master's thesis, University of Texas at Austin, 1939); Mamie B. Vielock, "Texas Women Campaign for Suffrage" (Master's thesis, St. Mary's University, 1949); Glenn K. Polan, "Minnie Fisher Cunningham" (Master's thesis, Sam Houston State University, 1968); and Sharon E. Strawn, "Woman Suffrage: The Texas Movement, 1868–1920" (Master's thesis, Hardin-Simmons University, 1982).

44. Humphrey, ed., *Texas Suffragist*, 78–112 (quotation at 81).

45. Ibid., 80; Christian, *History of the Texas Federation of Women's Clubs*, 363.

46. "Autobiographical Notes," box 2F80, Margie E. Neal Papers, CAH-UT; Humphrey, ed., *Texas Suffragist*, 80; *Austin American*, June 26, 1918.

47. Eleanor Flexner, *Century of Struggle: The Woman's Rights Movement in America* (1959; rept. New York, 1979), 288–90; "Report of Texas Equal Suffrage Association," 1917, in Winegarten and McArthur, eds, *Citizens at Last*, 153–55. *Woman Citizen*, Dec. 15, 1917, p. 53, and Aug. 17, 1918, p. 238. See Sarah Hunter Graham, *Woman Suffrage and the New Democracy* (New Haven, 1996), 103–5, on NAWSA's war work.

48. "Report of Texas Equal Suffrage Association," 154; Elizabeth York Enstam, "They Called it 'Motherhood': Dallas Women and Public Life, 1895–1918," in *Hidden Histories of Women in the New South*, edited by Virginia Bernhard et al. (Columbia, Mo., 1994), 93; Baines, *Houston's Part in the World War*, 148; *Woman Citizen*, Nov. 17, 1917, p. 476, May 11, 1918, p. 478.

49. William A. Link, *The Paradox of Southern Progressivism, 1880–1939* (Chapel Hill, N.C., 1992), 119–20; Minnie Fisher Cunningham to Carrie Chapman Catt, June 20, 1917, 1/8, Cunningham Papers.

50. Rena Maverick Green to Lavinia Engle, June 28, 1917, box 3, folder 10, McCallum Papers (part 1); Green to Minnie Fisher Cunningham, Sept. 24, 1917, ibid.

51. *San Antonio Express,* Dec. 1, 2, 1917, and Jan. 9, 1918; Green to Cunningham, Dec. 6, 1917, Jan. 19, 23, 1918, Feb. 3, 1918 (quotation), 4/47, Cunningham Papers; Harrol B. Ayres, "Democracy at Work: San Antonio Being Reborn," *Social Hygiene* 4 (Apr. 1918): 211–17.

52. Green to Cunningham, Jan. 4, 1918 (first quotation), Jan. 19, 1918 (second quotation), 4/47, Cunningham Papers.

53. *Austin American,* Sept. 30, 1917.

54. For details of the suffrage bargain, see Judith N. McArthur, "Minnie Fisher Cunningham's Back Door Lobby in Texas: Political Maneuvering in a One-Party State," in Marjorie Spruill Wheeler, ed., *One Woman, One Vote: Rediscovering the Woman Suffrage Movement* (Troutdale, Oreg., 1995), 315–24.

55. Ibid., 325–31; WCTU Minute Book, 1917–18, Houston Central, Rockwell Brothers Records, CAH-UT, esp. entries for Apr. 2, May 9 (quotation), and Sept. 12, 1918.

56. M. M. Crane to Hobby, Feb. 2, 1918, box 3N98, folder 4, Crane Papers (first quotation); Thomas B. Love to Hobby, Jan. 26, 1918, Love Papers (second quotation).

57. *Austin American,* Jan. 7 (Curtis quotation), 1918; Humphrey, ed., *Texas Suffragist,* 100, 102–3. See also *Texas White Ribbon,* May 1918, copy in box 2J192, Rockwell Brothers Records, in which Curtis claimed that the German ambassador had sent messages to the Kaiser from a powerful wireless radio transmitter on the roof of Adolph Busch's daughter's house in New York.

58. Hortense Ward to Minnie Fisher Cunningham, Jan. 10, 1918, 13/193, Cunningham Papers; Cunningham to Charles Metcalfe, Jan. 28, 1918, 14/213, ibid. See Philip N. Cohen, "Nationalism and Suffrage: Gender Struggle in Nation-Building America," *Signs* 21 (Spring 1996): 707–27, on suffrage leaders' embrace of nationalism as a strategy that minimized gender conflict and emphasized a complementary partnership with white men.

59. Ward to Cunningham, Dec. 22, 1917, Jan. 10, 1918, 13/193, Cunningham Papers; Humphrey, ed., *Texas Suffragist,* 102.

60. *Dallas Morning News,* July 3, 1918 (Hobby quotation), June 30, 1918 (Campbell quotation). On the progressives' campaign strategy, see Gould *Progressives and Prohibitionists,* 239–41.

61. Quotation appears in Hortense Ward to Minnie Fisher Cunningham, Dec. 22, 1917, 13/193, Cunningham Papers.

62. *Ferguson Forum,* Aug. 1, 1918; President's Report, 1914, box 11, file 8, McCallum Papers (part 2). See Graham, *Woman Suffrage,* chap. 4, on NAWSA's strategy of building a suffrage "machine."

63. Minnie Fisher Cunningham to Carrie Chapman Catt, July 31, 1917, 1/8, Cunningham Papers; Charles Metcalfe to Cunningham, Feb. 18, 13, 1918, 14/213, ibid.; Jane McCallum, "Activities of Women in Texas Politics," in *Texas Democracy: A Centennial History of Politics and Personalities in the Democratic Party, 1836–1936,* 2 vols., edited by Frank Carter Adams (Austin, 1937), 1:481.

64. *Austin American,* June 29, 1918; *Dallas Morning News,* July 11, 1918 (for Fort Worth); G. C. Groce to M. M. Crane, July 9, 1918, box 3N98, Crane Papers; Mrs. L. F. Beuckenstein to Minnie Fisher Cunningham, July 7, 1918, box 3, folder 4, McCallum Papers (part 1); Belle Crichett to Edith Hinkle League, July 1, 1918, ibid.

65. C. F. Richardson to Walter White, July 2, 1918, reel 19, Houston Branch files, *Papers of the NAACP* (University Publications of America, microfilm); *Houston Post*, July 4, 9, 12, 13, 1918. By comparison, approximately 14,400 white women registered. The pro-Hobby *Post* reported daily registration totals for white women in front-page stories, mentioning the black women only occasionally and in round numbers.

66. Steven A. Reich, "Black Texans and the Fight for Citizenship, 1917–1921," *Journal of American History* 82 (Mar. 1996): 1478–1504.

67. Richardson to White, July 2, 1918 (quotation); Dr. O. C. Garrett to Mary White Ovington, Dec. 12, 1920, reel 19, Houston Branch files, *NAACP Papers.*

Conclusion

1. Kathryn Kish Sklar has developed this point in "The Historical Foundations of Woman's Power in the Creation of the American Welfare State, 1830–1930," in *Mothers of a New World: Maternalist Politics and the Origins of Welfare States*, edited by Seth Koven and Sonya Michel (New York, 1992), 68.

2. [Anna J. H. Pennybacker] to Mrs. Thomas Winter, Dec. 27, 1918, Pennybacker Papers.

3. Anti-Saloon League, *The Brewers and Texas Politics*, 2 vols. (San Antonio, 1916), 2:887.

4. *Home and State*, Dec. 2, 1911; June 15, July 13, 20, 1912.

5. May Baines, *A Story of Texas White Ribboners* (n.p., [1935?]), 116; *Texas White Ribbon*, May 1914, pp. 5–6; Texas Woman's Christian Temperance Union, *Thirty-fifth Annual Convention*, 1917, copy in box 19, folder 280, Cunningham Papers.

6. Elna Green, "'Ideals of Government, of Home, and of Women': The Ideology of Southern White Antisuffragism," in *Hidden Histories of Women in the New South*, edited by Virginia Bernhard et al. (Columbia, Mo., 1994), 105, and Elna Green, *Southern Strategies: Southern Women and the Woman Suffrage Question* (Chapel Hill, N.C., 1997), 93–94.

7. See for example, *Houston Daily Post*, Apr., 11, 1915; *Ferguson Forum*, May 15, 22, 1919. Numerous mailings from the Men's Organization Opposed to Woman Suffrage are preserved in box 9, folder 4, McCallum Papers (part 1).

8. "Plan of the Texas Association Opposed to Woman Suffrage," box 9, folder 11, McCallum Papers.

9. Mrs. James B. Wells, "The Truth about Wage-Earning Women," *Houston Daily Post*, May 16, 1915; Mrs. George F. Arnold, "Woman Suffrage Has Been Defeated," ibid., June 7, 1915; TAOWS, "Woman Suffrage and the Liquor Question," box 9, folder 11, McCallum Papers; "Why I Am Opposed to Woman Suffrage," Mrs. James B. Wells Biographical File, CAH-UT. The earliest reference to race that I have found is a statement by Pauline Wells in the *Fort Worth Star Telegram*, Apr. 6, 1918.

10. Nancy F. Cott, "Across the Great Divide: Women in Politics Before and After 1920," in *Women, Politics, and Change*, edited by Louise A. Tilly and Patricia Gurin (New York, 1990); Anne Firor Scott, *The Southern Lady: From Pedestal to Politics, 1830–1930* (Chicago, 1970), chap. 8.

11. Emma Louise Moyer Jackson, "Petticoat Politics: Political Activities among Texas Women in the 1920s" (Ph.D. diss., University of Texas at Austin, 1980).

12. Steven A. Reich, "Black Texans and the Fight for Citizenship, 1917–1921," *Journal of American History* 82 (Mar. 1996): 1510; Ruthe Winegarten, *Black Texas Women: 150 Years of Trial and Triumph* (Austin, 1995), 195–96; Fannie C. Potter, *History of the Texas Federation of Women's Clubs, 1918–1938* (Dallas, 1941), 183, 193–94.

13. Glenda Elizabeth Gilmore, *Gender and Jim Crow: Women and the Politics of White Supremacy in North Carolina, 1896–1920* (Chapel Hill, N.C., 1996), 177; Margie E. Neal, Autobiographical Notes, box 2F80, Neal Papers, CAH-UT.

14. Potter, *History*, 89, 145, 182, 209; *Dallas Morning News*, Nov. 26, 1926.

Index

Priscilla Art Club (Dallas), 89
progressivism: women's contributions to, 2, 144
Prohibition, 115–16, 118–19, 132–34, 138
prostitution, 4, 83–87, 121, 136–37; at military bases, 127, 130–32
public schools: in Texas, 57, 61, 64. *See also* compulsory education; Conference for Education in Texas (CET)
pure food legislation, 41–44, 52

Reppert, Vernice, 135
Richards, Ellen S., 31–34, 45, 54
Ring, Elizabeth, 109
Rockefeller, John D., Jr., 86
Roosevelt, Theodore, 58–59
Ruiz, Vicki, 83
Rumford Kitchen, 32
Runge, Johanna, 66, 67
Runge Free Kindergarten (Galveston), 66
Rusk Settlement (Houston), 79

Sampson, Mrs. Edward, 112, 115
San Antonio Council of Mothers, 73, 100
San Antonio Equal Franchise Society, 97, 100, 105, 106, 108, 136–37
San Antonio Federation of Women's Clubs, 72, 109
San Antonio Light, 73
sanitation, 33–34, 45–46, 56, 58, 63
Saunders, Ida, 26–27
school boards: women as candidates for, 70–75, 101, 143
school improvement: clubwomen's role in, 4, 56, 58–63, 73
Scott, Anne Firor, 2
segregation, 5, 87–88
settlement houses, 4, 79–83, 88–89, 96
Sewell, May Wright, 11
"sex hygiene." *See* social hygiene movement
Shaw, Anna Howard, 11, 97, 108, 111, 135
Sheltering Arms (Houston), 88
Sheppard-Towner Act, 147
Sinclair, Upton, 41
Sklar, Kathryn Kish, 2
Smith-Lever Act, 48–51, 143, 165n53
"social economics," 4, 10, 41, 78, 79
Social Hygiene, 127, 131
Social hygiene movement, 85–86, 96, 130
Southern Committee (NAWSA), 15, 110
Southern Education Board, 63, 64, 65

Southern women: antebellum culture, 2; rise of political activism, 3, 143–44; and public space, 5
Speer, Elizabeth, 131–32
Stanton, Elizabeth Cady, 11, 102
State Council of Women of Texas, 13–14, 22, 32. *See also* Texas Congress of Women
Stoddard, Helen, 35–37, 44, 52
Stone, Lucy, 11, 99
suffrage. *See* woman suffrage movement

TACWC. *See* Texas Association of Colored Women's Clubs (TACWC)
tag days, 80
Talbert, Mary B., 141
Talbot, Marion, 31, 33, 35
Taylor, Bride Neill, 1, 142
TCM (Texas Congress of Mothers). *See* Texas Congress of Mothers and Parent-Teacher Associations (PTA)
telephone operators, 90–91
TERA. *See* Texas Equal Rights Association (TERA)
Terrell, Mary Y., 22–29, 107
TESA. *See* Texas Equal Suffrage Association (TESA)
Texas A&M University, 35, 38, 43–44, 50
Texas Association of Colored Women's Clubs (TACWC), 17, 89, 141, 148–49
Texas Association Opposed to Woman Suffrage, 146–47
Texas Brewers Association, 145
Texas Club Woman, 85
Texas Conference of Charities and Correction, 88
Texas Congress of Farm Women, 47, 49
Texas Congress of Mothers (TCM). *See* Texas Congress of Mothers and Parent-Teacher Associations (PTA)
Texas Congress of Mothers and Parent-Teacher Associations (PTA), 61–64, 66, 69, 86, 100, 108, 132; and married women's property laws, 102–3, 180n21; and child welfare, 124–27
Texas Congress of Women, 1, 12–14, 110, 143
Texas Equal Rights Association (TERA), 12, 15, 97–99, 101, 109–11, 116
Texas Equal Suffrage Association (TESA), 105–17, 130, 132, 135–40, 147
Texas Farmers' Alliance, 12

JUDITH N. MCARTHUR, lecturer in history at the University of Houston–Victoria, is coeditor of *Citizens at Last: The Woman Suffrage Movement in Texas* and coauthor of *A Gentleman and an Officer: A Military and Social History of James B. Griffin's Civil War.*